A Treatise on the Right of Property in Tide Waters

A Treatise on the Right of Property in Tide Waters

and in the Soil and Shores Thereof to which is added an Appendix, Containing the Principal Adjudged Cases

JOSEPH K. ANGELL

BeardBooks
Washington, D.C.

Reprinted 2001 by Beard Books, Washington, D.C.
ISBN 1-58798-105-X

Printed in the United States of America

TO

NATHANIEL SEARLE, Esq. LL. D.

THE

FOLLOWING TREATISE

IS INSCRIBED AS A MARK OF RESPECT

AND ESTEEM,

BY HIS FRIEND AND

HUMBLE SERVANT,

THE AUTHOR.

PREFACE.

The attention of the author was incidentally drawn to the subject of the present work, when he was occupied in preparing his work on *water courses*, which was published nearly two years since. The latter (it will be recollected) related solely to *inland* streams, in which there is no ebbing and flowing of the tide. After completing the work referred to, it occurred to him, that an exposition of the principles which relate to the right of property in tide waters, would not only be useful to the profession, but to the public generally, and would also especially invite the attention and patronage of those whose estates are contiguous to such waters.

The only work that has hitherto been published, which has professed to discuss systematically the main principles involved in the present subject, is the celebrated treatise of Lord Hale, entitled "*De jure maris, &c.*" which is one of the manuscripts that were collected and published by Francis Hargrave, Esq. and comprise the interesting volume called "Hargrave's Tracts." This production of Lord Hale is obviously the result of very great research, and embodies many very ancient and important precedents. On this account, and also on account of his uncommon qualifications as a lawyer, his treatise has been received as leading authority, both in England and in this country.

Many years, however, have elapsed since the treatise of Lord Hale was written, and, as might be expected, many adjudications on the subject to which it relates, have subsequently been reported. The principles of the common law in relation to the subject, have also in several respects been very materially modified and altered in this country, by our *Charters*, our *Statutes*, and our *Customs*. These circumstances, it is presumed, will afford a sufficient apology, for soliciting, in this instance, the attention of the profession, and of the public, to a subject which was so ably and profoundly investigated by the learned author above mentioned.

6 *College-street, Providence,*
August 12, 1826.

TABLE OF CONTENTS.

CHAPTER V.

CHAPTER VI.

CHAPTER VII.

CHAPTER VIII.

CHAPTER IX.

Table

OF

CASES, &c. IN THE APPENDIX.

INTRODUCTION.

In commencing an exposition of the legal rules and principles which relate to the subject of the present work, the attention is very naturally first attracted to the *open sea;* with regard to which, it is only necessary to observe, that the well established rule respecting the right of property therein is, *from its nature it cannot be possessed.* And hence it is, that the sea is regarded as the common property, and is denominated the common highway of nations.

The dominion of a nation may, however, extend so far from the land as is necessary for its own safety. And although history, both ancient and modern, affords many instances in which a much greater extent has been arrogated:

although, for example, the naval strength of England has encouraged its monarchs to attribute to themselves the whole sea which surrounds their island, even as far as the opposite coasts; and the republic of Venice asserted her claim to the empire of the Adriatic; yet it is not consistent with sound and well founded principle to establish a right of so enlarged an extent, without the express or implied consent of other powers. (*a*)

It is admitted by all the writers upon maritime and international law, that every nation has jurisdiction to the distance of a *cannon shot*, or maritime league over the waters adjacent to its shores. (*b*) This rule has also been adopted by the Supreme Court of the United States. (*c*)

It is a matter of importance, and sometimes of difficulty, to establish the line of demarcation, between what is called the "main sea" or "ocean," and the *county*. This question is more a question of fact, than of law, and is determinable by evi-

(*a*) Selden's *Mare Clausum*, L. 1. b. 2. Vattel, 191.

(*b*) Bynk. Qu. *Pub. Juris*, 61. 1 Azuni, 204. S. 15. Ib. 185. L. 4. Vattel, 207.

(*c*) 2 Cranch. 187, 234. 1 Circuit Rep. 62.

dence of a local nature. In general it is said that such parts of the sea are deemed to be within the bodies of counties, *where persons can see from one side to the other.* And lord Hale in his treatise, *De jure maris,* says that the arm or branch of the sea which lies within the *fauces terræ,* where a man may *reasonably discern* between shore and shore, is, or at least may be within the body of a county, and consequently subject to the jurisdiction of the *sheriff.* (*d*) Hawkins, however, considers the line more accurately confined, by other authorities, to such parts of the sea, where a man standing on one side of the land, *may see what is done on the other.* (*e*) And the reason assigned by lord Coke, in the Admiralty case (*f*) in support of the coroner's jurisdiction, where a man is killed in such places, *because that the county may well know it,* seems rather to support the more limited construction.

In the arms and inlets of the sea, and also in the sea itself, so far as the right of national do-

(*d*) Harg. Tracts, 10. vid. also, 3 Bla. Com. 106.

(*e*) 2 Hard. ch. 9.

(*f*) 13 Rep. 52.

minion extends, the sovereign power not only exercises a right of jurisdiction, but also *a right of property or ownership.* To consider the latter is the design of the following chapters.

A TREATISE.

CHAPTER I.

THE ROMAN AND ENGLISH LAWS, IN RELATION TO THE RIGHT OF PROPERTY IN THE SEA, AND ARMS OF THE SEA.

As it is so very obvious that the principles adopted by the common law, respecting the subject which is to be discussed, were suggested by the jurisprudence of the Romans, it may be proper in the commencement, to refer the attention of the reader to the latter. The right to the sea, &c. is treated of by the civilians, under the title *de rerum divisione*. The following extracts from this title, in the Institutes of Justinian, will suffice for the present purpose.

Et quidem naturali jure communia sunt omnium hæc: aer, aqua profluens, et mare et per hoc littora maris. Nemo igitur ad littus maris accedere prohibetur. (*a*)

"And truly by natural right, these be common to all; the air, running water, and *the sea*, and hence the *shores of the sea*. Nobody is therefore prohibited to come to the sea shore."

Flumina autem omnia, et portus publica sunt, ideoque jus piscandi omnibus commune est in portu fluminibusque. (*b*)

"Also all *rivers* and *ports* are public, so that the right of fishing in a port and in rivers is common to all."

Littorum quoque usus publicus est et juris gentium, sicut et ipsius maris, et ob id cuilibet liberum est casam ibi ponere in quam se recipiat: sicut retia siccare et ex mari deducere. (*c*)

"And by the law of nations the use of the shore is also public, and in the same manner as the sea itself, and for this reason any person is at liberty to place a cabin there, in which he may harbor himself, and for the like reason to dry nets and draw them from the sea."

It most clearly appears then, to have been the established rule of the imperial law, that the sea and its branches, and also, the shores of the same, were subject to be used in common by the people

(*a*) Ins. L. 2. T. 1. S. 1.

(*b*) Ib.

(*c*) Ib.

generally: every person being equally entitled to their benefit, for the purposes of fishing, drying and drawing nets, navigation, &c. They were in fact by the Roman jurists expressly denominated *res communes*, and were considered as *res omnium*, in respect to their *use and benefit;* but with regard to *their property*, as *res nullius. Proprietas autem eorum potest intelligi, nullius esse.* (*d*)

In this respect, it will appear, that the Roman law has been very much surpassed, by the common law of England. For although, as will presently be shewn, the sea, &c. according to the provisions of the common law, are as public and common, as they were among the Romans; yet it is not only the policy of the common law to assign to every thing capable of occupancy and susceptible of ownership a legal and certain proprietor— but also to make those things which from their nature cannot be *exclusively* occupied and enjoyed, the property of the *sovereign*.

Indeed, in England, the *king* is regarded as *universal occupant*, and the presumption is, that *all* property was originally in the Crown. Hence it is said that all lands are holden mediately or immediately from the Crown, and that the king has the *absolutum et directum dominium*. This however is but a *fiction* of law adopted not for the aggrand-

(*d*) Ib. Taylor's Sum. of Rom. Law, 246.

izement of the throne, but for the good of the people. For it will be recollected that the right of the people of England to their lands, does not depend upon, nor in fact was ever derived from any royal grant. *(e)*

To the king, therefore, is not only assigned the sovereign dominion over the sea adjoining the coasts, and over the arms of the sea; but in him is also vested the *right of property* in the *soil thereof*. *(f)*

Thus it was resolved in the case of the *royal fishery in the river Banne*, that the sea is not only under the dominion of the king (as is said 6 *R.* 2. *Fitz. Protect.* 46—the sea is of the legiance of the king as of his Crown of England;) but it is also his proper inheritance, and therefore the king shall have the *land* which is gained from the sea, *Dyer* 15. Also the king shall have the grand fishes of the sea, *(whales and sturgeons,)* which are royal fish. And all *ports* and *havens* which are *ostiæ et januae regni*, appertain to the king, because he is *custos totius regni*. *(g)*

Thus too in the case of the Attorney General *v.* Richards, in the Exchequer *(h)* the information

(*e*) 1 Brac. L. 3, 120. 2 Bac. Abr. 177. 2 Roll. Abr. 168. 2 Bla. Com. 14, 104. Harg. Tracts, *de jure maris, &c.*

(*f*) Ib.

(*g*) Case of the Royal Fishery, App. 35.

(*h*) Attorney General *v.* Richards. App. 9.

stated that by the royal prerogative, *the sea and sea coasts, and as far as the sea flows and reflows, between the high and low-water marks*, and *all the ports and havens of the kingdom*, belong to his majesty, and ought to be preserved for the use of his majesty's vessels and others, and that his majesty has the right of superintendency over them for their preservation.

"Touching our *Mare Anglicum*," (says Mr. Serjeant Callis, *(i)* "in whom the interest therein is, and by what law the government thereof is, the king hath therein these powers and properties: 1 *Imperium regale*. 2 *Potestatem legalem*. 3 *Proprietatem tam soli quam aquæ*. 4 *Possessionem et proficuum tam reale quam personale*."

But although the dominion and property of the sea and tide waters are in the Crown, yet the water is of common right public, (as among the Romans,) for every subject to navigate, and to fish in, indiscriminately and without interruption: with the exception only of *royal fish*, the king's right to which, is created by the consideration of his guardianship of the seas, and of his protection thereof against pirates. *(k)*

(*i*) Callis on Sewers, 39.

(*k*) Besides the foregoing authorities, vid. 5. Com. Dig. 102. 10 Rep. 141. Sid. 149. Salk. 357. Lord Fitzwalter's case, 1 Mod. 105. Rex *v*. Smith, App. 130. Sir Henry Constable's case, App. 140.

And although the property *of the soil* is in the Crown, to high-water mark; yet the shore, or the land which is between the high and low-water marks, is also of common right public. (*l*) The maxim being, *Rex in ea habet proprietatem, sed populus habet usum ibidem necessarium*, (*m*) the king has the property, but the people have the necessary use.

The right of property in the tide waters of England appears to be vested in the king, not merely on the principle before mentioned, of his being the universal occupant, but also as the fountain from whence in contemplation of law all authority and privilege proceed. In him all rights of a public nature may be considered, *prima facie*, to reside, and from him emanate to his subjects, who by virtue of their subjection become entitled to the free and uninterrupted exercise of what is regarded as an inherent privilege. Among these inherent privileges (as will presently be shewn,) are the rights of fishing and navigating in and upon the sea, &c. which are classed among those public rights often known by the denomination of *jura publica*, or *jura communia*, and are thus contradistinguished from *jura coronæ*, the private rights of the Crown.

It may be observed, that the important doctrine

(*l*) Ib.

(*m*) Callis on Sewers. 53.

that public rights and such things as are materially dependant on them, cannot be alienated by the Crown, was established at a very early period. The rule as laid down by Bracton is, that those things which relate particularly to the public good, cannot be given, sold, or transferred by the king or separated from the Crown; "*Res fiscalis dari non potest, nec vendi, nec ad alium transferri a principe vel a rege regnante et quæ faciunt ipsam coronam, et communem utilitatem respiciunt.*" (*n*) The same rule was also admitted by the feudal law: "*Res ad coronam regis, vel utilitatem publicam pertinentes inter sacras numerantur; neque recte in feudum dantur et quasi sacræ dicuntur.*" (*o*) Hence the people of England are not only, *prima facie*, entitled to the use of the sea, &c. for the purposes hereafter to be considered, but their right in this respect cannot be restrained or counteracted by any royal grant, on the ground that the king is the legal and sole proprietor. In favor of this view of the subject, we have the Treatise of lord Hale, and also the opinion of one of the present judges of the king's bench, (Mr. J. Bayley) who says, "many of the king's rights are, to a certain extent, for the benefit of his subjects, and that is the case as to the sea, in which all his subjects have the

(*n*) Bract. L. 2. c. 5. s. 7.
(*o*) Craig. *Jus Feud.* L. 1.

right of navigation and of fishing, and the king can make no modern grants in derogation of those rights." (*p*)

It would at first appear, to be a regular consequence of the foregoing doctrine, that the proprietor of the upland contiguous to the shore, has no greater right to the shore than others, who have no interest in the upland. And this to a certain extent, is most undoubtedly a correct principle; but is nevertheless to be understood with some degree of restriction, and is fully and particularly explained in Chapter VIII.

It necessarily follows, too, from the doctrine which has been advanced, that anything which tends to interrupt the common use of the water, or shore, or to impair in value the privileges naturally incident to the same, and to which the public have an inherent right, is a public injury. These privileges consist in *fishing* and *navigating*.

I. Fishery in the sea, &c. as it constitutes a great source of sustentation, is in every country considered of very great importance, and by the common law it is well settled that no citizen can be excluded from an equal and fair participation in the benefit to be derived therefrom, so long as it remains unrelinquished by the public, or so long as no particular and exclusive right has been

(*p*) Blundell *v.* Catterall, App. 160.

acquired by usage or prescription. (*o*) "Though the king," (says lord Hale) "is the owner of this great waste," (meaning the sea, &c.) "and as a consequence of his property, has the primary right of fishing in the sea, and the creeks and arms thereof; yet the common people of England have regularly a liberty of fishing in the sea, or creeks, or arms thereof, as a public common of piscary, and may not without injury to their right, be restrained in the exercise of it, unless in such places, creeks, or navigable rivers, where either the king, or some particular subject has acquired a property exclusive of this common liberty." (*p*)

The principle, as laid down by lord Hale, is expressly recognized in the case of Warren *v.* Mathews (*q*) and in Carter *v.* Murcot. (*r*) In the last case, it was said by lord Mansfield, that a man *may* have an exclusive privilege of fishing in an arm of the sea; but that such right is not to be presumed, it must be *proved*. And Mr. J. Yates observed, that he knew a case to fail, wherein an exclusive right was claimed, because no prescription was proved; and in that case it was determined, that the right of fishing in the salt water was common to all. The case of the Mayor and Commonalty of Orford

(*o*) Vid. Chap. 6.

(*p*) Harg. Tracts 11.

(*q*) Warren *v.* Mathews, App. 159.

(*r*) Carter *v.* Murcot, App. 32.

v. Richardson, in the King's Bench, and in error in the Exchequer Chamber (*s*) was also determined wholly on the ground, that every subject, *prima facie*, has a right to fish in an arm of the sea.

With the common law of England on this subject corresponds the ordinance of Louis XIV. section 47 (*t*) which provides as follows: "We declare the fishing in the sea to be free and common to all our subjects, whom we allow to fish, as well in the high sea, as upon the shore, with the nets and engines specified in this ordinance."

As to the right of taking *shell fish* on the shore between the high and low-water marks, after the reflux of the tide; this seems to be included in the general proposition that the right of fishery is common; and it is not controverted by any authority. On the contrary, the court in the case of Bagott *v.* Orr (*u*) expressly recognised the doctrine, that it is a right common to every subject to take shell fish on the shore, by digging up the soil.

As the right of fishing in the sea and in all tide waters is a right which is, *prima facie*, common to all, it follows that an actual appropriation or manucaption must be made, to complete the right of property; and that when fish are taken, they become the exclusive property of him who has

(*s*) Mayor, &c. of Orford *v.* Richardson, App. 105.

(*t*) Sea Laws 357.

(*u*) Bagott *v.* Orr, App. 20.

taken them, unless they are afterwards restored to their native element. Thus, Bracton and Fleta, the first writers on this subject, lay it down as common law, that fishes generally are, "*animalia quæ in mari nascuntur quæ cum capiuntur captoris fiunt.*" (*v*) Occupancy may in fact be said to relate to fish as well as to all other animals *feræ naturæ*, and the very principle that the fish belong to him who takes them, implies an antecedent want of ownership in the fish, and therefore in a qualified sense they may be considered as the property of no one, though by the common law, the right to any thing which has no other owner, by the operation of a legal fiction, is vested in the Crown.

As to the question whether or not the common right of fishing in the sea, &c. affords to the public any right to pass over the land which is conterminous—it may be observed, that rights of way can only be claimed by *usage*, or by *grant*, or by way of *necessity*, arising out of a grant. On the ground of necessity, it might at first seem, that the liberty of passing over private soil to a public fishing place may be legally claimed by the people at large, and it has been often suggested that the law would not give to every man the right to fish in the sea, &c. and at the same time deny to him the means of going there. And it has in fact been adjudged that

(*v*) Bract. L. 1. c. 12. s. 10. Fleta. L. 3. c. 2.

a right to *wreck* (by grant or prescription) thrown upon another's land, will carry with it a right of way over the same land to take it. (*u*)

It is important to recollect, however, that in all cases where a way is claimed by *necessity*, it is considered a good plea that the plaintiff has *another* way. (*w*) Besides which, if any right of passage over estates adjoining the salt water did exist, as a necessary incident to the right of fishery, its importance, it may reasonably be presumed, would have caused it to be treated of, and that the right would have been somewhere defined with precision—that is, whether it extends to horses as well as men, and to what number of horses, &c.

It is said, it is true, in *Fitzh. Barre* 93, which cites the *year books* of 1469, "That the fishers who fish in the sea, may justify their going upon the land adjoining to the sea, because such fishery is for the commonwealth, and for the sustenance of all the kingdom." But in *Brooke's ab. tit. Customs*, 46, the case is more fully stated, and shews that the doctrine was laid down on a question which arose upon a *custom*. The action was trespass for *digging* land, and the defendant pleaded, that it was four acres adjoining to the sea, and that all the men of *Kent*, from time immemorial, have used when they have fished in the sea, to dig

(*u*) 6 Mod. 149.
(*w*) Ib. 8.

in the land adjoining, and pitch stakes *for hanging their nets.* Lord Hale, also (*x*) considers it as founded upon a custom; for he observes, " Look at the book of 8 *Ed.* 4. 18. for the *custom of Kent*, for fishermen to dry their nets upon the land, though it be the soil of private men. Mr. Justice Holroyd, too, in the recent case of Blundell *v.* Catterall, (*y*) who had occasion to consider this old authority, regarded it as proceeding entirely from a particular custom.

It may also be observed that the current of authorities, too, as it relates to any interest or servitude which the public may legally claim in the land of an individual contiguous to the salt water, (the cases of Ball *v.* Herbert, (*a*) and Blundell *v* Catterall, (*b*) in particular,) is decidedly adverse to the right of fishermen to pass over the land of other persons, in order to get to the water. And however the interest of the public may be involved, yet it is an incontrovertible principle that *private rights shall not be infringed without a satisfaction being made to the parties injured.* If satisfaction then is necessary in such cases, and that satisfaction not defined, the right in question cannot be said to exist at common law.

(*x*) Harg. Tracts, 86.

(*y*) Blundell *v.* Catterall, App. 160.

(*a*) Ball *v.* Herbert, App. 233.

(*b*) Blundell *v.* Catterall. App. 160

From the authorities, therefore, and from the silence of legal authors, and from the extreme inconvenience to which individuals having landed property adjoining the sea would be exposed, if their lands were subject to the accommodation of the public, it may be fairly concluded, that however convenient a way may be over the land of an individual to the people at large in going to, and returning from any public fishing place, it cannot be properly claimed by virtue of the common privilege of piscary.

II. The common privilege of *navigating* the sea and its branches, is far more important than the common privilege of piscary. In the language of a celebrated writer, "the wisdom of God is highly to be admired, who has not granted all things to every land, but has distributed his gifts to several countries, that men having need of one another, might maintain society for their common good. Therefore, has he endowed man with knowledge and understanding to invent and build ships, to govern and guide them by those lamps of heaven and other instruments of his divine wisdom, enabling thereby the merchant to convey to all what any place affords." (*b*)

By the common law all arms of the sea, navigable rivers, &c. are considered as public highways.

(*b*) Molloy, 414

and to obstruct their passage, or render it dangerous, or inconvenient, by bridges, causeways, or embankments, or by throwing overboard ballast, or other substances from vessels, or boats, or in any other manner, are *nuisances* which any one may abate, and which will subject the offender to punishment. (*c*)

So effectually is the public privilege of navigating the tide waters secured against annoyance or interruption, by the common law, that the king, although he is the undoubted proprietor thereof, and in this character may grant the soil thereof; yet the king, or any person claiming under him, has no authority to obstruct the navigation. (*d*) Thus it was adjudged, that a corporation who were the conservators of a navigable river, and the owners of the soil, could not authorize their lessee to erect a wharf which produced inconvenience to the public, in the use of the river for the purposes of navigation. (*e*)

Indeed so tenacious is the law of the uninterrupted and safe exercise of the public right of navigation, that even when vessels are sunk by *misfortune* and *inevitable accident*, and without any fault on the part of the owner, a *buoy* must be placed over them for the safety of the public: and this

(*c*) 1 Russell on Crimes, 485.

(*d*) Harg. Tracts, 85.

(*e*) Rex *v.* Lord Grovesnor. App. 127.

was considered by lord Ellenborough, as the only proper and specific notice, which all understand and are bound to attend to. (*f*)

Thus, in an action on the case against the defendant for his neglect in not placing a buoy over his lighter which had been accidentally sunk in the river Thames, whereby the plaintiff's barge had struck against the lighter and been greatly damaged; the only question was, whether due notice had been given of the danger arising from the wreck of the lighter. No buoy it appears was placed over it until two or three days after, though a watchman was stationed near the spot, to warn all vessels to avoid it. When on duty, the watchman desired the people on board the barge, to keep off, but his admonition was disregarded. Under these circumstances, the plaintiff had a verdict. And the court held, that whenever any substance was sunk in a navigable river so as to create danger, a verbal communication, being liable to be misunderstood, was not a sufficient warning; and that it was a peremptory law of navigation, that a buoy should be placed over it. (*g*) In this case, however, though the party is liable for all special damage to an individual, occasioned by the want of proper notice, yet he is not liable to an *indictment* for not removing the wreck. (*h*) Indeed the

(*f*) 1 Camp. 515.
(*g*) Ib.
(*h*) Ib.

law does not seem very specifically to have designated the manner by which navigable highways are to be kept in repair, though it is laid down in Hawkins, that if a river be stopped, to the nuisance of the country, and none appear bound by prescription to clear it, the neighboring towns and those who have a common passage and easement therein may be compelled to do it." (*i*)

But if a town has been accustomed from time immemorial to preserve a free passage, it is then bound by prescription, as in that case the presumption is, that it was the condition of its creation or charter. (*k*)

As the public have no right to the adjoining land as incident to their right of fishery, so they have none as incident to the right of navigation. And although it seems to have been formerly understood that the banks of navigable waters were subject to be used by the public for the purpose of *towing* vessels, &c. yet in the case of Ball *v.* Herbert, (*l*) it was determined on great deliberation, that at common law no such right existed, but might be *acquired by usage.* This case related to the river Ouse, where the tide ebbed and flowed. In this respect, the common law is different from the civil law, as by the latter the public had the same right

(*i*) H. P. C. Ch. 75.

(*k*) Mayor of Lynn *v.* Turner, App. 103.

(*l*) 3 T. R. 253. Ball *v.* Herbert. App. 233.

to the banks for the purpose of towing, as to the water itself. (*m*)

It may so happen, that the public right of navigating the tide waters will interfere with the public right of fishery. It may happen for instance, that an individual in exercising his common right of piscary, by extending a seine across the channel of an inlet of the sea, may be incommoded by the passing of a vessel. To determine in such an event, which right should yield to the other, it will be necessary to consider with attention, the *nature* of the two rights. And an attentive consideration. will render it obvious, that the right of navigation necessarily supposes, that the passage *shall remain* free and navigable, and must, therefore, from the nature of the right, exclude every thing that will interrupt it.

The privileges of *fishery* and *navigation* in the sea, &c. are said to exist of *common right*. *Common right*, according to Sir Edward Coke, is only another epithet for *common law*. (*n*) And the *common law* of England is known by the various appellations of *right*, *common right*, *public right*, and *communis justitia*. When it is said, therefore, that a man has a thing by common right, it is always to be understood that he has it by the common law.

(*m*) Coop. Just. Tit. *de usu et proprietate riparum*.

(*n*) 2 Inst. Exposit. on *Magna Charta*. 6. 21.

And it is further held, that the common law is denominated common right, because it is the common birthright which the people have for the protection and safeguard of their privileges, &c. (*o*) And it is the excellency of the common law, says Sir Edward Coke, that the receding from the true institution thereof, introduces many inconveniences, and the observation of it is always accompanied with peace and quiet, the end and centre of all human laws. (*p*)

Admitting, therefore, that the right of property in the sea, &c. is, *prima facie*, vested in the king as the representative of the public, and that from him all liberties in contemplation of law are primarily derived, yet it cannot be construed that the king has any other legal tenure in the rights of fishery and navigation than belong to him in the character of *protector* of public and common rights. And hence it is that the king has no authority either to grant the exclusive liberty of fishing in any arm of the sea, or to do any thing which will obstruct its navigation. (*q*) The king, it is true, may grant the soil of any arm of the sea, &c. to an individual, but the right of the grantee so de-

(*o*) 2 Inst. 56.

(*p*) Epist. to 4 Rep.

(*q*) Harg. Tracts, 85. Warren *v.* Matthews, App. 179. Blundell *v.* Catterall, App. 160.

rived is always subservient to the public rights before mentioned.

These are, however, the *only* privileges connected with the sea, &c. which are considered as existing *de jure commune*, or of common right, or, in other words, which are independent of the control and prerogative of the Crown. Hence, *bathing* in the sea, &c. is not regarded as a common law right. Thus, in a very recent case, (*a*) where an individual had the exclusive right to the shore to low-water mark by a grant from the Crown, it was adjudged that the defendant was liable for passing with *bathing carriages*, from some place above high-water mark, across the part of the shore which had become private property, for the conveyance of persons to and from the water, for the purpose of bathing. In this case it was strongly urged, to be a right at common law, for all the king's subjects to bathe on the sea shore, and to pass over it for that purpose on foot, and with horses and carriages. One of the topics which was urged at the bar in favor of this supposed right, was that of *public convenience*. With regard to this topic, Mr. C. J. Abbott observed, "public convenience is, in all cases, to be viewed with a due regard to private property, the protection whereof is one of the distinguishing characteristics of the law of England." It is not to be

(*a*) Blundell *v.* Catterall. App. 160.

expected, however, that where the property of the shore remains in the sovereign power, any obstruction would be interposed to the practice of bathing, and it will not be questioned but that the practice is in itself innocent and lawful. (b)

CHAPTER II.

OF THE INTRODUCTION AND APPLICATION OF THE DOCTRINE OF THE COMMON LAW CONCERNING THE RIGHT OF PROPERTY IN THE SEA, &c. IN THIS COUNTRY.

THE general principles of the common law of England in respect to the right of property in the sea, &c. having been considered in the preceding chapter, the next inquiry is, as to their adoption and application in the United States.

It will be recollected that when the early settlers of North America left their native shores of Britain, to search for new countries and habitations, they considered themselves as British subjects, and behaved in that character. In the association

(b) Blundell v. Catterall, App. 160.

held at Cape Cod, by the first emigrants to New-England, on the 11th November, 1620, they acknowledged themselves the loyal subjects of king James. (*c*) They afterwards took possession of the country in the king's name, and treated and made war with the Indians by his authority. Instead of manifesting a disposition to institute a new and independent government, or to establish new laws of their own promulgation,—all the early settlers sought the protection of their native kingdom, and by general and common consent *adopted its existing laws.* The whole of a country possessed by a nation and *subject to its laws*, (says Vattel,) is the common country of all the individuals of the nation. (*d*)

The territory, therefore, which was discovered, acquired and possessed by the early settlers of this country, although it was separated from the principal establishment, or mother country, might be considered as a part of the British empire, and subject to the rules and provisions of the British system of jurisprudence. Hence, not only the jurisdiction of the British sovereign extended over the possessions which were acquired by the colonists from the native occupants by grant or conquest, but also his *jus proprietatis*, or right of property in all the tide waters included in these

(*c*) Chal. 102.
(*d*) Vattel, 166.

possessions existed, at least to the same extent, as in the tide waters of England.

But inasmuch as the king by virtue of his prerogative was authorized to create *political power* in this, as in all countries newly discovered and possessed by his subjects, (*e*) the colonies on receiving the royal charters, were invested with a *political character*, by which they succeeded to all the territorial interests, which had previously belonged to the sovereign power of the parent country. These charters, it is to be observed, were in the nature of *grants*, and were conferred by the king, on the idea that he was proprietor. (*f*) But as they respectively created *governments*, they were

(*e*) Cowp. Rep. 213.

(*f*) The Colonial governments of this country were of three kinds: first, *Charter* governments, by which the powers of legislation were vested in a governor, council, and assembly, chosen by the people. Of this kind were the governments of Rhode-Island and Connecticut. Secondly, *Proprietary* governments, in which the proprietor of the province was governor; who generally resided in England, and administered the government by a deputy of his own appointment; the assembly only being chosen by the people. Such were the governments of Pennsylvania and Maryland, and originally of New-Jersey and Carolina. Thirdly, *Royal* governments, where the governor and council were appointed by the Crown, and the assembly by the people. Of this kind, were the governments of New-Hampshire, Massachusetts, New-York, New-Jersey (after the year 1702) Virginia, the Carolinas (after the resignation of the proprietors in 1728.) and Georgia.

not construed as his other grants were; that is as not excluding arms of the sea, &c. but as *including* them. And thus the governments of the several colonies had ample authority to alter the established law with regard to their tide waters, or to grant an exclusive property therein, at their discretion.

If any doubt could be entertained on general principles, as to the property of the tide waters of this country being in the king before the charters were granted, it will be removed by referring to the charters. What is particularly alluded to, is the reservation of the right of fishery, which, (as will be shewn, in the following chapter,) is contained in several of the charters; the object of which, was to prescribe how far this important and, *prima facie* public right, might be restrained by any colonial enactment. By a reservation of this kind, it is clear that the king considered himself as the undoubted and legal proprietor of the tide waters; for if he had not thus considered, then to qualify his grants by such a reservation was manifestly absurd.

The property then of the tide waters of this country being in the Crown of Great Britain, previously to their alienation by charter, they were of course held by him as subject to the public use. There can be no doubt, therefore, that before the charters were granted, the arms, inlets and creeks of the sea of this country were public and common, and consequently could not be taken up or appropriated by any individual or corporation. Those to whom house lots for instance were granted, were the proprietors only to high water mark. (*g*)

It may be added, that not only the king as grantor, but also the *grantees*, that is the colonists, recognized the principles of the common law of England, as applicable to the tide waters of their newly acquired territory. This is most clearly indicated by an exercise of sovereign power (which appears among the earliest legislative acts of Massachusetts, after its charter was granted) with respect to the *shore*, or *flats of coves*, &c. The enactment alluded to was made in 1641, and transferred the public right to the soil flowed by the tide, with certain conditions and limitations, to the owners of the adjacent upland. (*h*)

It has been suggested, however, that by those grants which were made by the *Indians* (before the charters were granted) of the territory which included arms of the sea, &c. a right of property in such waters was transferred to the grantees, independent of the Crown. A grant of this kind, and under like circumstances, was made to the early settlers of Rhode-Island. In considering the effect of a grant so made, as it relates to the right

(*g*) Commonwealth *v.* Charlestown, App. 48.

(*h*) Anc. charters, &c. of Mass.

of property in salt and tide waters, it is proper to advert in the first place to the nature of Indian grants generally.

It was not unusual at the period of the early settlement of this country, for the European emigrants to purchase of the natives the land which they occupied. This seems, however, to have been a measure of policy which was resorted to *merely* with the view of avoiding hostilities. And the purchase of William Penn, which was the most remarkable transaction of the kind, was not considered to augment the strength of the title he had acquired by discovery. (*i*) Indeed it has been the established law among all civilized nations, that the American Indians were not to be regarded as independent communities, who had that fixed and permanent property in the soil, which is capable of alienation to private individuals. (*j*) All the treaties and negotiations also between the powers of Europe and the American continent, from the treaty of Utrecht in 1713, to the treaty of Ghent in 1814, have uniformly recognized the principle just mentioned, and have entirely disregarded the supposed right of the Indians to the territory included within their jurisdictional limits. (*k*)

(*i*) Penn *v.* Lord Baltimore, 1 Ves. 445.

(*j*) 2 Ruth. Ins. 29. Jefferson's Notes 126. Smith's Hist N. Y. 35. Montesq. Spir. Laws 1. 18. c. 11. 12. 13.

(*k*) An. Reg. 56. 233. Niles' Reg. 220

What is completely decisive, however, of the point now under consideration is, the case of Johnson *v.* M'Intosh, in the Supreme Court of the United States. In this case, the validity and effect of Indian grants was very fully discussed, and it was therein deliberately determined by Mr. Ch. J. Marshall, that a title to lands made by Indian tribes or nations, could not be recognized in the courts of this country. (*l*)

In the case of the Mohegan Indians, also, (which depended on the nature and extent of the reservations made by these Indians in their several deeds and treaties, and on the violation, by the colony, of rights thus reserved and secured) no assertion can be perceived that individuals might obtain a complete and valid title from the Indians. (*m*)

But there are some expressions contained in the Rhode-Island charter, and also in a letter addressed to the governors of the neighboring colonies by the king's command, which indicate the *royal approbation* of the title acquired from the Indians, and which therefore next demand attention.

The charter of Rhode-Island recites " that the said John Clark and others had transplanted themselves into the midst of the Indian nations, *and were seized and possessed, by purchase and consent of the said natives, to their full content of such lands.*

(*l*) Whea. 543.

(*m*) Ib.

islands, rivers, harbors and roads as are very convenient," &c. And the letter recites, "that Thomas Chiffinch and others having in the right of Major Asperton a just propriety in the Narragansett country, *by grants from the native princes of that country*, and being desirous to improve it into an English colony, &c. To determine the true meaning of these expressions, it may be proper to refer to the circumstances under which they were used. At or about the period when the Plymouth company surrendered their charter to the Crown, (1635) Roger Williams and his followers, on account of the religious dissensions in Massachusetts, came to what is now called "Rhode-Island and Providence Plantations," and purchased lands from the Indians.

The English government being too much occupied at home to bestow its attention on this new acquisition of their subjects, there existed no authority to arrest the settlement of the country, and if the Indian title was obtained, there was nobody to assert the title of the Crown. Under these circumstances, the Rhode-Island settlement was resorted to by many new adventurers, who with the former settlers acquired separate property in lands which they cultivated and improved, and who established a government among themselves, which no power in America could legally dispute. On the restoration of Charles II. this small society hastened to *acknowledge his authority*, and to solicit his approbation of their title to the soil, and to their jurisdiction over the country. A charter from the king, was afterwards granted, containing the recital before mentioned.

Under such circumstances, the most rational construction of the recognition by the king, of the Indian grant to the inhabitants of Rhode-Island, certainly appears to be, that they might retain and enjoy the territory they had purchased of the natives, according to the rules and provisions of the law of England; that is, that "the lands and islands" were to be held as private property, and the "rivers, harbors and roads," were to be enjoyed in common, until otherwise provided by the legislature; with the exception only of fresh rivers, which always belong to, and are transferred with the land over which they pass. And what appears conclusive on the subject, is, that although the king assented to the grant made by the natives, yet he at the same time asserted his prerogative in all the tide waters, by reserving to his subjects generally the right of fishery therein. The nature and extent of this reservation is more particularly noticed in the next succeeding chapter.

If the position, however, could be established, that by virtue of the Indian grant and the recognition thereof by the king, the tide waters included within the limits of the grant were made subservient to private ownership, it would then follow, that the grantee of every lot which was bounded by the water, held to the middle of the channel. In such a case, the same rule precisely would apply, as is applicable to fresh and inland streams; which is, that a man whose land is bounded by a river, holds to the *filum aquæ*, or central line of such river. The result of this position, therefore, if established, would be that the soil of Providence harbor, and of the other tide waters included within the limits of the Indian grant, are, by legal construction, vested in the owners of the adjoining land, in proportion to their respective interests. Thus in the State of New-Jersey, where the original grant of its territory by Charles II. was such as to convey the right of property in all the tide waters, every person whose land in that State, is bounded on a *bay*, for instance, has the undisputed right of property in the soil, *usque ad filum aquæ*, or to the middle of the bay, which is subject only to the *jus publicum* of navigation. (*n*)

Let us now advert to the construction and application which the common law with regard to the sea, &c. has received from the courts of this country since the period of the revolution.

In the supreme court of Massachusetts, there

(*n*) Vid. the Charter of New-Jersey, fully considered in the following chapter.

was an action of trespass for carrying a vessel through the plaintiff's dam, which was erected under a vote of the town of Scituate, and which flowed a landing place where vessels were usually built. The defendant justified under the *common right* to pass on such waters, and the court held that it was a good justification. (*o*)

Another precedent of the same court, was where an inhabitant of Salem was indicted for a nuisance in erecting a wharf in Salem harbor, and extending it beyond the limits proscribed by the old colony law above referred to, by which the navigation was affected. He was ordered to pay a small fine, and the precept to abate the nuisance was stayed on his engagement to do it himself. (*p*)

In the case of the inhabitants of Arundel *v.* M'Culloch, in Massachusetts, the court say, "it is an unquestionable principle of the common law, that all navigable waters belong to the sovereign, or in other words to the *public*, and *that no individual can appropriate them to his own use, or confine or obstruct them.*" (*q*)

In the case of Adams *v.* Frothingham, in the same State, the principle was recognized by the court, that at common law all the *soil* and *waters* in the tide rivers or waters belong to the king in

(*o*) Sul. on Land, Tit. 286.

(*p*) Ib.

(*q*) Inhabitants of Arundel *v.* M'Culloch. App. 96.

England, and to the government here, below high-water mark; *and that therefore towns and proprietors in this country owned their lands only to high-water mark, and not below it.* (*r*)

In the recent case of the Commonwealth *v.* Charlestown, in the same State, Mr. Ch. J. Parker said, "by the common law it is clear that all arms of the sea, coves, creeks, &c. where the tide ebbs and flows, are the property of the sovereign, unless appropriated by some subject, by virtue of a grant, or by prescriptive right, which is founded on the supposition of a grant. The right, however, of fishing in such places, or sailing over them in boats, *is common to all the subjects*, but liable to be restrained and regulated by the sovereign power." (*s*)

In the State of New-York, the same principle has not only been recognized by the courts as to the sovereign and public right of property in all the tide waters and soil thereof; but it has also been decided by the supreme court of that State, that no separate and exclusive right to the same, can be maintained by any town, by virtue of an act of the legislature which extends the limits of the town over such waters.

Thus in Palmer *v.* Hicks, (*t*) in error; Hicks as

(*r*) 3 Adams *v.* Frothingham, App. 1.

(*s*) Commonwealth *v.* Charlestown, App. 48.

(*t*) Palmer *v.* Hicks, App. 123.

supervisor of the town of Flushing, in the court below, brought an action of debt against Palmer, the plaintiff in error, for the penalty prescribed by "regulation of the town, by which it was ordered that no person should be allowed to *rake clams* within the boundary line of said town. The plaintiff below averred, that the place where the raking of clams was thus prohibited was in the town of Flushing, and was *the property of the freeholders and inhabitants of the town*, and that Palmer, the plaintiff in error, did rake clams within the bounds of the town, whereby an action had accrued. That the place where the clams were raked, by the plaintiff in error, was within the town of Flushing, was admitted. But the objection of the plaintiff in error, was that *the town of Flushing had no right to pass a law to regulate the taking of clams. Per curiam.* "The town of Flushing *must shew a right of property* to the lands in the bay, in order to entitle them to make rules to regulate the use of those lands. We will not presume a grant of lands under navigable waters, to the owners of the adjacent soil, without evidence of long exclusive possession and use to warrant such presumption. No grant has been shewn, *nor was any fact proved, from which a grant was to be presumed.* The act extending the bounds of the town over the bay and into the sound or East river, so as to include the islands southward to the main channel, was merely for the purpose of *jurisdiction, and is no evidence of a grant of property in the soil covered by the water.* All the ground under the navigable waters of the Hudson river, is within the boundaries of some town, for the purposes of civil and criminal jurisdiction; but it does not follow that the lands under the water, belong to the towns situated on the river. The judgment below must be reversed."

It was also adjudged in the same State, that an act of the legislature which empowered the city of New-York to regulate wharves, &c contained no implied grant of the soil under the water. (*u*)

In the court of *Oyer and Terminer* at Philadelphia, in 1785, in the case of Respublica *v.* Caldwell, an indictment was sustained for the erection of a wharf, on the ground of its being an encroachment upon the public property. (*v*)

In Connecticut, the taking of fish between high and low-water mark was adjudged to be a *common right.* (*w*)

The principle of the common law upon which the public right to the free navigation of salt and tide waters rests, has never been controverted in this country; and it is clear that no power less

(*u*) Mayor, *&c.* of New-York *v.* Scott, App. 99.

(*v*) Respublica *v.* Caldwell, App. 126. and vid. the case considered at large in chap. 8.

(*w*) Peck *v.* Lockwood, App. 116.

than the legislature, can authorize any use of such waters inconsistent with this right. Upon this principle it is that so many acts of the legislature have been made, authorizing the building of bridges over tide and navigable waters. (*x*)

These judicial determinations and opinions, it will be perceived, are in accordance, so far as they go, with the principles laid down in the preceding chapter, as to the sovereign and public right to the arms and inlets of the sea, and to the soil and shores thereof. But in most of the Atlantic States, the common law doctrine has been in some respects very materially altered and modified by *statutes*, *grants* and *usage*. These alterations and modifications will be more particularly noticed in chapters vii. and viii.

The common law doctrine that the right of fishery gives no right or interest in the adjoining land, has also been recognized in this country, as it was laid down in the preceding chapter. This will appear by the case of Cortelyou *v.* Van Brundt (*y*) in the State of New-York, and the case of Coolidge *v.* Williams (*z*) in Massachusetts.

In White *v.* Whittier, also cited in the abridgment of Mr. Dane (*a*) the defendant claimed the

(*x*) Commonwealth *v.* Charlestown, App. 48. In. of Arundel *v.* M'Culloch, App. 96. Post *v.* Munn, App. 110.

(*y*) Cortelyou *v.* Van Brundt, App. 63.

(*z*) Coolidge *v.* Williams, App. 59.

(*a*) 2 Dane's Abr. 702.

right of going over the plaintiff's land to the Merrimack river, but he relied on prescription, and also that he had a wharf on the river, and therefore a way of necessity to it, and no right of way was pleaded as incident to the right of fishery.

The next question which is suggested by the subject of this chapter, is, how far the right of property in the tide waters of the several Atlantic States is affected by the powers given to the general government.

By virtue of the royal charters (as has been shewn) the colonial legislatures of this country were invested with the same right of property in the tide waters included within their respective jurisdictional limits, which, anterior to the charters, was in the British sovereign. Of this right there has been no relinquishment to the general government of the United States—though by the very act of confederation, it may be fairly implied, that so far as it relates to *navigation*, the tide waters of every State were to be free and open to the citizens of all the States. And by the Constitution, (art 1, sect. 8,) power is expressly delegated to Congress "to regulate commerce among the several States." Subject to this general liberty of navigation, and to this power of Congress to superintend the commercial interests, the Atlantic States may be said to retain the same proprietary interest in their water, which was derived from the charters of the king of Great-Britain; inasmuch as it has never been granted, and inasmuch as it is provided by the amendment to the Constitution (art. 10) that "the powers not delegated to the United States by the Constitution, nor prohibited by it to the States, are reserved to the States respectively."

The several Atlantic States may therefore be considered with regard to their tide waters, to correspond, in relation to the general government, to an individual who has acquired the right of soil in an arm of the sea by a grant from the sovereign power. For, in the latter case, the public are entitled to an easement in such arm of the sea, for the transportation of goods, merchandise, &c. in boats, vessels, &c.; and the sovereign power may prescribe rules to preserve this public easement unimpaired. No person, however, except the grantee of the soil himself has a right to appropriate any part of the soil to his own use; and even the grantee cannot so exercise his right of property as to injure the navigation, any more than the person who has the fee simple of a road is authorized to obstruct its passage. Or, as it is expressed by Lord Hale, (*b*) "the *jus privatum* of the proprietor is subject to the *jus publicum* of the community." So the *jus privatum* of each State, in its tide waters, (or in other words the right of property therein con-

(*b*) Harg. Tracts. 32. Vide also chap. 6.

ferred by the charters) is subject to the *jus publicum* of the United States, which is a free and uninterrupted passage for all the citizens of the United States. The government of the United States, it is true, possess to a certain extent, the right of *empire and jurisdiction*, over the waters of the whole country. But the subject now under consideration is the *right of property*. And it appears that this right of property was given to the States by the king, when they were his colonies, and that it is still retained. And it being still retained, Congress can have no other power to interfere with it, than the one above-mentioned. And Congress not being authorized to interfere with it, except only to preserve a freedom of navigation, it follows, *a fortiori*, that they cannot interfere with it in any State, to the particular injury of such State.

CHAPTER III.

THE PUBLIC RIGHT OF FISHERY IN THE SEVERAL STATES, HOW AFFECTED BY THE ROYAL CHARTERS.

It has been shewn, that before the charters were granted to the respective colonies, the right of fishery in the salt waters of each, belonged, of common right, to all the king's subjects indiscriminately. This right in some of the charters was expressly reserved, in its full extent; in others, but partially reserved, and in others again, there was no reservation. They in fact may be arranged as follows:

First. The charters which contained a reservation of the right of fishery to all the king's subjects, without exception.

Secondly. The charters which contained a reservation of this right, in favonr only of particular subjects.

Thirdly. The charters which contained no reservation.

I. In the charters to the colonies of New-England, was reserved to the *king's subjects*, " the trade of fishing upon the coasts of New-England, in the seas thereto adjoining, or in *any arms of the said seas*, or *salt water rivers*, where they have been accustomed to fish." These are the words made use of, and they clearly amount to a reservation to *all* English subjects of the common right to fish, so that the subjects of one colony had still an undoubted right to fish in the salt waters of the other colonies. By the revolution, the remaining British subjects lost the right so reserved, and it of course became the common right of the people of the United States. And by the treaty of peace, between this country and Great-Britain, the subjects of neither nation have a right to fish in the waters of the other.

As to the expression, "they have been accustomed to fish," how far it is applicable, must always remain a question of fact. There can, however, be but little doubt, but that the people of one State have a right to fish in the salt waters of another State, in the charter of which the reservation of the right was general. There can be but little doubt, for instance, but that the inhabitants of Rhode-Island may lawfully fish on the sea-coasts of Massachusetts, though they may be excluded from fishing in the *counties* thereof by the general court of Massachusetts.

In the charter of Charles II. to Roger Williams, and the inhabitants of the Rhode-Island colony, the king relinquished his prerogative right to whales and sturgeons.

II. In the charter granted to lord Baltimore, was contained the following saving or exception, "saving always to us, our heirs and successors, and to all the subjects of our realms of *England* and *Ireland*, of us, our heirs and successors, the liberty of fishing for sea fish," &c. (*a*) Here it will be observed, the reservation is limited to the subjects of the *realms of England and Ireland.* Accordingly it became a question in Maryland, whether the inhabitants of that State, or of any part of America, were entitled to the right of fishing, so saved and excepted in lord Baltimore's charter. This question was proposed to Daniel Dulany, Esq. in the year 1768, (who was a very able and learned lawyer, and at one time the Attorney General in Maryland,) for his opinion. The opinion he gave, may be found in the Appendix of the first volume of the Reports of *Harris & M'Henry*, p. 564; the most material part of which, is as follows:

"The term '*regnum*,' in the original charter, or *realm*, does not extend to America, in the proper and legal signification of the word, nor could it be intended to extend to America."

"Maryland is no part of the realm or kingdom of England, but is a part of its *royalty*, or of the dominions belonging to it; realm or kingdom is that which gives to the head, or governor the title or denomination of "king."

(*a*) Vid. the Charter, Sect. 16.

"The people of Maryland are the subjects of the king of England, not his subjects of or in the realm, or kingdom of England, but in the dominions belonging to it. This is the proper and strict sense of the words, and corresponds with the nature and regular operation of a saving or exception."

"When the charter of the Province was framed, it was thought that extensive fisheries might be carried on here, as a matter of great consequence in the national trade and navigation. As extensive legislative authority was conferred by the charter, under which, regulations might have been made, (if not controlled by the saving) less favorable to the *English* and *Irish*, than the inhabitants here; but it is not to be supposed that acts of assembly would be wanting, to put the people here upon as good a footing, as any other, and therefore there seems to be very little reason for the notion, that the distinction is unfavorable to the people of Maryland, when it only imports that the liberty is secured to one, against the attempts of the other, and yet leaves to the latter the right of exercising it, in what manner they please, not affecting the liberty of the former, if the provincial legislature should think it for the public benefit. And since an act of assembly may confer the same liberty and privilege to the inhabitants of Maryland, that is contained in the saving, may regulate, restrain or control it, as the general interest may require, I apprehend that the saving is rather favorable to the inhabitants here than otherwise, according to the above interpretation."

Admitting this exposition of Mr. Dulany to be correct, which seems too obvious to be disputed, however favorable it may be to the people of Maryland, it must be regarded as unfavorable to the inhabitants of the other States. For as the inhabitants of the other States were not originally included in the saving, and the reservation not extending to them, they were of course debarred the liberty of exercising any piscarial privilege afforded by the waters of Maryland. And it would therefore, be superfluous for the legislature of Maryland, to enact any law to prohibit the citizens of the other States from fishing in its waters. In fact, as the persons to whom the reservation was confined, lost the right thus reserved by the revolution, it became the common right of the inhabitants of Maryland only.

III. By the grant of Charles II. to his brother the Duke of York, of the territory including what is now *New-Jersey*, he conveys to his said brother, his heirs and assigns, "all the said lands islands, soils, *harbors*, *rivers*, *waters*, *fishings*, *&c.* and all other *royalties*, profits, &c. to the same belonging and appertaining, *together* with full powers of government." Here then was as full and ample a grant as the king had authority to make, containing no saving, exception or reservation whatever.

In June following, the Duke of York granted all the tract of land which now forms the State of New-Jersey, to *lord Berkley* and *Sir George Carteret,* their heirs, &c. with all *waters, &c.* as in the grant of Charles II.

From the two aforesaid grantees of the Duke of York, or their assigns, all *titles* in New-Jersey are derived, by patent, deed or survey. These grants describe the premises, and convey the fee, with all the rights and privileges of the original proprietors. And lands bounding on rivers, bays and streams of water, are usually described as bounded by the same. This description of boundary is common to all waters, whether fresh or tide waters.

The construction in New-Jersey, as to the *extent* of such boundaries, has always been the same, both as to fresh and tide water rivers, in respect of *private* ownership and privileges, viz: that the middle of the channel was the line of boundary. Hence, the citizens of other States, are not only excluded from fishing in the waters of New-Jersey, but persons whose lands are bounded thereon, have always claimed and exercised the right of *several,* or exclusive fishery in front of their lands, as well in rivers where the tide flows and reflows, as in fresh and inland rivers. And this right of exclusive fishery has, from the earliest times been enjoyed and *alienated* like any other species of property. It descends to heirs, is devised, conveyed, leased and partitioned, and subject to dower, curtesy and all the incidents of estates in fee. Trespass is sustained by the courts for intrusions thereof, and ejectments on the possession and title, as in other real property.

The legislature, however, in order to preserve the uninterrupted privilege of navigation, in creeks, rivers, &c. have declared them to be *public highways*, and enacted penalties against obstructing them. (*b*)

On the whole, it may be said, that in New-Jersey, by virtue of the original charter of Charles II. the proprietors of lands bounded on rivers or waters, of whatever description, have the exclusive legal right to the possession and enjoyment of *fisheries* established in front of, and on their own shores. But that in the exercise of this right of occupation and enjoyment, they are regulated from time to time by acts of the legislature. With regard to these regulations, it may be observed that they are all *affirmative* of the right of several fishery, in front of and within the lines of land of the respective owners, or occupiers, bounding on the river.

The laws of the State also regulate the manner in which the owners, or occupiers of fisheries shall determine the *boundaries* of their respective fisheries, and require a description of them to be en-

(*b*) Vid. 4 An. Law Reg. 1286.

tered in the clerk's offices of the several counties. (*a*)

Thus it appears, that in ascertaining and defining the exact limits of the rights and interests connected with the arms and inlets of the sea, to which the States and the individuals of this country are entitled, it is in a great degree essential, to have recourse to the charters of government they received, when they were dependant on the Crown of Great-Britain.

CHAPTER IV.

WHAT IS MEANT BY AN ARM OF THE SEA, AND BY THE SHORE; AND THE RULE FOR DETERMINING HIGH WATER MARK CONSIDERED.

Arm of the Sea. It was said by Lord Coke, in Sir Henry Constable's case, (*b*) that "an arm of the sea is where *the sea or tide flows and reflows.*" By this definition, it appears that all the branches of the main ocean, or those parts of the sea which extend into some inlet or angle of the land, are

(*a*) Vid. 4 Ann. Law Reg. 1290.

(*b*) Sir Henry Constable's case. App. 140.

arms of the sea. Hence they may properly be said to include what are commonly called *bays*, *roads*, *creeks*, *coves*, &c. And as they are considered to extend as far into the interior of a country, as the water of fresh rivers is propelled backward by the ingress and pressure of the tide, a *navigable river* is also considered as an arm of the sea, and is so defined by Lord Hale, in his treatise before referred to. But as there is an important distinction between the legal and the popular import of the term "*navigable*," as applied to rivers, and as we are in the course of the present discussion, to consider the term with regard only to its legal import, it becomes necessary to explain this distinction.

In the case of the *Royal Fishery of the river Banne in Ireland* (*c*) it was resolved as follows: "There are two kinds of rivers, navigable and not navigable. Every navigable river, so high as the sea ebbs and flows in it, is a royal river, and the fishery of it is a royal fishery, and belongs to the king by his prerogative; but in every other river not navigable, and in the fishery of such river, the ter-tenants on each side have an interest of common right. The reason for which is, so high as the sea flows and ebbs, it participates of the nature of the sea, and is said to be a branch of the sea, so far as it flows.

Indeed, no part of the law is more clearly set-

(*c*) Case of the Royal Fishery, App. 35.

tled, than that to determine, whether or not, a river is navigable, a regard must be had to the ebbing and flowing of the tide. For those streams of water which are of public use for inland navigation, *above* the line to which the tide ordinarily flows, are strictly not navigable, though they are *public highways*, for the purposes of transportation; and nuisances and obstructions therein may be punished by indictment. In the latter, it will be observed, the bed and shores of the river are the exclusive property of the owners of the adjoining banks; but in the former, the soil thereof is the property of the sovereign, and subject to the public use. The line of demarcation between the navigable river and the public highway, or in other words, between the public and private right to the soil, being established by the tide at high-water. (*c*)

The foregoing distinction, which has never been controverted in England, and which has been recognized in many cases in this country, (*d*) it will be proper to remember whenever the term "navigable river" may be mentioned, in the course of the treatise.

(*c*) Harg. Tracts, 8, 9. Callis 78. Carter *v.* Murcot, App. 90. Miles *v.* Rose, App. 109.

(*d*) The cases on the subject in this country, are Adams *v.* Pease, 2 Conn. Rep. 481. Shaw *v.* Crawford, 10 Johns. 236. Palmer *v.* Mulligan, 3 Caines, 307. People *v.* Platt, 17 Johns. 195. Hooker *v.* Cummings, 20 Johns. 90.

It should also be recollected that although the water is fresh at full tide, yet the river is still an arm of the sea, if it *flows and reflows.* For it was once ingeniously urged, in Rex *v.* Smith, (*e*) that the river Thames above London bridge, was not navigable, (although it was flowing and reflowing) as the tide beyond that limit was occasioned by the pressure and accumulation backward of the fresh water. But this distinction was by lord Mansfield pronounced new and inadmissible. The river Connecticut, for example, is consequently for a considerable distance from the sound, and above where the water is salt, an arm of the sea, and as such, the bed and shores thereof, as well as the water itself, are *prima facie*, public.

Notwithstanding the foregoing distinction is so well settled both in England and in this country, yet it was positively rejected in Pennsylvania. What is particularly alluded to is the case of Carson *v.* Blazer, (*f*) in which the court decided that the river *Susquehannah* in that part of it where there was no flow of the tide, had all the attributes of an arm of the sea, and that the soil thereof was not the property of the owners of the adjoining banks, but of the Commonwealth. Or, in other words, that it was not only a public highway, but *navigable.* This decision, however, seems in a great

(*e*) Rex *v.* Smith, App. 180.
(*f*) 2 Binney, 475.

measure to have been founded on a particular custom and usage of the State.

Shore. We next proceed to consider what is to be understood by *the shore* of the sea and its arms. In common language, the word "shore" is used to convey the idea of land which is in the vicinity of the water. Callis in his reading upon the statute of sewers, in describing the shore, introduces the verse from the 13th chapter of St. Matthew, wherein it is said, our Saviour "went into a ship and sat there, and the whole multitude sat on *the shore*, and he spake unto them." (*g*) From this passage the learned author infers, 1st. That the shore was the *dry land*, because they sat thereon. 2d. That it was a great quantity of ground, for thereon was a multitude of people. 3d. That it was near the brink of the water, because they heard Jesus speak unto them from the ship.

The shore of the sea and its arms was by the civilians, denominated *Littus maris.* Both the English and Latin names, therefore, appear to be derived from the sea itself, as participating *more* of its nature than of the land, though it may be said to participate in some measure of both. In legal construction, it may be said to be *that space of land which is alternately covered and left dry, by the rising and falling of the tide.* Or, in other words, that space of land which is between the

(*g*) Callis, 55.

high and low-water marks. (*h*) And this space as has been shewn, is *prima facie*, public.

How high-water is determined. The next question then is, what is to be considered as the high-water mark; as it is well known, that the tide rises much higher on some occasions, and at some seasons of the year, than it usually does.

By the Roman law, it seems, high-water mark was determined by the highest tides, and the shore was understood to include the land *as far as the greatest wave extended itself in the winter.* Thus in the Institutes, *Est autem littus maris, quatenus hibernus, fluctus maximus excurrit.* (*k*) And in the Digest, *Littus publicum est eatenus qua maxime fluctus exaestuat.* (*l*) In a note in Callis on sewers (*m*) also, it is said "all the space which is covered and discovered during the new and full moon, and as far as the tide extends at the high flood of March, shall be reputed to be the sea shore." This note refers to the ordinance of Lewis XIV. (*n*)

But by the common law, as it is laid down by lord Hale (*o*) and others, the soil which is overflowed by high spring tides, or by extraordinary tides at

(*h*) Harg. Tracts, 12.
(*k*) Ins. L. 2. T. 1. s. 3.
(*l*) Dig. L. 50. T. 16. s. 112.
(*m*) Callis, 55.
(*n*) Sea Laws, 347.
(*o*) Harg. Tracts. 12.

any time, does not properly come under the denomination of shore, and consequently the sovereign and public right is not of that large extent. The rule which lord Hale lays down and which is now understood to prevail, is that the shore is that land only which is usually overflowed *by ordinary tides*. And this he says was ruled in the exchequer chamber about 12 Car. 1. on prosecution by information for lands in the county of Norfolk, also in Sir Edward Heron's case, 15 Car. B. R. and also in an *ejectione firmæ* for the town of Cowes in the Isle of Wight, 17 Car. 2.

The rule as advanced by lord Hale, is not only well established in England, but has been recognized in this country. In the case of Storer *v.* Freeman, in Massachusetts, (*o*) one of the questions was as to a boundary mentioned in a conveyance which was a line running *to the shore*, and thence *by the shore;* and whether the land (by virtue of such description) was conveyed between high and low-water mark. "The sea shore," (Mr. C. J. Parsons observed,) "must be understood to be the margin of the sea, *in its usual and ordinary state*. Thus when the tide is out, (he continued) low-water mark is the margin of the sea; and when the sea is full, the margin is high-water mark. *The sea shore is therefore all the ground between the ordinary high-water mark and low-water mark.*"

(*o*) Storer *v.* Freeman, App. 149.

So in the case of the Commonwealth *v.* Charlestown, (*p*) the court understood the rule of the common law to be that the sovereign and public right extended only to ordinary high-water mark.

It was contended in argument in the case of Cortelyou *v.* Van Brundt, in the supreme court of the State of New-York, (*q*) that the rule of the civil law as above mentioned, was the proper rule to be adopted in that State. The reason offered was, that the State was granted by the Dutch government, and at the time of the grant, the civil law prevailed in the *Seven United Provinces.* The court, however, recognized the doctrine of the common law as laid down by lord Hale.

It may be considered, therefore, as perfectly well established that the shore is the land which lies between the high and low-water marks in *ordinary tides*, and that the ordinary high-water mark is the line of boundary between the right of the public and the property of the conterminous or adjoining upland. This is unquestionably the best rule which could be adopted. For if the shore was supposed to include any part of the land covered by the sea, it would then have no definite limit in that direction. So on the other hand, if it was supposed to include any part of the upland, there would be the same objection. The ordinary high-

(*p*) Commonwealth *v.* Charlestown, App. 48.

(*q*) Cortelyou *v.* Van Brundt, App. 63.

water mark, in fact, prescribes the most definite line of demarcation between public and private rights, and thus has the effect to promote (in the language of Sir Wm. Blackstone, (*r*) "the grand ends of civil society and the peace and security of individuals, by assigning to every thing capable of ownership a legal and determinate owner."

CHAPTER V.

OF MARINE INCREASES AND THE RIGHT TO SEA WEED.

THERE are four kinds of marine increases, or additions made to the land of the sea.

1. The first is the increase *per projectionem*, which happens when the sea by casting up sand and other substances makes an accession to the land, and shuts itself out beyond its former limits. As a general rule, the accession so made belongs to the sovereign, as it is no more than a part and parcel of the *fundus maris*, or bottom of the sea, which as has been shewn was previously the property of the sovereign. (*a*)

To the above rule, however, there is this impor-

(*r*) 2 Bla. Com. 14.

(*a*) Harg. Tracts, 14. 28. Callis 51. 4 Com. Dig. 418.

tant exception. If the increase is slow and secret, and is so gradually and insensibly occasioned as renders it impossible to perceive how much is added in each moment of time, it then belongs to the proprietor of the land to which the accession is made, who is often denominated the *riparian* proprietor, from the latin *ripa* or bank. This is called *alluvion*; and therefore alluvion may be said to consist only in slow, petty and imperceptible increases. And in such increases it is understood the sovereign has no property, the maxim of the common law being "*de minimis non curat rex.*" Besides which the right to alluvion is founded on the equity, that as the riparian proprietor is exposed to the danger of loss by the impetuosity and sudden encroachment of the sea, he ought as an equivalent to have the chance of gain. (*b*)

The common law on this subject is clearly copied from the civil law. Indeed, Bracton quotes the very words of the Institutes, which are as follow: *Quod per alluvionem agro tuo flumen adjecit jure gentium tibi adquiritur. Est autem alluvio incrementum latens. Per alluvionem autem id videtur adjici quod ita paulatim adjicitur, ut intelligi non possit quantum quoque temporis momento adjiciatur.* (*c*) The literal translation of which is thus, "*what the river adds by alluvion to your estate, becomes yours by the law of nations. Allu-*

(*b*) Ib. and Emans *v.* Trumbull, App. 90.

(*c*) Ins. L. 2. T. 1. s. 20. and Bract. L. 2. Ch. 2.

luvion is a latent increase. That seems to be added by alluvion which is so added by degrees, that you cannot know how much in each moment of time."

The definition of alluvion in the French law corresponds with the one just given. That is to be an increase of land which is made *peu a peu*, or by slow degrees by the earth which the water brings there. *Accroissement de terrien qui se fait peu a peu sur les bords de la mer des fleuves et des rivieres par les terres que l'eau y apporte.* (*d*) But when the augmentation is suddenly made, it belongs to the sovereign as by the common law. "*Il n'en seroit pas de meme d'une augmentation, arrivee, subitement a un heritage par un debordement ou par quelqu' autres cas fortuit. Cette augmentation appartient au roi dans les rivieres navigables et aux seigneurs hauts justiciers dans les rivieres non navigables.*" (*e*)

The case of the Marquis de Bouzols and M. de Chamflour, on the 15th of April, 1774, in one of the Chambers of the Parliament of Paris, and the case between the Chapter of Lucon and M. Champagne, determined on the 22d of February, 1769, turned chiefly on the distinction between augmentations made slowly by alluvion, and those which are suddenly created, and *the first* (it was decided) *belong to the adjacent proprietor*. (*a*)

(*d*) Gugot's Repertoire Universelle, 118.

(*e*) Ib.

(*a*) 5 Amer. Law Journ. 167.

Another case was decided in the Parliament of Paris in 1765. The Marquis of Langeron owned a fief, to which was attached the right of *haute justice* upon the Loire, by virtue of which he claimed all the alluvions on that river, as being attached to his domain. His pretensions were, however, disallowed, and the land formed by the alluvion of the river, was adjudged to the nuns of Marcigny, who claimed it as the *riparian proprietors*. (*h*).

But although to constitute alluvion, the rule is that the increase must be secret and insensible, (*incrementum latens*,) yet this must be supposed to relate to the process of formation. For if it is an increase at all, after it is made, it must of course be discernible and sensible to the eye, or else it could never be made the object either of property, or discussion. To shew, therefore, that an accession made to the land of the riparian proprietor, *per projectionem*, is not alluvion, and is not his property, it is not enough to shew, how extensive the accession has been, but it must be shewn, how much has been deposited *in each moment of time; quantum quoque temporis momento adjiciatur*. In the celebrated controversy respecting the *batture*, at New-Orleans, when it was urged, that the batture was not alluvion, because its increase was perceptible, after every swell of the Mississippi, it elicited from Mr. Livingston the fol-

(*h*) Amer. Law Journ. 167.

lowing very pertinent and elegant reply: "When the ingenious counsel can analyse the different deposits, separate the sands of the Red river, the rich mould of the Missouri from the clay and other various soils which the Mississippi receives from a thousand tributary streams; when he can dive into its turbid eddies, watch the moment of the precious deposit, and date the existence of each stratum of its increase; then this first branch of the authority he has cited may be applicable to his cause." (*i*)

In the case of Adams *v.* Frothingham (*k*) in Massachusetts, it was adjudged that whatever addition is made to shores of rivers, bays, coves, &c. by alluvion from natural causes, or from a union of *natural* and *artificial* causes, belongs to the owners of the shores. This decision was made in reference to the old colony law, that was mentioned in chapter ii. which annexed the flats to the adjacent upland, to the distance of one hundred rods from the high-water mark. And whatever increase happens within these limits, and from whatever cause, is very properly assigned to him who owns the soil, to which the increase is attached.

One of the most important cases ever decided on the subject of alluvion, or perhaps any other sub-

(*i*) Vid. the examination of the Title of the U. States to the Batture, by Edward Livingston, Esq. 2 Hall's Law Journ. 307, and App. 197.

(*k*) Adams *v*. Frothingham, App. 1.

ject of property, either as it relates to the value of the soil in controversy, or to the elaborate, learned and able discussions which it produced, or to the public ferment and excitement which it occasioned, was the case before alluded to, respecting the batture in the city of New-Orleans.

Battures are certain portions of the bed of the river Mississippi, which are left dry when the water is low, and are covered again, either wholly, or in part, by the annual swells. The batture, which was in this case the subject of controversy, was very considerable in extent, and had existed from time immemorial in front of the suburb of St. Mary. But for the aid of the natural depositum of the materials which constituted this batture, it was said, that New-Orleans would probably never have existed, or that it would have been built but very slowly. The earth which it afforded, it was impossible to find elsewhere in the vicinity, so that the whole city, with its levees and streets, was completely dependant on it for its growth, safety, and protection.

The suit was brought in the superior court of the territory of Orleans, by Jean Gravier, against the corporation of New-Orleans. It was a fact of public notoriety, that before the plaintiff set up his claim to the batture, which was in 1804, the inhabitants of New-Orleans had always enjoyed the liberty of gratuitously taking from the batture all the earth which they required for their buildings, and that the Spanish government had ever taken the earth for public uses, such as raising the streets and repairing the levees of the city. It was further proved that the Spanish government and the French government, which had preceded, had always evinced a settled determination to preserve to the inhabitants of New-Orleans, the free use of the batture, so useful and indispensable, not only for obtaining earth there, but to supply various other necessities not less urgent. To have permitted any individual to have appropriated the batture to himself, would have also devoted the population of the city to ravaging epidemics, and been of great detriment to the navigation and commerce. Accordingly, the Spanish government constantly opposed the forming of any establishment on the batture, and at different times caused to be demolished the houses and other buildings which divers persons had ventured to erect there, at different periods.

In this situation of affairs, Louisiana was ceded to the United States. The great increase of commerce which succeeded this change of dominion, rendered it still more necessary to leave the batture free to the public, as it had till then been. This consideration suggested to Gravier, who was the former proprietor of the plantation on which the suburb St. Mary had been formed, the idea of raising a claim, which before he had not thought of, and prompted him to maintain, that *batture being real alluvions, the one in dispute belonged to him, as he had been the proprietor of the land which immediately bounds it.* And the Court declared, that the corporation of New-Orleans was destitute of any legal title against him, and *maintained him in the possession and enjoyment of the batture.*

Although the corporation were by this decision excluded from all kind of right to the batture, yet it did not follow that Gravier was the legitimate proprietor. And it afterwards became a question whether Gravier, as the riparian proprietor, or whether the United States, were entitled to the batture. For the very able arguments and opinions which were given on this question, the reader is referred to 2 Hall's Law Journ. 295. And for the defence of Mr. Jefferson, in taking possession of the batture, when President, in behalf of the United States, and for Mr. Livingston's very able, learned and spirited reply to this defence, the reader is referred to 5 Hall's Law Journ. 1 and 113. (*w*)

2. The second kind of marine increase is *per relictionem*, or by *reliction*, which is an increase by the retreat, or recess of the sea. This in some parts of the world has been known to take place suddenly, and for a very great extent. Lord Hale informs us that "sometimes the ocean, especially

(*w*) Vid. also the opinion of Mr. Livingston as to the right of the U. States, App. 197.

the narrow sea between England and France and the Netherlands, leaves the English shore in a very considerable measure; possibly by reason of some superundation on the other eastern shore." (*h*)

The general rule is, that the land which is thus relicted and left dry, by the receding of the water, is the property of the sovereign, as being a part and parcel of what was previously the demesne of the sovereign. And the *jus proprietatis*, or ownership of the soil which is covered with water, is not changed merely because the water has receded from it. (*i*)

But if the soil when covered with water belonged to a subject, then after it is relicted, it still continues to belong to him. As if an individual has acquired by grant from the sovereign (or by prescription, which supposes a grant,) (*k*) the exclusive right of property in the soil of any arm of the sea, &c. and the water should afterwards recede from it, the soil will still be his. (*l*)

So if an individual has land near the shore, which is inundated by the encroachment of the sea, and is afterwards left dry, he still retains his property therein. Inundations of this kind seldom

(*h*) Harg. Tracts, 30.
(*i*) Ib. 14. 15. 30. 31. 3 Roll. Abr. 168.
(*k*) Vid. Chap. 6.
(*l*) Harg. Tracts, 15.

occur in this part of the world to any considerable extent, and are fortunately much less common than in some parts of Europe. One instance, however, occurred but a few years since, in this country, in which the land for a great space from the shore was flooded by the water from the ocean. What is here alluded to, is the memorable storm and high tide, which happened on the 23d September, 1815, when many warehouses on the sea coasts of New-England and buildings of almost every kind, floated away, and were demolished, and when vessels were driven from their fastenings, and in the town of Providence were seen navigating the streets at the distance of many rods from the ordinary high-water mark. In such cases, no man is considered as losing his property in his land; and on its being left dry, he has the sole right to it. (*m*)

So also an individual whose land is inundated or taken away by the encroachment and violence of the sea, may *regain* the same by his *own art or industry*, and continue his property therein. And this, says lord Hale, "was held by Cooke & Foster, M. 7. Jac. C. B. even when the land was inundated for the space of *forty years*." (*n*)

The two following precedents, in illustration of this subject, are cited by lord Hale.

Rot. Parliamenti 8. *E.* 2. *m.* 23. *pro willielmo*

(*m*) Harg. Tracts.
(*n*) Ib.

Burnello. Philip Burnell, father of William, being seized of the manor of Hacchesham, near Greenwich, died his heir within age during his minority. *Aqua Thamissæ magnam partem terræ et prati manerii prædicti ac aliarum terrarum contiguarum superundavit.* The bishop of Bath and Wells, by agreement with the king, was to stop the breach at his own charges, and was to hold the land for seven years, to reimburse the charges. This he did, and the land was regained and the bishop held the land for his seven years and three years over them. Burnell desired relief for his land against the bishop. The answer was, *Sequatur versus episcopum ad communem legem;* let him proceed against the bishop at common law. Which answer, lord Hale says, would not have been given, if the king had gained any title by the inundation. (*o*)

The other precedent was, *P.* 18. *E.* 2. *Rot.* 174. *B. R.* in which on the same account, one hundred acres of marsh ground, parcel of the manor of Stebunhith, was regained from the Thames and enjoyed accordingly. (*p*)

It will appear, therefore, that in general no new property is acquired in relicted land, and that the former proprietors are only allowed to retain and regain what was previously their own. If the soil

(*o*) Harg. Tracts. 15.

(*p*) Ib.

belonged to the sovereign before the reliction, it is his afterwards. On the other hand, if it had been acquired by a subject when covered with water, it belongs to him after the water has receded from it. And if an individual's land has been inundated, he may regain it by any work which will shut out and exclude the water. And this is not only agreeable to law, but to reason and justice.

But as the rule is that in *slow* and *imperceptible* increases, they accrue to the owner of the land to which they are annexed; it follows that although the soil was originally the property of the sovereign, yet if it is so gradually relicted as not to be observed, it accrues to the owner of the land and not to the sovereign. But a gradual reliction of this kind it would seem can but seldom, if ever, happen, without some degree of *alluvion*. And it has already been shewn, that if the alluvial character predominates, it is regarded as a part of the land with which it has become incorporated.

3. The third kind of marine increase is *per insulam*, or by a newly discovered island arising in the sea, or the arms thereof. Such island is of course, *prima facie*, the property of the sovereign, as it before constituted a part of that soil in which the sovereign has the right of property. For generally, when islands are created, it is either by the desertion of the sea, or by the collection and exaggeration of sand and other substances, which in

process of time become discoverable, as *terra firma* environed by the water. (*q*)

The same exception, however, holds with respect to islands arising in arms and inlets of the sea, as holds in regard to the general rule of acquisition by reliction. That is, although of common right, and in common presumption, they belong to the sovereign, yet when the interest of the soil has been acquired by prescription, or grant by an individual, the island which may happen within the limits of such private ownership, will be vested in the latter. (*r*) If, for instance, the west side of a salt water creek belongs to the estate of the west side, and an island should arise on the west side of the *filum aquæ*, or central line of the channel, the property of the island will belong entirely to the owner of the estate on the west side. And if the east side of the creek belongs to an estate on the east side, *usque filum aquæ*, and an island should happen between the east side of the river and the *filum aquæ*, it will belong to the owner of the estate on the east side. And if an island arises exactly in the middle, it is then to be equally divided; but if one part approaches nearer to one side of the creek than it does to the other, the greater part will belong to the owner of the neighboring estate, according to its approximation thereto. To establish therefore how

(*q*) 2 Bla. Com. 251. Callis 45. Harg. Tracts, 17. 36.
(*r*) Ib.

great an extent of property in the island belongs to the adjoining estates, the vicinity and remoteness of the island to and from the shores are to be the guide to determine. (*s*)

So if the water should by chance environ a part of the upland, and thus form an island; the property of the land so environed and insulated remains unaltered, and continues in him to whom it before appertained. (*t*)

By the Roman law, islands which were created in the sea, &c. became the property of the *first occupant*, the reason of which rule will be understood by referring to what was said with regard to the distinction between the Roman and English laws, in chapter i. Thus it is laid down by Justinian: *Insula, quæ in mari, nata est, (quod raro accidit) occupantis fit, nullius enim esse creditur.* (*u*)

4. The fourth kind of marine increase is *per avulsionem*, or by avulsion. Avulsion is where, by the immediate and manifest force and violence of the water, the soil is taken suddenly from one man's estate, and carried to another's, and hereby a new property is constituted *only* by *acquiescence*. For it is regarded as the property of the first owner, unless it shall have continued on the other's land

(*s*) 2 Bla. Com. 251. Callis 45. Harg. Tracts 17. 36. Swift's Dig. 111.

(*t*) 2 Bla. Com. 251. Callis 45. Harg. Tracts 17. 36.

(*u*) Ins. L. 2. T. 1. s. 22.

for so long a period, that it has coalesced and become incorporated with the soil. (*v*) And the Roman law provided, *that if the impetuosity of a river should sever a part of your estate and adjoin it to that of your neighbor, it is certain that such part will still continue yours.* (*w*)

Sea weed. Whatever is naturally adapted to fertilize the earth, and render it capable of affording an ample remuneration to the husbandman, is, in every enlightened and agricultural community, regarded as of great importance. Hence it is that the marine substance, known by the name of "sea weed," is so very highly valued in this country. This substance is now very generally sought after by all who cultivate the lands in the vicinity of the ocean. And when it is also considered, that along the whole of the vastly extensive range of shore, which intervenes between Maine and Florida, great quantities of this fertilizing material are thrown up and deposited by the flux and reflux of every tide; the question as to *who is entitled to sea weed*, is a question of no inconsiderable interest.

It seems to have been the general rule, that when any substance is thrown from the sea upon the shore, by the operations of nature, the first occupant, if he did not commit a trespass, by going over the adjacent land, is the absolute owner. And by the Roman law, it was expressly provided

(*v*) Bract. 221. Callis 24. 21. 2 Bla. Com. 262.

(*w*) Coop. Just. L. 2. T. 1.

that all substances found on the sea shore, became the property of the finder. Thus it is said in the institutes, "*item lapilli, et gemmæ, et cetera quæ in littore maris inveniuntur, jure maturali statim, inventoris fiunt.* (*x*)

So by the laws of Oleron, (Art. 34.) "If any man happens to find any thing, in the sea, or in the sand on the shore, in floods or in rivers, if it be precious stones, fishes, or *any treasure of the sea, which never belonged to any man in point of property*, it belongs to the first finder." (*i*)

It seems that in Normandy, however, at the time when the ordinance of Lewis XIV. was established, (1681) the right to sea weed when thrown on shore, was claimed both by the owners of the land adjoining the sea, and by the public. (*k*) To prevent all future disputes on the subject by making the law certain, the ordinance provided as follows: "We allow all persons indifferently, in all places and times, to take the *sea ware* cast ashore by the tide upon the sands, and carry it whither they please." (*l*)

Whether or not sea weed thrown on shore, is the property of the owner of the land by the common law, has not been treated of by any writer. In lord Hale's treatise, the only instance in which the

(*x*) Ins. L. 2. T. 1. s. 18.

(*i*) Sea Laws, 164.

(*k*) Ib. 357.

(*l*) Ib.

word *sea weed*, is used, is where he mentions the constant and uninterrupted taking of it by the proprietor of the adjoining estate, as one of the usual means of shewing that the space between high and low-water marks, is a part and parcel of the estate. "The shore" (he says,) "may be part and parcel of a manor, and the evidences to prove this fact, are commonly these; constant and usual fetching gravel and *sea weed* and sea sand, between the high and low-water mark, and licensing others so to do." (*m*) This passage would seem to indicate that the learned author considered the public to be, *prima facie*, entitled to sea weed. For if he had not so considered it, then the circumstance of its being exclusively taken by the lord of the manor, could not be received as a proof of his adverse right of property in the shore.

There are, however, good reasons and good authority for considering the owner of the land contiguous to the shore as having the sole and exclusive right to sea weed, which are as follow:

It is a well established rule of the common law, that if animals *feræ naturæ*, make nests or burrow in the land of any person, and have young ones there, the owner of the land has a property in them, *ex ratione soli*, until they fly or run away. (*n*) If the property of unfledged young birds is then

(*m*) Harg. Tracts, 27.

(*n*) 2 Bla. Com. 393.

assigned to the owner of the land, it would seem, a *fortiori*, that inanimate substances thrown there by nature, like sea weed, must also belong to him.

Again, on the same principle that the proprietor of an estate adjoining the sea has the exclusive right to *sea sand* thrown up by the sea, he has the exclusive right to the *sea weed.* That he has the exclusive right of the former by the common law, may perhaps be inferred from the Stat. 7. Jac. 1. (Harg. Tracts, 26.) which provides, *that the people of Cornwall and Devonshire, may take the sea sand for the improvement of their land, and shall not be hindered by the owners of the land adjoining.* It appears that by this Statute a peculiar privilege is granted to the inhabitants of Devonshire and Cornwall; which peculiar privilege it would have been absurd to grant, if all the people of England had been entitled to it by the common law. If the public then have no right to the sand thrown up by the sea and deposited between high and low-water marks, it follows that they have no right to the sea weed so thrown up and deposited.

Lastly, it has already been shewn, that all the gradual accessions, or *alluvions,* belong to the owner of the soil. Now it is a fact of very general notoriety, that both sea weed and sea sand, thrown up by the sea, are deposited *gradually.* On this principle, it certainly seems no more than proper. to consider sea weed as an incidental advantage, arising from the drift of the sea, to which the owner of the upland has a perfect and exclusive right. And as he is exposed to the loss, by inundations, so he ought to have the benefit.

The latter view of the subject is fully supported by the case of Emans *v.* Trumbull, (*o*) in the supreme court of the State of New-York, when the question, who had the right to sea weed, was directly before the court. The opinion of the court was given by Mr. C. J. Kent, in the following words: "Sea weed thrown up by the sea may be considered as one of those marine increases arising by slow degrees, and according to the rule of the common law, belongs to the owner of the soil. The rule is, if the increase be by small and almost imperceptible degrees, it goes to the owner of the land; but if it be sudden and considerable, it belongs to the sovereign. Sea weed is supposed to have accumulated gradually. The slow increase, and its usefulness as a manure, and as a protection to the bank, will upon every just and equitable principle, vest the property of the weed in the owner of the land. It forms a reasonable compensation to him for the gradual encroachments of the sea, to which other parts of his estate may be exposed. This is the sound reason for vesting the maritime increments in the proprietor of the adjoining land. The *jus alluvionis*, in this

(*o*) Emans *v.* Trumbull, App. 90.

respect, ought to receive a liberal encouragement in favor of private right."

As the principles upon which the above case was determined, appear so obviously rational, and at the same time so perfectly conformable to the rules and analogies of the law, and as the question in controversy, was decided by a court of such great authority, and by one of the most eminently legal men of the age; the decision will, no doubt, be received as fully establishing the law in this country, with regard to the right to sea weed.

CHAPTER VI.

RIGHTS ACQUIRABLE IN SALT AND TIDE WATERS, AND IN THE SOIL AND SHORES THEREOF, BY PRESCRIPTION AND CUSTOM, AND BY GRANT.

ALTHOUGH it has been made to appear, that, *prima facie*, the sovereign has the right of property in salt and tide waters, and that they are also for the public use; yet there are many maritime interests to which an exclusive right may be acquired by prescription, custom and grant.

1. *Prescription and custom.* Though prescription and custom mean nearly the same, and are both created by *usage*, yet there is this difference:

the former is merely a *personal* usage, as that A. B. and his ancestors, or those whose estate he hath, have been used time out of mind to enjoy a certain advantage or privilege. Custom, on the other hand, is a *local* usage, that is, relating to a particular *place*, or *district*. The origin and evidence in both are the same, and both must be established on uninterrupted usage, *longa, continua et pacifica.* (*a*)

To constitute a good prescription, or custom, the usage must have been continued *time out of mind*, which in England is considered to be antecedent to the reign of Richard I. (*b*) But in the case of Rust *v.* Low. (*c*) it was held by Mr. C. J. Parsons, that this country has now been settled long enough, to allow of the time necessary, to prove a prescription. Indeed, in England, if a right has been exercised a considerable number of years, the presumption is, that it has existed from time immemorial. On this principle it was decided (in Hill *v.* Smith) (*d*) that *toll* taken for *forty* years was evidence of a prescriptive right. And in Chad *v.* Tilsed (*e*) where an embankment had been continued forty years across a small *bay*, it was held by Burrough, J. that

(*a*) Vid. 1 Bla. Com. 75. 2 do. 263.

(*b*) Ib.

(*c*) 6 Mass. 40.

(*d*) 10 East 476.

(*e*) Chad *v.* Tilsed; App. 43.

though the erection of the bank forty years ago, would not of itself confer a title; yet from such erection unopposed, and the subsequent uniform usage, *prior* usage to the same effect might be presumed, so as to entitle the owner to an action of trespass, *quare clausum fregit.*

As it respects rights of a *private* nature, *twenty* years uninterrupted enjoyment is in general sufficient to create a right, (*f*) as a right of way, the right to divert a water course, and many other incorporeal hereditaments. (*g*) This rule, however, has application to private rights *only*; for the interest of society, requires that the disturbance of privileges of a public nature should be suppressed, though of longer standing. (*h*) Besides, in every case of acquiring a right to an incorporeal hereditament, the use and possession in the first instance are a *usurpation* of the right of some other person, and an action would always lie until the twenty years were elapsed. But in the case of rights relative to the sea, &c. which are common to all, the use and possession of any one person is *lawful*, and the mere lawful exercise of a common right for twenty years, cannot, on any well settled principle, be regarded as conferring any exclusive right. Thus it has been expressly decided, that a right of

(*f*) 2 Wms. Saund. 175. n. (2)

(*g*) Bealy *v.* Shaw, 6 East, 208.

(*h*) Vooght *v.* Winch, 2 Barn. & Ald. 662.

several fishery cannot be acquired in the sea and in navigable rivers, merely by virtue of a quiet and uninterrupted use of twenty years. (*i*)

But by *prescription*, an individual may acquire an exclusive or several fishery in any arm of the sea, &c. or within certain limits in and upon the sea itself. Thus in the case of the Prior of Stoke, P. 4. E. 1. B. R. Surry, cited by Lord Hale (*j*) the Prior brought trespass for fishing in the waters of Sturmer. The defendant justified that he fished in his own waters, in a part of the county of Suffolk, where he and his ancestors were *always accustomed* to fish.

Lord Mansfield, in the case of Carter *v.* Murcot (*k*) said if any one could shew a right by prescription, to fish in an arm of the sea, he may then exercise an exclusive right, though the presumption is against him, unless he *can prove* such a prescriptive right. This doctrine, his Lordship said, was agreeable to what was laid down in Lord Fitzwalter's case. (*l*)

It was on the above principle, that the case of Bagott *v.* Orr (*m*) was decided, in which it was adjudged, that the general right of every subject to fish in arm of the sea, might be abridged, by the

(*i*) Chalker *v.* Dickinson, App. 70.

(*j*) Harg. Tracts, 19.

(*k*) Carter *v.* Murcot, App. 32.

(*l*) Lord Fitzwalter's case, 1 Mod 105.

(*m*) Bagott *v.* Orr, App. 20.

existence of an exclusive right, in some individual.

The same principle is also recognized in the case of the Mayor and Commonalty *v.* Richardson. (*n*) This was trespass for fishing in the plaintiff's fishery, and the defendant pleaded, that the place was an arm of the sea, in which every subject had a right to fish. The plaintiff, in his replication, claimed an exclusive right by prescription, and traversed the general right. The court held that the defendant ought to take issue on the traverse, and ought not to traverse the prescriptive right claimed by the plaintiff: the first traverse being a material one, which put in issue the true question in dispute.

A right of fishery acquired by prescription is divisible; that is, it may be lost as to part, and preserved as to part. Accordingly, it was adjudged in the case of Rogers *v.* Allen, (*o*) that an exclusive right to dredge for *oysters* might subsist in a navigable river, as appertinent to a manor, although the public had the right to the *floating fish*.

In the same case it was ruled, that the prescription must be proved to be as extensive as it is laid. So that if the right is shewn to exist in three out of four places, and not in the fourth, the variance is fatal; notwithstanding the alleged trespass is committed in a part of the water where the sole

(*n*) Mayor, &c. *v.* Richardson, App. 105.

(*o*) Rogers *v.* Allen, App. 136.

and exclusive right of fishery prescribed for, is proved to exist. But if the prescriptive right is shewn to be *more ample* than what is claimed, the party prescribing will not fail in consequence. (*p*)

Though a several fishery in an arm of the sea, may be prescribed for and may pass as a privilege appertinent to an estate, (*q*) yet a prescription for *common* of fishery therein, as appertinent to an estate, is bad. Thus in Ward *v.* Creswell, (*r*) the court held, that as all the subjects of England might of common right fish in the sea, &c. a prescription for it as appertinent to a particular township was void, and as absurd as a prescription would be for travelling the king's highway, or for the use of the air, as appertinent to a particular estate.

Piscarial rights, which are acquired by prescription, are not confined to the mere liberty of fishing, but may also give an interest in the soil, as where weirs are made use of for taking fish; which are of necessity fixed to the soil. The following ancient precedent among others, is cited by lord Hale. (*s*) "The Abbot of Tichfend impleaded the burgesses of Southampton, *quod diripuerunt gurgitem suam apud Cadeland. Burgenses*

(*p*) Hob. Rep. 64.

(*q*) Rogers *v.* Allen, App. 136.

(*r*) Ward *v.* Creswell, App. 155. Vid. also Vin. Abr. Tit. Piscary, B.

(*s*) Harg. Tracts. 20.

respondent, quod ipsa gurges levata fuit ad nocumentum domini Regis et villæ Southampton, et quod batelli et naves impediuntur, quo minus venire non possunt ad portum villæ predictæ. Juratores dicunt quod a tempore quo, &c. non fuit ibi, aliqua gurges, sed antiquitus solebant stare pali, per quod credunt, quodtunc fuit prostrata gurges eadem occasione qua modo, eo quod fuit ad nocumentum transeuntium."

In Rastall's entries, trespass in Piscary, pl. 4. prescription for several fishery *in aqua maritima fluente et refluente in seisonabili tempore cum 7 stallis separatis separalis piscariæ fixis pro retibus.*

In 7 Rep. 15. it appears that the Abbot of Abbotsbury before the dissolution of the Abbey, had the *right of soil* in an arm of the sea, and that it came to the king by the dissolution of the monastery.

The exclusive right to fish in any water will, of itself, give no right or privilege in the adjoining land which is above high-water mark. Nor will prescription in any case, give a right to erect a fishing hut on another's land, for building is a mark of title, which requires the higher evidence of corporeal seisin and inheritance; whereas prescription applies only to incorporeal hereditaments. (*t*)

Piscarial rights, of whatever nature, and in whatever manner acquired, are always subservient

(*t*) Cortelyou *v.* Van Brundt, App. 68.

to the rights of the public, that is to the right of navigation. "For the *jus privatum*," (says lord Hale,) (*n*) "that is acquired to the subject, either by patent or prescription, must not prejudice the *jus publicum*, wherewith public rivers and arms of the sea are affected for public use."

In an action for disturbing the plaintiff's fishery in the river Tweed, it was proved that the defendant's ship was moored against a rock on a bank of the river where she delivered her cargo, and that the plaintiff was prevented by the situation of the ship from taking so many fish, as he could otherwise have done. It appeared also, that ships frequently lie there waiting for a wind. Wood B. "A navigable river is a public highway, and all persons have a right to come there in ships and to unload, moor and stay as long as they please. Nevertheless, if they abuse that right, so as to work a private injury, they are liable to an action. The question will therefore be, whether the defendant has abused his right. *The privilege of the plaintiff must be subservient to the right of the public.* It would be of very mischievous consequence if the owner of a fishery could prescribe to the public, how, and where, they are to moor in a navigable river. The only case I remember like this, was, where a man obstinately refused to move his ship from opposite a wharf, although it would have

(*n*) Harg. Tracts. 22.

been just the same, if he had moved a little one way or the other; and therefore he abused his right, and the plaintiff recovered. The defendant had a right to moor and remain where his ship lay, so long as convenience required. Yet, if he acted wantonly and maliciously, for the purpose of injuring the fishery, the plaintiff is entitled to a verdict, but not otherwise." *(o)*

The doctrine just advanced as to navigable and piscarial rights, and as to the paramount nature of the former, was recognized in the supreme court of New-Jersey, in the case of Post *v.* Munn. *(p)* The court in this case, held that the master of a vessel was not obliged to slacken his sail, or change his course, or yield the channel to a fishing net. But if the owner of a vessel, under the pretence of exercising his right to navigate, should go out of his course to run upon a net, or should lie in wait till the net was spread, and then proceed to annoy it, or if he should unnecessarily anchor on fishing ground, or otherwise loiter about it, in these, and all cases of the same nature, he is answerable in damages.

It may be laid down, then, as the established rule, that the right of navigation, though superior, does not take away the right of fishing; but that it only limits it, and limits it so far, as it interferes with its own fair, useful and legitimate exercise.

(o) 1 Camp. 517.
(p) Post *v.* Munn. App. 110.

Not only the exclusive right of fishery in salt and tide waters, but also the exclusive right to the *shores* and *soil* thereof, may be acquired by prescription and custom. Hence, all those marine increases which were stated in chapter v. as *prima facie*, belonging to the sovereign power, may become the property either of an individual, or of a particular town or district.

That the shore and soil covered with water, may belong to a subject, appears by the charter of Alan de Percy, to the monks of Whitby, in which the bounds of the possessions belonging to the Abbey, included many salt water creeks; and yet they were granted by a subject. (*x*)

The right to the shores and soil of salt and tide waters, may not only be acquired in gross by an individual in the manner above-mentioned, but may also be *a part and parcel of an adjoining estate*, as appears by Sir Henry Constable's case. (*y*)

To prove a private ownership in these cases, the evidence according to lord Hale, is the constant and usual practice of taking the gravel and sea weed, between the high and low-water marks, and licensing others to do the same; enclosing and embanking against the sea, &c. Thus in a late case in England, (Chad *v.* Tilsed, before mention-

(*x*) Ib. and vid. Miles *v.* Rose, App. 109; and Blundell *v.* Catterall, App. 160.

(*y*) Sir Henry Constable's case, App. 140.

ed,) (z) where the proprietors of certain lands had without opposition, for forty years asserted and exercised by an embankment, an exclusive right to the soil of a bay; it was held by the court that such usage was evidence, whence *anterior* usage might be presumed.

It was observed in chapter v. in respect to *alluvion*, that if any *sudden* accession was made to the land adjoining the shore, it *prima facie*, belonged to the sovereign. Usage, however, may make it the property of the owner of the estate to which it is annexed; as was the case in the claim made by the Abbot of Peterborough to thirty acres of land thrown up by the sea, which was questioned at the suit of the king. The judgment was in favor of the Abbot, on the ground of the custom which prevailed in that part of the country, that the lords of manors bounding on the sea appropriated to themselves all alluvial increases. (*a*)

The following important precedent in relation to the interest which may be acquired in arms of the sea, &c. by usage, is afforded by the treatise of lord Hale. (*b*)

In Scaccario Car. upon the prosecution of Sir Sackville Crow, there was an information against Mr. John Smith, farmer of lord Barclay, setting

(z) Chad *v.* Tilsed, App. 43. Miles *v.* Rose, App. 109.

(*a*) Harg. Tracts. 29.

(*b*) Ib. 34.

forth that the river of Severn was an arm of the sea, flowing and reflowing with salt water, and was part of the ports of Gloucester and Bristol, and that the river had left about *three hundred* acres of ground near Shinbridge, and therefore. they belonged to the king by his prerogative.

Upon the evidence, it appeared by unquestionable proof, that the Severn in the place in question, was an arm of the sea, flowed and reflowed with salt water, and was part of the ports of Gloucester and Bristol, and that within time of memory these were lands newly gained and inned from the Severn; and that the very channel of the river did, within time of memory, run in the very place where the land in question lies, and that the Severn had deserted it, and the channel then run above a mile towards the west.

On the other side, the defendant claiming under the title of lord Barclay, alleged the following matters whereupon to ground his defence.

1st. That the barons of Barclay, were from the time of Hen. 2, owners of the great manor of Barclay.

2d. That the river Severn, *usque filum aquæ*. was time out of memory parcel of that manor.

3d. That by the constant custom of that country, the *filum aquæ* of the river of Severn, was the common boundary of the manors on either side of the river.

When this state of the evidence was opened, it was insisted on, that the river in question, was an arm of the sea, a royal river, and a member of the king's port, and therefore, lay not *in prescription* to be part of a manor. But the court overruled this exception, and admitted that even in such a river, though it be the king's in point of interest, *prima facie*, yet it may be by prescription and usage, time out of mind, *parcel of a manor*.

Upon which the defendant proceeded to his proofs, and insisted upon many badges of ownership, as follow:

That the lords of the manors adjacent to this river, and particularly those of that manor, had all *royal fish* taken in the river, opposite to their manor, *usque filum aquæ*.

That they had the sole right of salmon fishing.

That they had all wrecks cast between high and low-water marks.

That the lords of the manors adjacent had ancient fishing places, and weirs within the very channel.

That they had from time to time, granted these fishing places by lease, &c.; and that they were constantly enjoyed and rent paid by the lease holders.

That by common tradition and reputation, the manors on either side of the Severn, were bounded one against another, by the *filum aquæ*.

That the increases happening by the reliction of the river, were constantly enjoyed by the lords adjacent.

The above facts being effectually established, the court and the king's attorney-general, and the rest of the king's counsel were so well satisfied with the defendant's title, that they moved the defendant to consent to withdraw a juror, to which he agreed, and thus the matter rested.

This important and solemn trial for the right to a royal river, in a port and part of it, fully proves what has been laid down, viz. that it may be acquired as private property by usage.

There is a *limit*, however, to the interest which may be created in salt and tide waters by usage. The civilians say with truth, *nihil præscribitur nisi quod possidetis:* nothing can be claimed by prescription, unless it can be possessed. An individual, therefore, cannot acquire by prescription any more of the sea, than he can reasonably possess. And those parts of the sea, which may require a naval force to protect them, do not lie within the extent of private acquisition or possession. (*c*)

But although an individual may have the property of an arm of the sea, &c. by the means and to the extent above-mentioned, yet the sovereign must, of course, be supposed to have the right of empire or government over it. The people also

(*c*) Harg. Tracts 32.

retain the *jus publicum* of passing and repassing with every kind of water-craft, and may therefore remove all obstructions to the navigation. For the *jus privatum* of the owner or proprietor, is subject to the *jus publicum* to which the community are entitled, in the same manner as the soil of an highway: that is, although it is the freehold of an individual, yet it is controlled by a right of passage which must not be prejudiced. (*d*)

2. *Grant.* The same interests in salt and tide waters which may be prescribed for, and claimed by custom, may of course be granted, as prescription and custom are founded only on the supposition of a grant. And as there is no better exposition of an express grant than the usage under it, the grant may by such means become materially enlarged. Therefore, where an individual claimed the right to have an embankment in a certain part of an arm of the sea by virtue of a grant of *wreck*, (Chad *v.* Tilsed,) (*e*) the court held, that as wreck must rest upon the soil, the usage might determine to what extent the place in question had been deemed soil, and the plaintiff had a verdict.

But without an uninterrupted usage to the contrary, no greater interest can be claimed than what has been expressly granted. A right of fishery, for example, may be granted, without conveying any

(*d*) Harg. Tracts, 36.
(*e*) Chad *v.* Tilsed, App. 43.

right of property in the soil. So where the crown granted, by virtue of its prerogative, a part of the river Thames, where navigable, and an arm of the sea, to the citizens of London, by charter, it was acknowledged that the ground and soil of the river did not pass. And in consequence, another charter was obtained, by which the king granted to them the *solum et fundum* of the river. By virtue of the latter grant, the city of London afterwards received rents of those who fixed posts, or made whaves in and upon the soil of the river. (*f*)

It is, perhaps, almost superfluous to remark, after what has been advanced in the preceding chapters, that the power of granting an exclusive property, in salt and tide waters, is originally vested *only* in the sovereign. As this power may at any time be exercised by the sovereign, so it unquestionably may be *delegated* to any town or other corporation. When it is considered that the sovereign power, or in other words, the legislatures of this country are accustomed to pass acts in relation to salt and tide waters for various purposes, it is important to understand in what cases such acts may be construed as conveying, or authorizing a conveyance, of any right therein.

The right of civil and municipal government over arms of the sea, navigable rivers, &c. may be granted by the legislature of a State, without con-

(*f*) Case of the river Banne. App. 55.

veying any right of property therein, or without abridging in any manner their common and public use.

Thus, in the case of Palmer *v.* Hicks, (*g*) before mentioned, it was held by the supreme court of the State of New-York, that an act of the legislature which extends the bounds of a town over salt and tide waters, is merely for the purpose of *jurisdiction*, and is no evidence of a grant of the right of property in the soil covered by the water.

And where the authority is delegated by the legislature to the corporation of a city, for example, to grant a property in the salt water to the proprietors of the adjoining lots, the corporation in such a case, are only made attornies for the public, and cannot claim by implication, any interest for themselves.

Thus in the case of the Mayor, Aldermen and Commonalty of the city of New-York *v.* Scott, (*h*) (which was to recover a certain amount for *wharfage*,) it appeared that the corporation having granted away the whole of the land flowed by the tide, to which they were entitled by their charter, applied to the legislature, for an act to authorize them to run streets or wharves in front of the water lots already granted. The legislature enacted that the proprietors of the lots, on the front of

(*g*) Palmer *v.* Hicks, App. 123.

(*h*) Mayor, &c. of New-York *v.* Scott, App. 99.

which, the streets or wharves were to run, might fill them up, and make piers according to directions of the corporation. On non-compliance, the corporation were to be at liberty so to do, and receive the wharfage to their own use. It was also further provided, that the corporation might grant to such proprietors in fee, a common interest in such piers, in proportion to the breadth of their respective lots, under such restrictions, and within such limits as the mayor, &c. might deem just and proper. It was held by the court, that no implied grant to the corporation was contained in the act of the legislature, and that the corporation were only authorized to grant *as attornies for the public.*

Where a legislative act contains a general prohibition of fishing in certain places, and afterwards on the false representation of an individual that his own exclusive fishery is included in the act, the legislature are induced to suspend the prohibition as it relates to his alleged private right; it cannot be construed as a grant by the legislature to such individual of any exclusive right of fishery; and therefore, by a repeal of the act, the individual has only a common right to fish with others. (*i*)

In Peck *v.* Lockwood, (*k*) the declaration stated that the defendant entered upon the plaintiff's land, dug up the soil and destroyed the sedge herb-

(*i*) Chalker *v.* Dickinson, App. 74.

(*k*) Peck *v.* Lockwood, App. 116.

age, &c. growing thereon, and took therefrom great quantities of oysters, clams, and other shell fish. The land described in the declaration, consisted of a tract of upland, and about seven acres of sedge flats, contiguous thereto, which were overflowed at high water, but which were above low-water mark, so as to be entirely overgrown with sedge. It appeared on trial, that the defendant, at the time mentioned in the declaration, entered upon such flats, and dug up the soil, and carried away a quantity of *clams*. The plaintiff *established his title to all the soil in question*, to the satisfaction of the court, by conveyances, and also by forty years' possession. Notwithstanding which, the court decided, that the defendant, by virtue of the general principle of the common right of fishery, had a right to fish there, not only at full tide, but also to take *shell* fish there, at *low water*, and for this purpose, to *dig up the soil.*

Now, although it is an incontrovertible principle of the common law, that the fishery in the sea, &c. is, *prima facie*, public to high-water mark, yet as has been shewn, this right may be abridged by the existence of an exclusive right in some individual. And what better evidence, (it may be asked) is there to establish this exclusive right in this country, than the evidence of title to the soil. On the principle of ownership of the soil it is, that the owners of land bordering on *fresh* rivers, have the right of exclusive, or several fishery therein, in front of their lands. And Lord Hale, in treating of piscarial rights, which are acquired by individuals in arms of the sea, &c. says they may be either a liberty without the soil, or in concomitance with the soil; or otherwise they arise from the *propriety of the soil.* (*l*) It would seem, therefore, that in the case referred to, the evidence was fully adequate, according to common law principles, to vest the exclusive fishery of the place in question, in the plaintiff.

The same comment may be applied to the case of Brink *v.* Richtmyer, in the State of New-York. (*m*) In this case, the plaintiff claimed the exclusive right of fishery, by virtue of a grant made by the legislature, of a place called *Green Flats,* which consisted of about forty acres of soil, usually flowed by the tide. The interpretation which the court gave to the grant was, that the public were not thereby excluded from the fishery.

In the two last mentioned cases, the court relied on the principle of the common law, that by the king's grant of the soil in an arm of the sea, the exclusive right of fishery will not pass as an incident. (*n*) But it is conceived that there is an important distinction in such cases between *royal* and *legislative* grants. And although the king cannot

(*l*) Harg. Tracts, 18.

(*m*) Brink *v.* Richtmyer, App. 29.

(*n*) Vid. chap. 1.

alienate the public right of fishery, it being one of those rights inherent in his subjects, which he is not authorized to destroy, or restrain; yet it will not be denied, that parliament is vested with the power of alienation. Indeed it has been amply shewn, that an exclusive right of fishery may be acquired by *prescription* in an arm of the sea, which prescription is founded only on the supposition of a grant, and as the king cannot grant the fishery, the prescription must of course suppose a parliamentary grant. If the public right of fishery then, in an arm of the sea, is subservient to the will and power of parliament in England, it must, on the same principle, be subservient to the will and power of the legislatures in this country. There can, in fact, be no question but that the legislative power may destroy a common right, by prohibiting the use of it entirely, or by converting it into an exclusive right. Thus a right of way, either by land or water, may be shut up by law, and the use of it prohibited and discontinued. So the public right of fishery in salt and tide waters may be interdicted altogether by the legislature, or converted into an exclusive or several fishery. (*o*) The legislature, in fact, are the public, and no one can deny the authority of the public to relinquish what belongs to them, without at the same time denying that it does belong to them.

(*o*) Chalker *v.* Dickinson, App. 74.

It being then too clear to admit of controversy that the legislature may grant an exclusive fishery in an arm of the sea, it would seem to follow, that a legislative grant of the soil, would carry with it the right of exclusive fishery.

CHAPTER VII.

OF THE ALTERATIONS AND MODIFICATIONS OF THE COMMON LAW DOCTRINE, AS IT RESPECTS THE RIGHT TO THE SEA, &C. WHICH HAVE BEEN EFFECTED BY STATUTE AND BY USAGE, IN THIS COUNTRY.

As it appears by the preceding chapter, that the general principles of the common law appertaining to our topic of discussion, are subject to be altered, and restricted in their application, by the effect of usage and by the acts of the sovereign power; it is now proposed to point out to what extent, they have been so altered and restricted, in the respective Atlantic States.

Massachusetts. It appears that the statute law and usages of this State have made several material alterations of the common law in relation to rights in and to salt and tide waters. By the old colonial law before alluded to, it was ordained, "that every inhabitant, who is a householder, shall have free fishing and fowling in any great ponds, bays, coves and rivers, *so far as the sea ebbs and flows*, within the precincts of the town where they dwell, unless the freemen of the same town, or the general court have otherwise appropriated them: provided that no town shall appropriate to any particular person, or persons, any great pond containing more than ten acres of land; and that no man shall come upon another's property without their leave, otherwise than is hereafter expressed; the which clearly to determine, it is declared, that in all creeks, coves and other places, above and upon salt water, where the sea ebbs and flows, the proprietor of the land adjoining, shall have propriety to low-water mark, where the sea does not ebb above *one hundred rods*, and not more, wheresoever it ebbs further: provided that such proprietor shall not by this liberty, have power to stop, or hinder the passage of boats, or other vessels, in or through any creek, or cove, to other men's houses or lands; and for great ponds lying in common though within the bounds of any town, it shall be free for any man to fish and fowl there; and may pass and repass on foot, through any man's property for that end, so he trespass not upon any man's corn or meadow."

This old and important law, although it was annulled with the *charter* under which it was enacted, seems by the reported adjudications of the State to have been since constantly practised upon as the common law of the State, in regard to its harbors, beaches, flats, and wherever the tide ebbs and flows, as well as to fishing and fowling, taking sea manure, &c. as the *right of soil* in flats; also, in regard to great ponds, &c. Many actions, have already depended on this law, of various kinds; as actions on the *case*, wherever the householders' privilege has been disturbed, or invaded; actions of *trespass*, when the ground of the owner of the adjoining upland has been trespassed upon, and sometimes *real actions* to recover the soil or ground, where the tide ebbs and flows, whenever taken possession of, and claimed by another. (*p*)

The above act seems so far to have varied the common law as to confine free fishing and fowling to a *householder*, and his right to the *limits of the town*. But whether the practice has been confined as to person and place, is questionable. This act also, seems to have altered the common law, as it limits the *right of passing* over the *lands of others*, to great ponds, by exempting from this right, all tillage and mowing land, and thereby allowing persons to go over pasture, &c. Hence, going over other men's lands to fish and fowl in other waters than great ponds, remained as at common law, and

(*p*) Vid. 2 Dane's Abr. 694.

has so been generally understood. (*q*) The most material alteration made in the common law by this act, is in extending the right to the soil and all benefits in or upon it, of the adjoining upland to *low-water mark*. The cases which have arisen under this part of the law, we shall have occasion to consider in the following chapter.

It appears that many parts of the extensive flats in Massachusetts, and the rights belonging to them, belong to proprietors in common and undivided, and are often claimed by individuals by *prescription* and *custom*, against such proprietors. How these proprietors came into existence, and how they exist, as they do in every part of the State, as also in Maine, we are indebted for our information to the 2 vol. of the valuable work lately published by a citizen of the State. (*r*)

"They came into existence and have existed in Newbury (till 1764, including Newburyport,) as in other places. In Newbury, as in other places, in the early settlements, proprietors, commoners and towns were often confounded. When our ancestors first came to America, it was usual for the legislature to grant a township, say six miles square, to a number of *proprietors*, or *grantees*, in fee, to hold as *tenants in common* and undivided, of the township granted, and a great proportion of the

(*q*) Vid. 2 Dane's Abr. 694.
(*r*) Ib. 698.

land in Massachusetts and Plymouth colonies, were originally granted by the colony legislature in this way; as the grantees sold off, or set off in *severalty*, lots and parts, they remained proprietors in common of the residue, not sold or set off; and so they have continued, till in some towns, there is a small residue left, held undivided by the original grantees, their heirs and assigns; and in some towns no residue, and where none, there ceases to be there any proprietors or commoners. As these legislative grants of townships have ever been construed *tenancies in common*, on the death of a proprietor his heirs have come in to be proprietors of his undivided part, whenever he has not devised it, but died seized intestate; and if devised, his devisees have come in: So as a proprietor has usually had power to sell and convey his undivided part, or any part of it, in such common and undivided lands; and many such conveyances have been made, the proprietors or commoners, in all our old towns, especially, have become very numerous. In the sea ports, the *flats ground* generally remained the longest undivided, or not set off, because except a few wharf and store lots, they were a long time, and large portions of them are still worth buying, or being set off. These commoners, too, have generally acted and sold their lands, or several farms and building lots as *corporations* on a special law. Hence it is now difficult, in most places, to prove who are these commoners and proprietors; and often in early times they acted in the name of the *town*, as was the case in Newbury, till the year 1700, and in regard to some of the flats ground there, it long since became difficult in many places to prove the legality of their meetings, in which they made the grants. The second grant the plaintiff claimed under in this case," (Adams *v.* Frothingham) (*s.*) "was made Feb. 9, 1721, 1722, by the proprietors as a *corporation;* and was twelve rods of *upland*, four long and three rods wide, and bounded northerly by Merrimack river, at *high-water mark*, and extended up four rods above it. As this grant was expressly bounded by *high-water mark*, and the *flats ground* separated from the upland above, by the express act and intent of the parties, it was not held by the court, and not much urged by the plaintiff's counsel, that the said *colony law* annexed any flats to it; but it was said by the defendant's counsel, and admitted by the court, that this law was never to be so construed as to violate the contracts of the parties; and so as to unite what they evidently meant to keep separate."

And such a construction was given to a grant of the same kind, in the case of Storer *v.* Freeman. (*t*) But in this case it was adjudged, that when the

(*s*) Adams *v.* Frothingham, App. 1.

(*t*) Storer *v.* Freeman, App. 149.

grantor owns both the upland and flats, and grants the upland, and it is uncertain if his deed includes the flats, the law will extend his grant to *low-water mark*, and include the flats agreeably to the old colonial law. On the other hand, if the boundary is made certain (as in Adams *v.* Frothingham) the colonial law does not apply. And in all uncertain grants, it is a rule of law to construe them against the grantor.

By the first part of the old colonial law, as above recited, it seems to be intended "that no man shall come upon *others' property* without their leave," in *any case*, otherwise than afterwards to be expressed in the act, "the which clearly to determine," the act goes on to annex the flats to the upland, *sub modo*, and subject to passages to men's houses and lands, and then concludes, by expressly confining a man's right to go over *another's land*, to fishing and fowling in *great ponds.*

"It is a reasonable construction of the colony law," (says Mr. Dane) "to say that the owner of flats shall not use it so as to hinder persons passing to and from their houses and lands, in boats and other vessels, over such flats, when covered with the tide: and that the last clause in this law, respects only persons going to fish or fowl in *great ponds*, as to which only they must go *on foot*, through another's land, and so as not to tread down his *grain* or mowing; corn and meadow being named only by way of example. Then the act as to passing over other men's lands to fish and fowl, and to sail in boats, being confined to flats ground, when covered with the tide, and to great ponds; every other passing over other men's lands, to other purposes; that is, except as to *great ponds*, is out of the act." (*u*)

It is regarded as a part of the common law of the State of Massachusetts also, and derived from the old colonial law before recited, that towns may appropriate the fishery within the limits of the town, if it has not been appropriated by the legislature.

In the case of Coolidge *v.* Williams, (*v*) which related to the subject of fishery, the following points were decided:

1st. That towns adjoining on or extending across a *navigable* river, may own the soil of the *flats*, or even of *channel*, if a grant has been obtained of the government, but the property of the *fish*, and also of the *tide waters* is in the public.

2d. By the common law of the State, towns may appropriate the fish, if not appropriated by the legislature.

3d. To take fish, no one can, lawfully, go on another's land without license.

4th. That if no appropriation is made of the

(*u*) 2 Dane's Abr. 700.

(*v*) Coolidge *v.* Williams, App. 59.

fish, any citizen can take them, so that he trespass not on another's soil.

5th. When two towns adjoin a river, the citizens of each may take the fish swimming in their *tide waters*.

6th. Putting the seine into the river on the *Cambridge* side, and extending it across the river over the *flats*, on the *Watertown* side, and there drawing the seine on shore the *Cambridge* side, with the fish in it, is a fishing on the Cambridge side and lawful.

New-Hampshire. A very small part of this State, it will be recollected, is contiguous to the sea or its arms, and there has not as yet been any adjudication, or legislative act which has established any alteration of the general doctrine of the common law in regard to its tide waters. (*w*)

Rhode-Island. In this State, there has never been any adjudication, establishing any new or important principle at variance with the common law. The general understanding has, however, been, that the proprietors of land bounded on the tide waters, may embank the same, and hold and occupy such embankments, as a part and parcel of their conterminous upland, *if no detriment to the navigation.* And accordingly, an *usage* has prevailed from the first settlement of the State, to the present time, to make embankments, subject to

(*w*) 3 An. Law Reg. 47

the abovementioned restriction, without any interference on the part of the legislature, until the year 1822, when the General Assembly passed an act relative to the harbor and public waters of the town of Providence, which is as follows:

"Sect. 1. *Be it enacted, &c.* That the town of Providence be, and the said town hereby is authorized and empowered to prevent encroachments or obstructions, in the harbor of said town, in the cove above the bridge, and in the other public waters thereof; and to make such laws, rules and regulations, for the preservation of the said harbor, cove and waters, from encroachments and obstructions, as said town shall think proper, from time to time, to make and enact.

Sect. 2. That the proceedings of said town, on the 13th and 24th days of July, and the 29th day of August, A. D. 1815, relative to the defining and ascertaining the bounds of said harbor, be approved and established, and the boundaries and lines mentioned and described in the report of the committee be, and the same are hereby established; except only that the course from a stake at Simmons' wharf to the bluff, near the corner of John Corlis' farm, stated to be in said report, south, fifteen and an half degrees east, be corrected according to the plat made by the said committee, to the course of south, nine and an half degrees east.

Sect. 3. That if any person or persons shall encroach upon any part of the said harbor, as defined, ascertained and established in and by the next preceding section of this act, by erecting or placing therein any wharf, building, or other fixed obstruction, or neglecting to keep in good repair any wharf or lot adjoining the harbor, for the preservation of the channel, he, she, or they so offending, shall forfeit and pay a sum not less than fifty, nor more than five hundred dollars, to be recovered by action of debt, before any court proper to try the same; one half thereof to and for the use of the said town of Providence, and the other half thereof, to and for the use of the person or persons who shall sue for the same: and it shall moreover be lawful, for the town council of said town, to cause such obstruction to be removed at the cost and charge of him, her or them, who shall have so erected or placed the same, or caused the same to be erected, or placed as aforesaid.

Sect. 4. That if any person or persons shall violate any of the laws, rules or regulations, that may be at any time made by said town of Providence, for the preservation of the channel, and for the prevention of any encroachments or obstructions in the harbor of said town, or the cove above the bridge, or in the other public waters thereof, other than of the kind mentioned and described in the next preceding section of this act, he, she or they, shall forfeit and pay a sum not less than two.

nor more than twenty dollars for each offence, to be recovered by action of debt, before any justice or justices of the peace of the said town, one half thereof, to and for the use of the said town, and the other half thereof, to and for the use of the person or persons, who shall sue for the same." (*x*)

The fair construction of the statute just recited, would seem to be, that the owners of the land adjoining the salt water *below* the bridge, are licensed (if not forbidden by the town) to reclaim and possess the soil flowed by the tide, in front of their land, as far as the harbor lines, referred to in the 2d section of the said act. And with the view of preserving, effectually and securely, a free passage and navigation, *within* the aforesaid lines, it is not only made by the statute a fineable offence to obstruct the same, but the town of Providence are also empowered to make such rules and laws respecting it, as the said town may deem expedient.

It appears also, to be a fair construction, that the said town are entrusted with the conservancy of the *cove*, or water *above* the bridge, *and other public waters, within the limits of the town*, and in the execution of this trust, may at their pleasure, make regulations and laws to preserve them, for the benefit and health of the inhabitants of the said town, against all encroachments or obstructions.

Connecticut. In this State, it seems that the ad-

(*x*) Laws of R. I. 484.

joining proprietors on tide waters, have the exclusive privilege of wharfing and erecting piers on the front of their land. But as long as the soil covered by the tide, remains unappropriated, any person has a right to sail over it, without being liable for trespass. (*y*)

With regard to the right of *fishery*, the courts of this State have professed to adopt the principles of the common law, that is, in the sea and arms of the sea, the right is *common*. (*z*)

New-York. It appears that in New-York, the owner of lands bordering on a river, where the tide flows and reflows, is entitled to a several fishery in front of his land, by *usage*. (*a*)

The lands which the corporation of the *city* of New-York, under their charter hold, on Manhattan Island, and within the city, extend four hundred feet beyond low-water mark into the East river. To this right is annexed "the right, benefit and advantage of all docks, wharves, cranes and slips, or small docks within the city, with the wharfage, cranage and dockage, and all issues, rents, profits and advantages, arising, or to accrue, by, or from all, or any of them." (*b*)

The corporation having granted away the whole

(*y*) 1 Swift's Syst. 341.

(*z*) 3 Ann. Law Reg. 76.

(*a*) Ib. 141.

(*b*) Mayor, &c. of New-York *v.* Scott. App. 99.

of the land to which they were entitled, under their charter, applied in April, 1798, to the legislature, for an act to authorize them to run streets or wharves, of seventy feet width, in front of the water lots already granted. This, by a law of that month and year, (re-enacted on the third of April, 1801,) the legislature was pleased to grant; and by the same act, the proprietors of lots, on the front of which the streets or wharves might run, were to fill them up, and make piers, according to the directions of the corporation. On non-compliance, the corporation were to be at liberty so to do, and receive the wharfage to their own use. And it was further provided, that the corporation might grant to such proprietors in fee, a common interest in such piers, in proportion to the breadth of their respective lots, under such restrictions, and within such limits, as the Mayor, &c. might deem just and proper. (*c*)

New-Jersey. The law in New-Jersey with regard to the tide waters of the State, (with the exception of the public right of navigation,) is entirely the reverse of the common law. This is owing to the original charter; for a particular description of which, and the grants under it, the reader is referred to chapter iii.

Pennsylvania. In Pennsylvania, there are a

(*c*) Mayor, &c. of New-York *v.* Scott, App. 99.

number of *statutes* which regulate the right of fishery. (*d*)

Delaware. The right of *several* fishery in front of the land is exercised in certain parts of the tide waters of this State, by *usage*. (*e*)

Maryland. The rights of fishery in this State are adverted to, in the charter of the proprietary of Maryland; for which vid. chapter iii.

Virginia. By an act of this State, passed February 16, 1819, it is declared that hereafter the limits or bounds of the several tracts of land lying on the Atlantic ocean, the Chesapeake bay, and the rivers and creeks thereof within the commonwealth, shall extend to ordinary *low-water mark;* and the owners of said lands shall have, possess and enjoy, exclusive rights and privileges to and along the shores thereof, down to *ordinary* low-water mark: *provided*, that nothing in this act contained, shall be construed to affect any creek or river, or such part thereof, as may be comprised within the limits of any survey; and provided also, that nothing in this section contained, shall be construed to prohibit any person from the right of *fishing, fowling and hunting, on those shores of the Atlantic ocean, Chesapeake Bay, and the rivers and creeks thereof within the commonwealth, which*

(*d*) 3 An. Law Reg. 263.

(*e*) 4 Ib. 1066.

are now used as common to all the good people thereof. (*f*)

North-Carolina. In North-Carolina, there is no statutory provision in relation to the tide waters, nor any reported adjudications, establishing any important principle. (*g*)

South-Carolina. In South-Carolina, too, there has been no legislative act, nor decision, on these subjects. (*h*)

Georgia. The owners of lands in this State, bordering upon navigable waters, are entitled by *usage*, to the right of fishery. (*i*)

Alabama. In Alabama there has been no alteration of the common law. (*k*)

Mississippi. In this State, the doctrine of the common law prevails, without any alteration. (*l*)

Louisiana. The civil law, to which this State was subject, before it was ceded to the United States, now seems to prevail with regard to its tide waters. (*m*) The following extract is from the digest of the law, which is in force in the State of Louisiana, and which is modelled on the civil law.

(*f*) 3 An. Law Reg. 360.
(*g*) Ib. 222.
(*h*) 4 Ib. 862.
(*i*) 3 Ib. 444.
(*k*) 4 Ib. 583.
(*l*) Ib. 669.
(*m*) 5 Hall's Law Journ. 1. and 113.

"FISHERIES."

"Art. 3. Things which are common are those whose property belongs to nobody, and which all men may freely use, conformably to the use for which nature has intended them, such are air, running-water, the sea and its shores.

Art. 4. By sea shore, we understand the space of land upon which the waters of the sea are spread in the highest water during the winter season. (*n*)

Art. 5. From the public use of the sea shores, it follows, that every man has a right to build there a cabin to retire to, and likewise to land there, either to fish, or to shelter himrelf from the storm, to moor ships and to dry nets and the like; *provided*, no damage arise from the same to the buildings or monuments erected by the owners of the adjoining property.

Art. 6. Public things are those, the property of which belongs to a whole nation, and the use of which is allowed to all the members of the nation: of this kind are navigable rivers, sea ports, roads, highways, harbors, and the bed of rivers as long as the same is covered with water.

Hence it follows, that every man has a right freely to fish in the rivers, ports, roads and harbors.

Art. 8. The use of the shores of navigable riv-

(*n*) Vid. *ante* ch. 4.

ers, or creeks, is public; accordingly, every one has a right freely to bring his ships to land there, to make fast the same to the trees which are there planted, to unload his vessels, to deposit his goods, to dry his nets and the like." (*o*)

CHAPTER VIII.

THE RIGHT OF THOSE WHO OWN THE LAND ADJOINING THE SHORE TO MAKE EMBANKMENTS, SUCH AS WHARVES, &c.

Much of what is contained in the preceding pages, is doubtless, in a greater or less degree, applicable to the subject of this chapter. But as there are different views respecting it, and as there are few subjects in which the interests of individuals, and of the community, are more directly implicated, it is one which demands an attentive and particular consideration.

It is a fact of very general notoriety, that from the period of the first settlement of the United States, to the present time, the necessity of *wharves, quays, piers*, &c. has been experienced, for the lading and unlading of vessels; and that the ap-

(*o*) 4 An. Reg. 700.

propriation of land for such improvements, below the ordinary high-water mark, has been indispensable. It is as well and as generally known, that in the respective States, which lie along the margin of the Atlantic, there are many places where the tide ebbs and flows, (and which, therefore, according to the strict rule of the common law, are public,) that are of no navigable use, and in their original condition, without the aid of human art and industry, afford to the public not the slightest advantage of any kind. Flats, marshes, and other ground, which are covered with water only at full tide, are places of this description. The detriment which the community receive from the recovery, private appropriation, and occupation of such soil, is obviously but little, if any. So far from it, the result has proved that the public are thereby, in a very considerable degree, the gainers ; as they are thus accommodated with landing places, which are essential to every commercial depot, and are also accommodated with new thorough-fares, streets, avenues, &c. Indeed, among the multitude of improvements and works of art of a public nature, which command observation in the towns and cities of the Atlantic States, are the artificial embankments which have been made by enterprising individuals, or corporate companies, in and upon the soil which, in its natural condition, would have exhibited nothing more attractive or valuable than the offensive spectacle of an extended *waste*, alternately inundated and relicted by the entry and retreat of water from the ocean.

After these observations, it cannot appear singular, that an idea should have extensively prevailed, that the proprietor of an estate adjoining the salt water, might lawfully augment it, by embanking in and upon the water, so long as he did not encroach upon nor obstruct what is generally denominated the "channel;" or in other words so long as he did no injury whatever to the public. Hence it is, that the custom has been general to make accessions to land in this manner, without any suspicion of the want of right and authority so to do, and consequently without obtaining any formal and express sanction of the sovereign or legislative power. To shew that this idea is far from being erroneous, and that such a custom is by no means destitute of a legal foundation to support it, is the object of this chapter.

The first position is, that the principle which has been so frequently adverted to, viz: where the sea flows and reflows, the waters are, *prima facie*, and of common right public, *is to be restrained by a reference to public necessity and general utility.* This is no new suggestion; the same restriction was contended for by the eminent counsel in the case of the Commonwealth *v.* Charlestown, (*a*):

(*a*) Commonwealth *v.* Charlestown. App. 48.

but did not avail, because it was *inapplicable to the facts.* This case was concerning the right to build a bridge from Charlestown to Boston, without authority from the general court of Massachusetts, and thus prevent vessels from going so high up the river as they might otherwise have done. So that in fact, in this case, an *injury* was done to the people at large, by *an obstruction of the navigation.* And although the bridge was an accommodation to the public, yet the court very properly declined to assume the authority of determining which of the two was the *most* expedient, the bridge or the unobstructed navigation. But the cases, in relation to which it is here intended to restrict the application of the common law principle, are those cases only, where no privilege whatever is afforded to the public. Or, in other words, it is intended only to *confine the public right to what is of public use.*

It will be very readily admitted, by those who are most conversant with the nature and principles of jurisprudence, that there is no rule of law, however incontrovertible it may be, however clear to the understanding, and however self-evident may be the justice and propriety on which it is founded, but what is necessarily and in the nature of things more or less restricted in its application. If an example is required, let us take the rule of law which so very justly and wisely directs that no person shall enter upon another's freehold without consent. Now, if cattle, while the owner is driving them along the highway, should go into a cornfield, is not the owner of the cattle authorized to enter the cornfield and drive them away, without waiting to obtain consent; and thus prevent a destruction of property which delay would render unavoidable? Obstructions in highways and streets are very properly adjudged by the courts to be nuisances; yet in building, a man may deposit the materials for his house in a part of the highway or street, if he does not entirely obstruct it. To enforce the *strictum jus* in either of these cases, would prove in the greatest degree prejudicial, and would effectually counteract the very ends, which it is the design of the law to promote and establish. So it is contended, that although it is provided that the public have the right to all tide waters; yet that this rule requires a reasonable and limited construction, so as to restrict the public right to that from which the public may derive advantage. For what is there that can possibly appear in more direct opposition to sound reason and sound policy, (which are understood to constitute sound law) than to deny to an individual the opportunity to avail himself of what in its natural condition can be of but little or no use, to any one; but which, when reclaimed and converted to his private use, in the manner which is most for his advantage, affords to the *community* an accommodation, which otherwise it could never enjoy?

To present this subject fairly, and that it may be fully understood, let it be supposed that an individual should build out a wharf on Block Island or Martha's Vineyard, for the convenience of lading and unlading vessels or boats. No one is, surely, injured thereby, but on the other hand those who have occasion to go there and land goods and merchandise, derive from it a very great benefit. Now the individual who erects a wharf in Boston or in Providence, may do no greater injury to the public, than he who erects one on Block Island. As a public benefit, on the contrary, it is incalculably greater; for without wharves, a commercial town could never exist. Is the individual, then, to be indicted by a grand jury, and subjected to the expense of demolishing what is of vast utility to many, and a detriment to none? To such a question, common sense and common justice (and, as will presently be shewn,) the *common law of the land*, give a most decided negative. All that is insisted on (it will be recollected, is, that the design and intent of the rule of law, whether written or unwritten, is to be observed in every case; and that the design and intent of the rule of the common law which establishes a public right to the salt water, is only to protect the public in the enjoyment of any existing useful privilege, of which they may avail themselves.

It will now be shown how far the above position is supported by the authorities. The first authority is from the Roman law. The digest L. 43. T. 15. s. 1. provides, *Ripas fluminum publicorum reficere, munire, utilissimum est, dumne ob id navigatio deterior fiat: illa enim sola refictio toleranda est, quæ navigationi non est impedimento:* Or, in English, thus; "To repair and strengthen the banks of public rivers, is *most useful*, provided the navigation be not by that deteriorated; *for those repairs alone are to be permitted, which do not impede the navigation.*" In the same book of the Digest, T. 8. s. 8. is provided, *Adversus eum qui molem in mare projecit, interdictum utile competit ei, cui forte hæc res nocitura sit; si autem nemo damnum sentit, tuendus est is, qui in littore ædificat, vel molem in mare jacit.*' Or in English, thus; against him who projects a mole into the sea, the *interdictum utile* lies for him to whom this may possibly do injury; *but if nobody sustains damage, he is to be protected who builds on the sea shore*, or projects a mole into the sea."

Here, then, this position is fully supported by the law, from which it is said the common law on these subjects was derived. (*b*) And the principle now contended for, it appears, is most expressly and definitely laid down. "*If nobody sustains damage*," (says the Digest) "*he is to be protected who builds*

(*b*) Vid. ch. 1 and 5. and Bla. Com. 262.

on the sea shore," which is exactly the meaning and extent of the position.

The following extract from the treatise of Lord Hale, *de portibus maris*, (c) will doubtless be received as not less in favour of the position than the above extracts from the Digest. In speaking of nuisances in ports, by building too far into the water, he observes, "that nuisance, or not nuisance, in such a case, is a *question of fact*. It is not, therefore," he continues, "every building below the high-water mark, nor every building below the low-water mark, that is, *ipso facto*, in law a nuisance. For that would destroy all the keys that are in all the ports in England. *For they are all built below the high-water mark; for otherwise, vessels could not come at them to unlade; and some are built below the low-water mark.* And it would be impossible for the king to license the building of a new wharf, or key, whereof there are a thousand instances, if *ipso facto*, it were a common nuisance, because it straitens the port; for the king cannot license a common nuisance. Nay, in many cases, it is an advantage to a port to keep in the sea water from diffusing at large; and the water may flow in shallows where it is impossible for vessels to ride. Indeed, where the soil is the king's, the building below the high-water mark is a *purpresture*, an encroachment and intrusion upon the

(c) Harg. Tracts. 85.

king's soil, which he may either demolish, or seize, or arent, at his pleasure, but it is not, *ipso facto*, a common nuisance, unless, indeed, it be *a damage to the port and navigation.* In the case, therefore, of building within the extent of a port in or near the water, whether it be a nuisance or not, is *quæstio facti*, and *to be determined by a jury* upon evidence, and not *quæstio juris.*"

It appears then by the very best authority which could possibly be cited in relation to the present topic of discussion, that the most which can be made of an artificial embankment in and upon the salt water, where the water is usually shallow, is *merely* what is denominated a *purpresture.* Or, in other words, a petty intrusion or encroachment upon what is regarded as the property of the king, not amounting to a public nuisance. And such purprestures, it seems, the king has authority "to seize, demolish or arent at his pleasure." The inquiry, therefore, is here suggested, whether the king ever exercises this authority, and if so, under what circumstances and with what view? And here there is occasion to advert again to the general doctrine of the common law. By referring to chapter i. it will appear that in England, the right of property in the tide waters and soil thereof to high-water mark is, *prima facie*, in the king. It will also appear that they are nevertheless open to the free and uninterrupted use of the public. And that the king, although he is regarded as the legitimate proprietor, yet his character in this respect, is in a degree fictitious, inasmuch as he cannot exercise his ownership to the exclusion, inconvenience or injury of his subjects. He can therefore, be considered only as *guardian* and *trustee* for the benefit of his subjects. In this character, he is undoubtedly obligated to prevent all such appropriations of the sea shore, or of the banks of navigable rivers, as will impede navigation and injure the interests of commerce, and it is with this view, as we shall now proceed to shew, that complaints are made in behalf of the king for the purpose of removing purprestures or encroachments upon the *aquis regiis*, or royal, or tide waters. The tribunal by which the decisions were made, that are now about to be introduced is the court of exchequer.

It will be recollected that the *judicial* department of the English court of exchequer is subdivided into a court of equity and court of common law. The primary business of the former, is to recover any lands, tenements or hereditaments belonging to the *Crown*. (*d*) The method of suit, is by *information* filed by the king's Attorney General. One of the most usual informations is for encroaching upon the lands of the Crown without

(*d*) 3 Bla. Com. 44.

title. (*e*) Hence it will be perceived, that encroachments or purprestures upon arms and creeks of the sea, &c. are a proper subject for an information.

In the case of the Attorney General *v.* Philpot, in the exchequer, 8 ch. 1; the information stated the Crown to be seized of the river Thames where navigable, and an arm of the sea, for the use of ships resorting there; and that the Crown was also seized of the soil between high and low-water mark. That the defendant had lately encroached upon the soil of the king, and had thereby stopped the course of the river and rendered it less convenient for shipping and for their mooring in the pool. The information therefore, prayed that the encroachment might be declared a purpresture, and be abated as such. The defendants set up a defence that they had leave of the high admiral and that their encroachment was no damage to the shipping. The court directed a commission to inquire whether the fact complained of, was a purpresture. The commissioners returned that it was, and the encroachment was abated. (*f*)

In this case it will be observed that the ground of the information, was that the defendant had "*stopped the course of the river and rendered it less convenient for shipping,*" *&c.* In such a case.

(*e*) 3 Bla. Com. 261.

(*f*) Vid. the case cited in Ans. Rep. 607.

therefore, not only the high admiral, but even the king himself, had no authority to license the encroachment, it being an *annoyance to his subjects.*

In the case of the Attorney General *v.* Richards, (*g*) &c. Trin. T. 35. Geo. 3. the information stated that by the royal prerogative, the sea and sea coasts as far as the sea flows and reflows between the high and low-water marks, and all the ports and havens of the kingdom belong to his majesty, and ought to be preserved for the use of his majesty's vessels and others, and that his majesty has the right of superintendency over them for their preservation.

The information then proceeded to state that the defendants in 1784, erected a *wharf* or *key,* two docks and other buildings between high and low-water mark in Portsmouth harbor, adjoining to Gosport, so as both to prevent the boats and vessels from sailing over that spot or mooring there; and also to endanger further damage to the harbor by preventing the free current of water to carry off the mud. It was, therefore, prayed that the defendant might be restrained from making any further erections, and that those made might be abated, and the harbor restored to its ancient situation.

The defendants claimed to hold the soil of the place in question, under letters patent, 14th July.

(*g*) Attorney General *v.* Richards, App. 9.

8 ch. 1. These letters patent recited, that a commission had issued to the sheriff of Hampshire and other persons to examine all the mud banks and sea marshes within a certain district on the coast; and by a legal inquest to inquire and report whether any and what part of them might be recovered from the sea, without injury to any person. They made a return, certifying that certain mud lands and lands covered with the sea around the town of Gosport, might be recovered from the sea, to the great benefit of the nation, and without any injury or damage to any person. The letters patent, on the foot of this return, and in consideration of the services of the grantees and of the money to be by them expended in recovering from the sea the lands granted; and of the special favor, certain knowledge, and mere motion of the king, did grant to Mary Wandesford and William Wandesford, certain mud lands and lands overflowed by the sea, among others, certain lands overflowed by the sea, on each side of Gosport, and also discharged the same from all claim of *tithes* from the Crown, during seven years from the date of the lands being recovered and embanked from the sea, rendering a rent of four pence per acre for every acre recovered, till the year 1630, and from that period, the rent of one shilling. Two of the defendants also pleaded possession of the place in question, for more than sixty years.

It was much disputed in the evidence, whether the place in question was included within the grant or not? The defendants did not produce the conveyances and the deduction of title from the Wandesfords to the persons from whom they derived immediately their claim. They only produced the conveyance of this parcel of mud land to themselves, by persons stated in the conveyance to be entitled under the letters patent.

It was admitted that the defendants, or those under whom they claimed, had been in possession of a piece of mud land *adjoining* to the piece in question, for upwards of sixty years. The ground in question had never been recovered from the sea, till the erections complained of by the bill, and which were made after notice of the intention to dispute the right; but the defendants had held possession, by keeping floats of timber moored there for some time before.

Macdonald, chief baron, (after stating the case,) delivered the opinion of the court to the following effect:

It is clear that the right to the soil between high and low-water marks, is, *prima facie*, in the Crown. Then the *onus* of shewing an adverse title is thrown upon the defendants.

This they attempt to do, under the letters patent; but upon the whole evidence, as far as we can now trace the meaning of the grant, this spot does not seem to have been included in it. The return of the inquisition finds that the embanking the lands granted, would be of no detriment to any person. But that is not consistent with the evidence here, that the embanking would *hurt the harbor and prevent the passage of boats* up to the town of Gosport: then the inquisition and grant must have related to other lands, and the grant, in describing the parcels, gives the mud lands on each side of Gosport, studiously passing by the town; so that it does not appear that this land was ever meant to be granted from the Crown.

But the grant appears also to have been made for the sake of the public interest, in having this land brought into cultivation. The exemption of tithes for seven years shews the extent to have been, that it should be put into a state capable of producing titheable matter. The rent also proves the embankment, and regaining from the sea, to have been the condition and spirit of the grant. That has not been complied with.

But the defendants do not deduce their title from the grantees; they shew a title under A. and B. who they aver were entitled under the grant; but the *onus* of establishing their claim being upon them, they must shew how A. and B. derived that right. At present, it appears to be the conveyance by mere strangers.

They next went on the evidence of possession.

But it appears, that instead of their having possession, the Crown, has by its subjects, had possession of the place in question; and its being open as a public passage from 1629, precludes any right now to question the title of the Crown. If the grantees ever had any title, it has been abandoned. Upon the whole, we are of opinion, that the defendants have not made out any title to the soil of the place in question.

But it is argued, that the prayer of the bill being to abate the erections as a nuisance, the court can only consider that question, as alone supporting the relief prayed, and it is contended, that this court cannot give such a decree, or at least not without the intervention of a jury, the question of nuisance being, as laid down by lord Hale, a question of fact, and not of law. That may be where the question is of nuisance only, and the evidence doubtful. We do not hesitate to declare that the soil is the property of the Crown; and of course to decree, that these buildings be abated.

It will be observed, in this case also, that an essential injury of a public nature, is the cause of allegation. And although the defendants failed in establishing their right to the place in question by the grant on which they relied, yet it was not on this account alone, that the decree for abatement was obtained; but principally because the encroachment complained of had the effect, (to use the language of the bill,) "*to prevent boats and vessels sailing over the places or mooring there; and also to endanger further damage to the harbor.*" And such being the fact, the decree was made accordingly; for it will be recollected, it is not in the power of the king to sanction any thing, though on his own soil, which is a public annoyance. It should be remarked, too, that the information itself did not even pray, that the embankment might be declared to belong to the king, but merely charged a nuisance upon a particular spot, the soil of which, is the property of the king, by virtue of his royal prerogative. This case, therefore, as well as the preceding one, implies throughout, that the main design of informations in these cases, is to preserve the safety of harbors, and to protect the public in the full enjoyment of what they are by law, and of common right entitled to, *a free and unobstructed navigation.*

It will not be forgotten, that the object for which the above cases were cited, was to shew, that although the king, as proprietor, is legally empowered to abate encroachments upon the tide waters, whether nuisances or not, and consequently without the intervention of a jury; (*h*) yet that this power, whenever it has been exercised, has been with the view of preserving and promoting the in-

(*h*) Besides the authority of lord Hale on this point, which has been fully cited, vid. 18 Vesey, Jun. 218.

terests of his subjects, and the common good of the realm. To make this appear still more satisfactorily, we will now refer to the case of the city of Bristol *v.* Morgan.

In this case the bill stated the benefit of navigable rivers to commerce, and the right to have all purprestures therein abated. It was proved that the defendants had erected houses on the banks of the Avon, so as to straiten the river, and to incommode the passage to and from the shipping to the shore: that these houses also intercepted the commerce of the town and tended to defraud the revenue. The encroachment was ordered to be abated, on the ground of damage to the city.

Here then is not only proved that the encroachments had the effect "*to straiten the river,*" *&c.* but it appears that the ground on which the *decree was obtained*, was "*damage to the city.*" And it is particularly to be observed that notwithstanding the buildings were actually ordered to be abated, yet as the parties subsequently entered into a composition, the buildings *were allowed to remain.* (*i*)

It appears, therefore, that even in England, where the principles of the common law are usually most rigidly and scrupulously adhered to, and where prerogative rights especially, are respected with almost superstitious reverence, that encroachments or purprestures upon navigable and tide

(*i*) Ans. Rep. 607. and Harg. Tracts, 81.

waters, are allowed to remain, if they are no detriment to the public.

On the whole, the following points may be considered as having been thoroughly established.

1st. That in England every encroachment upon the salt water is not regarded as, *ipso facto*, a nuisance ; and whether it is a nuisance or not is *quæstio facti*, or a question of fact, and is therefore to be tried by a jury.

2d. That the king, as the legal proprietor of the tide waters, may abate every intrusion or encroachment thereon, whether the same is in fact a nuisance or not.

3d. That in exercising this power, he is supposed to act only in the character of conservator of the navigation, and as superintendent of the common interest of the nation.

The above points being established, it is left to the reader to determine, how far the position laid down has been supported.

There has been one case decided in this country, which it is admitted is at variance with what is here sought to be proved. This case, however, is by no means in our way, as it is so very easy to point out that the grounds on which it was decided, were mistaken by the court, both as to the law and as to fact.

In this case, (which was Respublica *v.* Caldwell, in the court of Oyer and Terminer, at Philadelphia, in 1785,) (*k*) there was an indictment for a *nuisance* in erecting a *wharf* upon the public property. The defendant offered witnesses to prove that the erection of the wharf had been beneficial to the public, and therefore was not to be regarded as a nuisance.

But M'Kean, C. J. delivered the opinion of the court, that the evidence was inadmissible for two reasons: *First*, because it would only amount to matter of opinion, whereas it is on facts the court must proceed, and the necessary facts are already in proof. *Secondly*, because it would be no justification; for, on the same principle that the defendant might carry his wharf twelve feet, he could justify extending it farther; or any other man might excuse a similar intrusion. Suppose, for instance, a street were sixty feet wide, twelve feet might be taken off, without doing any material injury to the public property, or creating any great obstruction; yet surely this will not justify a man's actually building upon, and assuming the property of the twelve feet that could be thus spared.

Now as it relates to the first ground on which the evidence offered was rejected by the chief justice, it is scarcely necessary (after the passage before cited from lord Hale's treatise) to make a single comment. And the reader must doubtless

(*k*) Respublica *v.* Caldwell, App. 126.

be convinced, that the chief justice disposed of the case before him, without consulting the best and most approved authorities.

As to the second ground, viz: "that on the same principle, the defendant might extend his wharf twelve feet, he might extend it farther," we answer that it is true, he might. But then he had no right to extend it twelve feet, nor even one foot, if it really, and in fact, was an injury to the public. So, on the other hand, if it really, and in fact, was no injury, he might lawfully have extended it sixty or any greater number of feet. And to determine whether or not it is really and in fact a public injury, is (as has been most clearly shewn) the province of the jury, "*upon evidence.*" The instance which the chief justice gave of *a street*, is by no means applicable. For if twelve feet are taken from a street, the public lose the opportunity of passing over so much of the street. But if a wharf is projected twelve feet beyond the high-water mark, it destroys no part of a passage way, for the wharf is confined to a spot which in its natural condition is susceptible of no passage. Besides, there is no doubt but that a man may emporarily exclude the public even from a certain part of a street, which he finds necessary as a place of deposit, for the materials of a building which he is erecting; (*l*) and this is founded on reasons of

(*l*) 1 Sergt. & Rawle, 219.

public policy. If a man, then, may appropriate to his own use, for a temporary purpose, a part of what is actually a common passage and a common convenience, on the ground of public policy; should he not be allowed, with the view of promoting the same important end, to appropriate permanently what is not calculated to afford to the public any convenience whatever? It is conceived, therefore, that our position is not only substantiated by authorities which are directly to the point, but also by *analogy*.

There have been two cases which relate directly to the projection of wharves upon the salt water, that came before the high court of Parliament. To these the attention of the reader is now invited.

In the case of Smart *v.* the Magistrates, town-council and corporation of Dundee, (*m*) which was an appeal from the court of sessions in Scotland, it appeared that the Crown of Scotland had, in very ancient times, granted to the corporation of Dundee, on the river Tay, the borough, with all the lands and pertinents, the privileges, profits, customs, ports, and liberties of the river on both sides, as freely in all respects as is possessed by the borough of Edinburgh over that of Leith, and in a word, as it seems, every right, power, and trust *which the crown could grant.* Smart, the

(*m*) 8 Brown's Parl. Cas. 119.

the proprietor of a lot, bounded, *per fluxum maris*, or the sea flood, admitted that the sovereign, as trustee, has a right to prevent all such appropriations of the sea shore, or the banks of navigable rivers as would impede navigation, or hurt the interests of commerce, either inland or foreign; and that all private persons, or corporations, having a grant of a port or harbor, possess to a certain extent, the same privilege as derived from the sovereign within a defined space. Still, however, he insisted on his right, as adjacent proprietor to ground, gained from the sea by its recess, or by his own industry in embanking, or by any other *opus manufactum not prejudicial to navigation, or the established right of others.* On the other hand, the corporation claimed, by *their grant*, a right to the sea shore adjacent to the town, in trust for the benefit of the community; to make harbors, basons and works for securing them, and wharves, wood yards and other repositories, for the accommodation of the trade; and for their different works, to take in sites from the water by embankment: in short, as standing in the place of the Crown, and succeeding to all the cares and powers of the Crown, in the territory and its waters, for the public good; *and for that object* were *now* engaged in making an embankment adjacent to the appellant's lot, for the benefit of navigation and commerce. They admit the general doctrine of the riparian right to the soil which may be acquired from a sea or river, by its receding naturally, or *by industry:* but that this does not apply to a tenement within a burgh, where the corporation is entitled to all the soil not expressly granted away: that the words "*per fluxum maris*" are but words of description, which were accurate, too, at the date of the grant, but have since become otherwise, by a change of character in the boundary, not in the area granted. They are a limitation of the subject of the grant, in the same way as a road would be, which, if removed farther off, would not carry the granted subject with it; the particular boundaries being named, not to limit the conterminous property, but the property granted.

The appeal was dismissed the House of Lords. No arguments of counsel, other than the written pleadings, nor reasons of the lords, are reported.

In this case, it seems, the proprietor of a lot bounded by the sea flood, admitting that the sovereign, as trustee for the public, had a right to prevent any such appropriation of the shore as would "*impede navigation, &c.*" still insisted on his own right as adjacent proprietor to ground gained from the water *by his industry in embanking*, if not prejudicial to navigation. The difficulty he had to contend with, however, appears to have been, that the soil of the place in question had been expressly granted to the corporation, which they considered they held as trustees, for the benefit of the community. Hence, the corporation had not only a right to control it, as in their discretion was most expedient, but were actually engaged in making an embankment adjacent to the lot of the appellant, for the benefit of navigation and commerce, upon the soil from which the water had receded. And what is important to observe, is, that the corporation themselves *admitted* the general doctrine of the riparian proprietor to soil which may have been reclaimed by his own industry. The circumstances, therefore, of this case, and the doctrine which was advanced by the appellants, and admitted by the respondents, authorize the strongest inference, that the principle of our position was perfectly well understood at the trial, to be the established and governing principle in *ordinary cases.*

The other case which came before the high court of Parliament, in relation to the subject now under consideration, is the Dean, &c. of Durham, appellants, and the member, &c. of Newcastle upon Tyne, respondents. (*n*) The points which were referred to the jury in this case, in the previous trial in the court of exchequer, were first, whether the respondents were entitled to the sole superintendency of the river Tyne, upon a part of which a wharf had been projected; and secondly, *whether the wharf was an injury to the navigation.* The inference to be drawn from this case then is,

(*n*) 8 Brown's Parl. Rep. 18. and App. 84.

that if it had been found by the jury, that the respondents had no exclusive control of the river, and that the wharf was no injury to the navigation; the appellants might have retained and occupied their wharf without molestation. It appeared however, (after every opportunity had been allowed to shew the contrary,) that the wharf was in fact a very serious public annoyance.

Is not the principle, then, fully recognized in England, that the doctrine of the common law, as it respects the public right to salt and tide waters, to be understood with the restriction, that the public right is to be confined to what is of public use? And does it not appear by the common, as well as the civil law, that *if nobody sustains damage, he is to be protected who builds on the sea shore, or projects a mole into the sea?*

2. The second position which is offered to support the right in question is, that *by the custom and usage of the country, the privilege of reclaiming and appropriating to private use a portion of the soil flowed by the tide, is a privilege appertinant to the conterminous or adjoining upland; and that, therefore, the proprietors of the conterminous upland may enclose and embank upon the water, provided such enclosures or embankments are of no actual injury to the public.* Supposing, therefore, the former position to be ever so exceptionable, and the authorities cited for its support to be ever so defec-

tive, the ground which is now taken, if it can be maintained, will afford a legal foundation for the right here contended for.

It will be recollected that the common law itself, is nothing more than general custom which has been long practised, and which was silently and gradually introduced. On the same principle that it has been so introduced, it may be withdrawn, and disuse is very justly considered as the *repeal* of custom. So among the civilians, laws were not only abrogated by the express declaration of the legislature, but also through *desuetude*, or by the tacit consent of all. (*o*) Indeed, in every production of human invention, (and more especially in those which relate to the transactions of mankind) it must of course occur, that changes and modifications therein will be effected by a series of years. The systems of one age have been consigned to oblivion, or have become the objects of mere historical remembrance in the next. And it is thus that the common law of England which, as a general rule, is the common and received law in this country, has been done away, or restricted in its application by the customs and usages of the country, as it relates to a variety of subjects. And it is also our pride and boast, that while the courts of this country, which are created to administer its jurisprudence, pay the utmost deference to English

(*o*) Dig. L. 1. T. 3. s. 32.

authorities, they seldom betray such an indiscreet or superstitious veneration, as tenaciously and rigorously to adhere to them when they can gratify the popular sentiment, and promote the *public good*, by respecting and enforcing what has been long and constantly practised.

Now if it is consistent that any custom peculiar to the country, can have acquired the effect of established law, the one in question must necessarily be received as such.

In the first place, it originated at the very earliest period of our country's history.

In the second place, it has been continued to the present time.

In the third place, it has not only been continued but has every year been more and more general in proportion to the progressive increase of trade and commerce.

In the fourth place, it is in itself reasonable.

And in the fifth place, it has in reality contributed in a most essential degree to public improvement, convenience and opulence.

But, it may be urged, that land can never be claimed as an *appertinence*, and that the only way to establish a legal title to it, is by the evidence of corporeal seisin or possession; and that custom and prescription relate only to rights of an *incorporeal* nature. To avoid the inconsistency which is implied in this objection, it may be answered, that one of those legal *fictions* are resorted to, which have been adopted in other cases, to remedy inconveniences, whenever reason and policy require the extension or limitation of any general legal axiom. The fiction which has been adopted with regard to the particular subject now before us, is that *the soil which is flowed by the tide, whether reclaimed from the water or not, is not land.* Should the reader be startled at this seeming anomaly, he will recollect the maxim *in fictione juris, semper subsistit æquitas.* (*p*) And it may be observed that the principle of the fiction here relied on, is certainly not more absurd or anomalous, than that a son killed in battle is supposed *to live forever*, for the benefit of his parents, which was a fiction adopted and encouraged for a certain purpose by the Roman law. (*q*)

In the case of Doane *v.* The Broad-street Association, (*r*) the action was to recover a part of India-street in Boston, formerly flats ground. The late Ch. J. Parsons, in giving the opinion of the court in this case, said expressly, "*we do not consider a wharf as land*, within the construction of the maxim, that land cannot pass as appertinent to land. *A wharf is a structure erected on a shore below high-water mark*, and sometimes extending

(*p*) 3 Bla. Com. 43.

(*q*) Ins. T. 1. L. 25.

(*r*) 6 Mass. 332.

into the channel, for laying vessels alongside, to load or unload; and on which stores are often erected for the reception of cargoes. To a structure of this description, and built for such a purpose, we are satisfied that flats, necessary for the use of the wharf, and usually occupied with it, *may pass as appertinent.*"

The general and well established principle, therefore, that land cannot be claimed as appertinant to land, will not be offered as an objection to the position which we are now endeavoring to establish.

We will now proceed to shew by authorities, that the right of making wharves and other embankments in and upon the salt water, (supposing it not to exist at common law,) has been created in this country by virtue of the general custom and usage.

The ancient colonial law of Massachusetts (to which we have before referred the reader,) which provided that the proprietor of land adjoining on the sea or salt water, shall hold to low-water mark, &c. it must be recollected, was annulled *with the charter* by the authority of which it was made. Notwithstanding this abrogation of the law, its provisions are still respected by the courts of Massachusetts, and are still in force as the *common law of the State.* For this we have the authority of Mr. C. J. Parsons, in the case of Storer *v.* Freeman, (*s*) who says, "an usage has prevailed from that time to the present, which now has force as our common law, that the owner of lands bounded on the sea, or salt water, shall hold to low-water mark," &c. On the same principle, it was adjudged in the case of Adams *v.* Frothingham, (*t*) that a proprietary grant of a piece of land to set a shop upon, was to be construed to extend to low-water mark. And on the same principle, also, several other cases have been decided by the supreme court of Massachusetts, which we will now consider.

In the case of Austin, *et. al. v.* Carter, *et. al.* (*u*) an action of trespass was brought against the defendants, for cutting down piers, on the flats in Charles river, a *tide and navigable* river, by the owners of the adjoining upland. In this case the court decided, 1st. That the proprietor of the land bounded on the sea has the exclusive right to low-water mark. 2d. That the authority of surveyors of highways, as such, is confined to highways on *land*, and does not extend to rivers such as Charles river. 3d. That though each individual inhabitant of Charlestown, and so of the State, had a right to pass and repass on the waters of Charles river, so long as the owner of the adjoining land leaves

(*s*) Storer *v.* Freeman, App. 149.

(*t*) Adams *v.* Frothingham, App. 1.

(*u*) Austin *v.* Carter, App. 19.

them open; yet he may, when he pleases, enclose, build and obstruct to low-water mark, *and exclude all mankind.*

And it is considered in Massachusetts, that the usage or common law of the country, will give a man a right to reclaim and appropriate the land below *low*-water mark, even if it is no inconvenience to the public.

Thus, in the case of Commonwealth *v.* Pierce, in 1790, cited in Mr. Dane's abridgment, (*v*) it appeared there was a small tide river in Salem, called "South river," and that Pierce had continued out his wharf to the channel, or near it, which was at a considerable distance from high-water mark, and quite up the river, towards the head of navigation. The court adjudged that wharves were useful and necessary to trade, and might, by the *common practice of the country*, be built out to low-water mark, or *further*, if not injurious to the public interest.

And in the case of the Commonwealth *v.* Charlestown, (*w*) Mr. C. J. Parker expressed his opinion, that the usages of the country would confine the public right to what might be of public use, and that in those waters which are *incapable of being navigated*, private property may be maintained.

In the case of the Commonwealth *v.* Crownin-

(*v*) 2 Dane's Ab. 696.

(*w*) Commonwealth *v.* Charlestown, App. 48

shield, it appears there was an essential injury done to the public, and therefore the verdict was very properly rendered against the defendant. The condensed substance of this case is given in Mr. Dane's abridgment, as follows. (*x*) In the year 1796, the defendant in this case was charged with obstructing, by his wharf, an ancient navigable river, being a *public highway.* A part of the wharf, it appeared, was below low-water mark. The defendant contended that although his wharf extended below low-water mark, it was no obstruction to the navigation, and no injury to the public; and that as the channel supposed to be obstructed, only led into a small dock, enclosed with wharves of private persons, the injury complained of, if any, could only be the ground of a *civil* action. The court adjudged, that it was no obstruction to build out a wharf; *if a sufficient passage way is left for the public.* The verdict was, however, against the defendant, as to the small part of the wharf which was in the channel. In this case, *the jury had a view,* and were satisfied that there was not a sufficient passage-way left for the public.

3. The third position is, that without any restriction of the doctrine of the common law, (which was the principle of the first position,) and without the usage of the country, (which was the principle of the second position,) the right to embank upon

(*x*) 2 Dane's Abr. 697.

any arm of the sea, &c. as belonging to the owner of the conterminous upland, is perfectly consistent and tenable.

To establish this position, let us consider the nature of public property. In all those things which are subject to public use, the prior right to their enjoyment belongs, (at least for a certain time,) to the *first occupant.* This right of occupancy is denominated by the writers on natural law, "*jus preventionis,*" or the "*right of prevention,*" which they say should be strictly observed in the use of property that is *common, and cannot serve at the same time for many.*" "By this term," (says Vattel,) (*y*) "we understand the right of him who first comes to this sort of things." "For example," (he continues,) "if I actually draw water from a public or common well, another who comes after, cannot drive me away to draw out of it himself, and he ought to stay till I have done. For I make use of my right in drawing that water, and nobody can disturb me; a second who has an equal right, cannot make use of it to the prejudice of mine: to make me have done by his arrival, would be to attribute to himself a greater right than me, and thereby to infringe against the law of equality."

To apply this doctrine to the subject of the sea, &c. the individual who first occupies a *fishing*

(*y*) Vattel. 175.

place, for instance, must be considered as having the exclusive right, so long as he is in the act of using it, and that while he is drawing his nets, &c. no one can by virtue of the common right, hinder or interrupt him. So also a ship which first takes possession of *anchorage ground*, may unquestionably retain it, until she is ready to leave it. It will not be denied, therefore, that an individual may, by virtue of his common right, take possession of the soil in front of his land flowed by the tide, and use it exclusively for his own private advantage. The only question there can be, is as to the *length of time* for which he is allowed to retain possession; and the only answer which can be given to this question, is, a *reasonable time.* Now to determine the question, as to what is to be regarded a reasonable time; the advantage which any other person might derive from a relinquishment of possession, seems to be the only certain and proper guide. If it is proved, then, that the space taken up by an embankment in and upon the salt water was never used by the public, and was in fact, never calculated to afford the public any privilege whatever, is it not perfectly reasonable and consistent with strict legal principles, that the embankment may be held and enjoyed by the projector and his assigns, *forever?*

It is conceived that the same principles will apply to this subject as is applicable to rights of common in ordinary cases. If, for instance, twenty persons have a common of pasture, it is clear that each commoner is obligated to exercise his right in such a manner as not to incommode the others. It is no less clear, that until he does incommode the other commoners, or does what may incommode them, by surcharging the common, or by any other inconvenience, they have no legal ground for complaint. So with regard to the present subject, if a man extends a wharf from his land into the water, and the navigation is not thereby deteriorated, the other commoners, to wit, the public, have no cause to complain. And as the public experience no inconvenience whatever, it cannot be construed that the projector of the wharf has arrogated to himself any thing more than the fair and legitimate exercise of the *jus communem* which he has as one of the public.

Again, it was provided by the Roman law, that any individual had permission to erect a fishing hut on the shore to subserve the purposes of fishing; "*cuilibet liberum est casam ibi ponere in quam se recipiat.*" (*a*) If this was allowed for such a purpose, it is presumed that it would have been for any other purpose connected with the use of the sea, &c. And if a structure of this kind was permitted to be erected at all for private advantage, it

(*a*) Ins. L. 2. T. 1. s. 1.

may be enquired why a structure of *shells, stones, and earth*, may not be erected for the same object, so long as it affords no obstruction to the *jus publicum* of the community. It may be added, too, that the right of navigation is vastly more important to the public than the right of fishery, and yet without proper landing places, it could be exercised comparatively to very little advantage.

But it may be urged that the embankment although it is no disadvantage whatever to the public, or to any individual, yet, as it is upon the soil which belongs to the State, the embankment may at any time be removed by the legislature. To this it is answered, that the property of the soil is vested in the State, with the view of protecting it against any occupation which would be prejudicial to the interests of the public; and that the property of the soil is held by the State, in the same manner as by the king in England, that is, in the character of *guardian* and *trustee*. (*b*)

It may also be urged, that if the right of embanking in and upon the sea, &c. is founded on the principle of prior occupation, it is then not confined to the owner of the upland to the exclusion of any other person who may *first commence* an embankment. The answer to this objection is as follows: should an individual who has no interest in the upland embank upon the shore between high and

(*b*) Vid. Ch. 1.

low-water marks, he would obviously interfere with rights of a *private* nature, as he would by such intervention shut out the owner of the upland from the water, to which the latter as *riparian proprietor*, is most unquestionably entitled. It is only in virtue of the right to the *contiguous soil*, (it will be recollected) that the owners of lands bounding on *fresh* rivers, possess the right of several fishery, which is a necessary incident, inasmuch as no other person can exercise it; and if the owner of the banks had no right to it, the privilege could not be enjoyed by any one.

Having, as it is conceived, established our three several positions, we will now advert to the question, which may be asked by way of suggesting an important objection, that if the right which has been discussed is admitted to exist at all, is there not a difficulty in determining to what extent it is to be exercised? To this question we give the following answer, which cannot fail to be satisfactory. The answer is, that every individual who projects a wharf or other embankment in front of his land, in and upon the tide waters, does it at his own risk, and must take care that it shall not be prejudicial to the public. If it is thought to be prejudicial, he unquestionably may be indicted for a public nuisance, and then the question whether or not the embankment, is *in fact*, a public nuisance, and consequently whether or not it may remain as an appendage to the conterminous upland, is a question to be determined by a jury of the country, upon evidence.

We now take leave of the particular subject before us, in treating of which it has been necessary to be somewhat elaborate, as doubts have from time to time been suggested as to the existence of the right we have endeavored to vindicate. That these doubts have resulted from a careless and superficial view of the subject, and that they are as ill-founded as they have been inconsiderately expressed, it is humbly conceived, has been most clearly and fairly demonstrated. And the right in question, to the extent contended for, with the ground of public expediency for its foundation, and authorized and supported by the provisions of the civil law, by the doctrine advanced by lord Hale, (who is universally allowed to have perfectly understood the subject,) by the cases decided by the English tribunals, by the long established and still existing usage of our country, and the adjudications which recognize this usage to be the *law of the land*; the right in question we say, must unquestionably be regarded as clear and incontrovertible.

CHAPTER IX.

OF WRECKED PROPERTY THROWN ON THE SHORE.

CONNECTED with the right of the shore, is the right to property, which is sometimes thrown thereon, by the disaster of shipwreck. This subject has been deemed of such importance, that particular provisions have been made respecting it, by the laws of many countries. In modern times, these laws have been dictated by a spirit quite the reverse of that exhibited by those savage customs which formerly prevailed among the northern nations of Europe, (and particularly on the shores of the Baltic,) permitting the inhabitants to seize on all the wrecked property they could find, as lawful prize. The inhuman *Drois de Bris sur le Naufrages*, was in barbarous ages very generally, and rigidly enforced in Europe, and especially among the Gauls. In those days, every stranger was treated as an enemy, and was not only robbed of his goods when in the distress of shipwreck, but was fortunate if he escaped the hand of the murderer. (*a*) As it is expressed by an ancient author, *in naufragorum miseria et calamitate tanquam vul-*

(*a*) Sea Laws, 153.

tures ad prædam currere. (*b*) It is worthy of observation, how very much the law of wreck has been altered, and its rigor gradually mitigated, in favor of the unfortunate proprietor.

In England, wreck is among the maritime revenues of the Crown, and was expressly declared to be the king's property by the prerogative statute of 17 Ed. 2. (*c*) It is no more than fair to presume that this prerogative of wreck, was founded on the general principle of policy and convenience. For if every person was permitted to carry away what he found upon the shore, the true owner would be likely to lose the opportunity of recovering his property. For the *benefit of the owner*, therefore, the law of England has consigned it to the custody of the sheriff, or proper officer of the Crown, by whom it is preserved, and to whom the owner is directed to make inquiry for the property he has lost. And at the time when the rightful claimant is despaired of, it is very properly applied to the augmentation of the public revenue. (*d*)

Wreck by the ancient common law was, where any vessel was lost at sea, and the cargo was thrown upon the land; and in such case the goods so wrecked were adjudged to belong to the king. But as this provision was consonant neither to rea-

(*b*) Vid. 1 Bla. Com. 285.
(*c*) Ib. Harg. Tracts, 37.
(*d*) Ib. note to 1 Bla. Com. 293.

son nor humanity, it was ordained by king Henry I. that if any person escaped alive out of the vessel, it should be no wreck. (*e*)

Afterwards, king Henry II. by charter, declared, if on the coasts of either England, Poicton, Oleron or Gascony, any ship should be distressed, and either man or *beast* should escape, or be found therein alive, the goods should remain to the owners, if they claimed them within three months; but otherwise should be esteemed a wreck, and should belong to the king or other lord of franchise. (*f*)

The charter of Henry II. was confirmed with improvements by Richard I.; who, in the second year of his reign, not only established the concessions of this charter, by ordaining that the owner, if he was shipwrecked and escaped, "*omnes res suas liberas et quietas haberet,*" but also, that if he perished, *his children*, or in default of them, his *brethren and sisters* might retain the property. And in default of brother or sister, then the goods should remain to the king. (*g*) It was in like manner that Constantine the great, finding that by the imperial law the revenue of wrecks was given to the princes' treasury, or *fiscus*, restrained it by an edict, and ordered them to remain to the owners, adding the humane expostulation, "*quod enim jus habet*

(*e*) 1 Bla. Com. 290. Harg. Tracts, 37, 38.

(*f*) Ib. 1 Rym. Fœd. 36.

(*g*) 1 Bla. Com. 291. Harg. Tracts, 40.

fiscus in aliena calamitate, ut de re tam luctuosa compendium sectetur?" (*h*)

The law, as laid down by Bracton, in the reign of Henry III. seems still to have improved in equity. For then, if not only a dog (for example) escaped, by which the owner might be discovered, but if *any certain mark was set on the goods*, by which they might be known, it was held to be no wreck. (*i*)

Afterwards, in the statute of Westminster the first, the time of limitation of claims, given by the charter of Henry II. (to wit, three months) is extended to a *year and a day*; and it enacts, that if a man, a dog, or a cat escape alive, the vessel shall not be adjudged a wreck. The animals just mentioned are only put for examples. And in Hamilton *v.* Davies, 2 Geo. III. it was held, that not only if any living thing escape, but if proof can be made of the property of any of the goods or lading which come to shore, they shall not be forfeited as wreck. The statute of Westminster further ordains, that the sheriff of the county shall be bound to keep the goods a year and a day, that if any man can prove a property in them, either in his own right, or by right of representation, they shall be restored to him without delay; but if no such property be proved within that time, they then shall be the king's. (*k.*)

(*h*) Cod. 11. 5. 1.

(*i*) Bract. L. 3. c. 3.

(*k*) 1 Bla. Com. 291. 2.

In case the goods are of a perishable nature, the sheriff may sell them, and the money received for the same, will be liable in their stead. (*l*)

To constitute a *legal* wreck, it is to be observed, the goods must *come to land.* If they continue at sea, they are distinguished by the barbarous names *jetsam*, *flotsam* and *ligan*. *Jetsam* is where goods are cast into the sea and there sink and remain under water: *flotsam* is where they continue to swim on the surface of the sea; and *ligan* is where they are sunk in the sea, but tied to a cork or buoy, in order to be found again. These, by the common law, are also the king's, if no owner appears to claim them; but if an owner appears, he is entitled to the possession. For if they are thrown overboard in order to lighten the ship, without any mark or buoy, the owner is not by this act of necessity construed to have renounced his property. (*m*) And agreeably to this was the Roman law, *Quæ enim res in tempestate, levandæ navis causa, ejiciuntur, hæ dominorum permannet. Quia palam est, eas non eo animo ejici, quod quis habere nolit.* (*n*) Each of these three is considered so distinct from wreck, that by the king's grant of wrecks, things *jetsam*, *flotsam* and *ligan* will not pass. (*o*)

Wrecks in their legal acceptation are in modern

(*l*) Plowd. 166. Molloy 263.

(*m*) 5 Rep. 108. 1 Bla. Com. 292. Harg. Tracts 41.

(*n*) Ins. L. 2. J. 1. s. 48.

(*o*) 5 Rep. 108.

days not very frequent; for if any goods come to land, it seldom happens, that the owner is not able to assert his property within the year and the day limited by the law. To preserve this property entire, and, if possible, to prevent wrecks altogether, the laws of England have most justly and humanely provided.

By the stat. 27 Edw. 3, if any ship be lost on the shore and the goods come to land, they shall be presently delivered to the merchants, paying only a reasonable reward to those who saved and preserved them. (*p*) This reward is entitled *salvage.*

By the common law, also, if any person, (other than the sheriff,) take any goods so cast on the shore, which are legal wreck, the owners might have a commission to inquire and find them out, and compel them to make restitution. (*q*) And by statute 12 Ann. C. 18. confirmed by 4 Geo. 1. C. 12. in order to assist the distressed, &c. it is enacted, that all head officers and others, of towns near the sea, shall, upon application made to them, summon as many hands as are necessary, and send them to the relief of any ship in distress, on forfeiture of £100; and in case of assistance given, salvage shall be paid by the owners, to be assessed by three neighboring justices. All persons who *secrete* any goods, shall forfeit their treble value:

(*p*) 1 Bla. Com. 293.
(*q*) F. N. B. 112.

and if they wilfully do any act, whereby the ship is lost or destroyed, by making holes in her or otherwise, they are guilty of felony without benefit of clergy. (*r*) Many other salutary regulations have also been made in England for effectually preserving ships of any nation in distress.

Though the governments of the States of this country when they were colonies, were understood to be exclusive of many royal prerogatives, yet the king considered himself as entitled to wreck. This is made to appear by the grant to Sir Ferdinando Gorges, of the province of Maine, in 1639, which grant includes the right to wreck. And as the king judged he could grant this right in one colony, he of course so judged, as relates to the other colonies. (*s*) If the king's prerogative of wreck, then, extended to the colonies, and was not relinquished to the colonies, (as for instance, his prerogative in royal fish was relinquished to Rhode-Island,) (*t*) the United States must have succeeded thereto, on the separation of the two countries.

By the seventh article of the Consular Convention with France, it was agreed, that when there shall be no consul or vice-consul of the king of the French, to attend to the saving of the wreck of any

(*r*) 1 Bla. Com. 293, 4.
(*s*) 3 Dane's Abr. 137.
(*t*) Vid. Rhode-Island charter.

French vessels stranded on the coasts of the United States, or not so near the place, &c. as the competent judge of the country may be, such judge shall immediately proceed to perform the office prescribed in the convention. The act of Congress, April 14, 1792, then directs "that the *district judge* of the United States, of the district in which the wreck shall happen, shall proceed therein according to the tenor of the said article, and in such cases it shall be the duty of the *officers of the customs,* within whose districts such wrecks shall happen, to give notice thereof, as soon as may be, to the said judge, and to aid and assist him to perform the duties hereby assigned to him." (*u*)

By the Convention and act above-mentioned, it appears that the federal government have actually exercised jurisdiction as to wrecks of *French* vessels. And as the jurisdiction of wrecks cannot properly be divided between the general and State governments, it would seem clearly to follow, that the general government must be understood to have the sole jurisdiction.

At common law, it seems, wrecks could be claimed only by action, in the courts of the county where they were found, (*v*) and by the express words of the Statute of 15 Rich. 2. the admiralty

(*u*) 2 U. S. Laws, 90.
(*v*) 5 Rep. 107.

could *not* take cognizance of wrecks. (*w*) The admiralty courts of this country, have, however, claimed and exercised a jurisdiction over this kind of derelict property, as well as over vessels and goods which have been abandoned, or have been found floating on the high seas.

In the case of Stephens, *et al. v.* Ship Argus, (*y*) in the district court of South-Carolina, an act of the State, was produced relative to goods wrecked, which gave occasion to consider the question of admiralty jurisdiction. The court held, that as incidental circumstances, necessarily flowing from, and dependent upon, the first cause of action, follow the original jurisdiction; and as the federal constitution gave to the district court *exclusive* cognizance over all civil causes of admiralty and maritime jurisdiction, the court had cognizance of wrecks.

As to the *amount of salvage to be awarded,* on the restitution of wrecked goods, the service rendered by the finder, the risk to which he was exposed in rescuing, and the value of the property saved, are the points by which in this, as well as in every other case of salvage, the decree as to the quantum of salvage must be regulated. One general rule, however, appears to run through all

(*w*) 4 Bac. Abr. T. Prerog. p. 159.
(*y*) Bee's Ad. Rep. 170.

the cases, and that is, the compensation must be *liberal.* This rule is undoubtedly established, with the view to the general interests of commerce, and to the interests of mankind in rewarding and encouraging generous and magnanimous actions.

However the ancient idea that wreck was the property of the Crown, may have been exploded in modern times, a very similar idea has certainly been preserved in the adjudication between salvors and claimants, as to the quantum which each shall retain of the thing saved. And such discretion has been assumed, as appears very much like acting under the principle, "*cujus est dare ejus est disponere.*" (*y*)

The case before mentioned of Stephens *et al. v.* Ship Argus, was a case in point as to the quantum of salvage to be awarded in the instance of wreck. This vessel, it appears, was wrecked on Charleston bar, and the goods were cast ashore on several islands contiguous thereto. Restitution was prayed, after such deduction for salvage, as the court might think reasonable. It appeared that the weather was tempestuous, and that great labor and exertion were necessary, first, to place the goods in a state of safety, and then to bring them to Charleston. All this was done by the salvors, without any assistance from the ship's crew. It appeared, also, that without great diligence, much

(*y*) Vid. 6 Am. Law Journ. 512.

of the cotton would have been washed off from the shore, to which it had drifted, and would have been again afloat at sea. The owners of these islands, and their negroes, were constantly employed for a considerable time, (in some instances for three weeks) in securing and drying the cotton; after which, it was carted with great labor, to distant landing places, from whence it was finally brought to Charleston. During the whole of this time the crops of those who were employed in rendering this service, were neglected. One of the salvors also lost a schooner valued at £250, which was employed in bringing a part of the cotton from a landing to Charleston, who libelled for salvage on that ground.

The opinion of the judge was thus given: "Here the service rendered was considerable. It is proved that the ship's crew abandoned the property, and the captain, who remained for some time on one of the islands, did not assist in any manner. Mr. Mair, by the papers and by hand bills, made known the situation of the vessel, and offered all due encouragement to such as would endeavor to save the cargo; yet no more than 35 bales of cotton, and 15 barrels of tar, were saved by these, or any exertions except those of the salvors, parties to this suit. They, unassisted but by their own negroes, saved 264 bags of cotton, 334 barrels of tar and a quantity of logwood, fustic, and mahogany, which sold for 600 dollars. The risk these persons run, was not, I think, so imminent as was contended. They exposed their health, indeed, and Mr. Lawton and his son were actually made ill by their exertions. Several respectable witnesses are of opinion, that the salvors run some risk of their lives in saving the cotton, and declare that they themselves would not have encountered the same, for the whole value of what was saved. The parties, however, seem to have dreaded sickness more than any thing else; and they might reasonably do so, for their labor must have been extreme. As to the value of what was saved, the sales amount to 12,999 dollars, chiefly arising from the cotton. The tar, &c. produced 1178 dollars; but these articles of inferior value, occasioned much more labor to the salvors than the cotton. Upon the whole, I think the libellants are entitled to receive as a compensation for their very meritorious exertions in this case, one third of the net proceeds arising from the sale of the cotton, and one half of the proceeds of the other articles."

As to the loss of the schooner, the court refused to allow any salvage on that ground, as the schooner was not lost in *saving* the goods, but in conveying them after they had been deposited in a place of safety to the agent of the owners.

In the case of the British consul *v.* Smith, the court was of opinion, that there was no difference between wreck and *derelict*, except that the property in one instance, is found on *land*, and in the other *at sea;* and in both, the original owners, whenever they can be found, have a paramount claim on payment of reasonable salvage. (*z*) To establish this paramount claim of ownership, the claimants, (according to Molloy,) (*a*) " must make their proof by the *marks* or *cocquets*, by the *book of customs*, or by *the testimony of honest men.*"

In the case of the two Catharines, which was shipwrecked in Narraganset bay, and her sails, rigging, &c. preserved by the exertions of the crew, a question was made at the bar, as to the liability of *underwriters* to the charge of salvage on a vessel which has been abandoned by the original owner. Mr. Justice Story declared his opinion, " that it must be borne by the underwriters." " It is not, (he continued) " like the ordinary charge of seamen's wages, which are a charge upon the ship owner, and are to be borne by the *freight;* but it is an expense in the saving of the materials of the ship, for the benefit of the underwriters, and as they exclusively receive the benefit, they are to receive it *cum onere*. The case of Frothingham *v.* Prince, (*b*) is directly in point; nor do I think, considering the circumstances of the case, that

(*z*) Bee's Ad. Rep. 180.
(*a*) Molloy, 274.
(*b*) 3 Mass. Rep. 563.

anything ruled by the court in Coffin *v.* Storer, (*c*) weakens the effect of the former decision. (*d*)

It was formerly made a question, whether or not wrecked goods *are liable for the payment of duties.* Chief Justice Holt, in 1 Ld. Ray. 388, was of opinion that they were not liable. "That wreck shall not pay custom," (he says) "has never been made a doubt since the case of Shepard *v.* Gosnold, in Vaughn, 159."

In the case of Sir Wm. Courtney *v.* Bower and Kingston, (*e*) the single question was, whether wrecked and *flotsam* goods were subject to pay duty. After this case had depended three or four years, and after several arguments at the bar, the judges delivered their opinions in solemn argument. Neville, Powell and Blencowe, were in favor of the plaintiff, (who was lord of the manor, and claimed the wreck by prescription,) and were of opinion that he ought not to pay custom. But Treby delivered his opinion for the defendants, (who were custom house officers,) that the plaintiff ought to pay custom. This case was also tried before Holt, C. J. at Exeter, he being then (1696) justice of assize there, and by the great importunity of the king's counsel, he permitted it to be found specially; but was most clearly of opinion.

(*c*) 5 Mass. Rep. 252.
(*d*) 2 Mason's Rep. 319.
(*e*) 1 Ld. Ray. 501, 502.

that no custom ought to be paid for wreck. Afterwards, error was brought upon this judgment in B. R. and after several arguments at bar by the counsel on both sides, the judgment of the common pleas was affirmed, without any other reason given by the court, than the authority of the case of Shepard *v.* Gosnold, above mentioned. (*f*)

But the rule that wrecked goods are not subject to duties, as above laid down, must be supposed to apply to those goods only which are *strictly* wreck, that is, where no owner appears in proper time to claim them. In such a case, the rule will very properly apply, for where no owner appears, the property of the goods is assigned to the king, and it would be absurd for the king to demand a duty out of that which is entirely his own. And where wreck is claimed against the king, by grant or prescription, the person claiming, (it seems by the above authorities,) shall have it in the same manner as the king has his, that is, as not chargeable with duty. (*g*)

Another question which may arise in relation to goods and merchandize thrown from the sea on the land is, how far they are liable to be forfeited for being removed, before the regular duties are paid thereon. To determine this question, we have the case of the United States *v.* The cargo of the ship

(*f*) 1 Ld. Ray. 501, 502.
(*g*) Molloy. 274.

Favourite, in the supreme court of the United States. (*g*) This was the case of a vessel deserted by her crew in the river Delaware. The court held, that the section of the act of Congress, for the collection of duties, which creates a forfeiture of goods not marked, nor accompanied by certificates, does not comprehend goods found on board of a vessel deserted by her crew, and in such a situation as to render it necessary to land them, on the nearest accessible part of the coast. Nor would the landing of goods under such circumstances without a permit, subject them to forfeiture, because forfeiture can only be applied to cases *in which the means that are prescribed for the prevention of a forfeiture*, may be employed. And the same rule the court held, applied to the *removal* of goods after they were landed.

(*g*) 1 Hall's Law Journ. 251.

APPENDIX.

ADJUDGED CASES.

3 Mass. Rep. 352.

ADAMS *v.* FROTHINGHAM.

This was a writ of right, in which the demandant claimed an undivided moiety of a certain parcel of land in *Newburyport*, bounded northwardly on *Merrimack* River. The writ was dated the 8th day of February, 1802, and alleges that *Zaccheus Perkins*, the demandant's father, was seized of the same within sixty years from the date of the writ, that on his death the same descended to her as his daughter and heir, and that the tenant deforceth her.

The demandant having obtained a verdict in the original action, the tenant brought his writ of review, upon which another trial was had before *Parker*, *J.* April term, 1806, when a verdict was again rendered for the demandant. The tenant moved for a new trial, for the misdirection of the Judge at the trial, and that motion came on now to be argued by *Dane* and *Putnam* for the tenant, and *Jackson* for the demandant, before *Sedgwick*, *Sewall* and *Parker*, Justices; the *Chief Justice* not sitting, as he had been formerly of counsel in the cause.

The report of the Judge, who sat in the trial, states that the demandant, to prove the seizin of her ancestor, read in evidence the copy of a vote of the town of *Newbury*, (1) passed 8 March, 1680, granting *William Noyes* a piece of land below high-water mark, to set a shop upon, and not exceeding forty feet in the front: also the copy of another vote passed 9 February, 1721, granting to the same *W. Noyes* another parcel of land above high-water mark, and bounded northwardly thereby.—The demandant then read a deed of *Parker Noyes* and his wife, who had the estate of the said *W. Noyes*, dated 10 November, 1740, of the same two parcels of land to *Zaccheus Perkins* her father.

On the 28th of April, 1741, the said *Z. Perkins* conveyed the same two parcels of land by deed to *Spencer Bennett*, who on the 2d of March, 1742, conveyed one half of the house which had been built on the upland, and of the land upon which it stood, by metes and bounds, together with one half of the land and flats below the house in quantity and quality, to the said *Z. Perkins*.

It appeared in evidence, by depositions in the case, that *Bennett* had in 1740 lived in a house on the premises, and built a shop below the house, on a wharf or breastwork also built by him; but it did not appear under whom he so occupied. It also appeared that the west end of the house and the land back of it was occupied under *Z. Perkins*, and that the flats below were used in common by the occupants of each part of the house.

It was also proved by the shifting of the channel of the river, the flats were much increased in extent since the year 1740.

The tenant produced in evidence a deed from a committee of the proprietors of *Newbury*, dated 15th of June, 1750, conveying, besides a piece of upland, "a piece of flats of forty feet "in breadth, running from the rear of *W. Noyes'* grant down "to the channel," to *Spencer Bennett*, under whom, by the

(1) The town of *Newburyport* constituted a part of *Newbury* until 1764, when it was incorporated by its present name.

deed of said *Bennett* to *James M'Herd*, and by deed of the heirs or devisees of *M'Herd* to the tenant, he claims to hold.

The tenant's counsel insisted at the trial, that *Z. Perkins* could have been seized of the flats only as they in fact existed at his death, and that none which had been made by *alluvion* could be recovered by the present demandant. The Judge directed the jury that, if *Perkins* was seized of the flats within sixty years, whatever increase there had been, rightfully accrued to the demandant as his heir.

They also contended that the grant of the proprietors to *Noyes* passed to him no more of the flats than were sufficient to set a shop upon. Upon this point the jury were directed that, by the legal construction of the grant, it extended to low-water mark; which appeared, by the evidence in the case, to have been the construction given by all who had occupied under said grant.

It was then contended that the deed from *Bennett* to *Perkins* did not necessarily create a tenancy in common: and that, if such was the legal construction of the deed, the jury might presume that a partition had been made by the parties. The Judge directed the jury that by virtue of the said deed, *Bennett* and *Perkins* became tenants in common, and there being no evidence of any holding in severalty, except of the upland, which severance was in conformity with the deed, there was nothing in the case from which a partition of the flats could be inferred.

Another point made by the tenant's counsel was that *Bennett*, having entered in 1740, and built a wharf, and afterwards having purchased of the proprietors, must be considered as having entered under the proprietors, and not under *Z. Perkins*. Upon this point the jury were instructed that *Bennett* having conveyed to *Perkins* in 1742, his purchase of the proprietors in 1750, provided he acquired any title by that purchase, inured to the use of *Perkins*, whom he had made, by his deed, tenant in common with himself.

Finally, the Judge directed the jury, if they were satisfied with the evidence of the demandant's title, as she had set it forth they might by their verdict find, that, to all the demanded premises above low-water mark, she had a better right to recover than the said *Frothingham* had to hold : and their verdict was accordingly. To all which opinions and directions the counsel for the tenant excepted.

Curia. This cause has been twice fully tried, once before a court competent to decide ultimately all questions of law, which arose in the trial, and the verdict has in both instances been in favour of the demandant, with the approbation of the court: yet as the new organization of the court intervened between the first and second trial, the tenant has the right to take the course he now pursues, and, if any misdirection of the Judge can be shewn, he will have the privilege of a third trial before another jury.

The points, in which the Judge is supposed to have mistaken the law, are particularly specified in his report of the case before us.

The *first* relates to his construction of the proprietary grant of 1680, which gives to *William Noyes*, under whom the demandant's ancestor held "*a piece of land below high-water* "*mark to set a shop upon, not exceeding forty feet in width.*" It is said by the tenant's counsel, that no more land passed by the grant, than was actually covered by such shop as the immediate grantee may have placed upon it; whereas the Judge directed that all the land and flats between high and low-water mark, of the width of forty feet, were the subject of the grant, provided they did not extend more than one hundred rods from the upland: and we are all of opinion that in this decision the Judge was correct. Whatever might be the construction of analogous words in a recent conveyance, made in times of precision and accuracy, and when considerable value is attached to flats in the beds of rivers, creeks and coves; it is obvious that to apply rigid rules of construction to transactions, which took place early after the settlement of the country, when conveyancing was little understood, and when the mud of a river or harbour was supposed to be worth nothing, would often be attended with injustice, and in many instances subvert the titles to property of almost incalculable value.

Whether a mere vote of a proprietary at the present day, without any deed or location in pursuance of such vote, would pass lands from such proprietary to an individual, not a member of the corporation, is questionable: but it is well known that almost all the titles, which have been derived from proprietors of townships, have nothing better to depend upon than a vote recorded in the proprietor's books; and where a possession was taken in conformity to the vote, and transmitted by the grantee to his heirs or assigns, titles so acquired have been respected and maintained in our courts of law.

Nor indeed can there be any doubt, that the construction given by the Judge, as to the extent of this grant, was conformable to the true intent of the proprietors in making the grant. By the statute of 1641, it was declared that the owners of upland should own the flats to low-water mark, unless these should exceed the distance of one hundred rods from the upland, in which case they were to be restricted to that distance. Under that statute, the proprietors of *Newbury* became the proprietors of all the flats in the river *Merrimack*, down to the channel, that being within the distance before mentioned.—Now it is very fairly to be presumed that in 1680 these proprietors were desirous to settle their township, and they were inviting mechanics and other valuable settlers by offering them advantageous situations upon the river, situations then of little consideration as to their value, though since become so important. *William Noyes* applied for a place below high-water mark, to set a shop upon, which was granted him. The object of *Noyes* in seeking such a place, must have been an access from the river to his shop. The proprietors take care to limit his extent upon the shore, confining him to forty feet.—But they do not limit him towards the river. Is it to be supposed that they intended to reserve the flats between the grantee's shop and the channel to themselves, and so have it in their power entirely to frustrate the manifest object of their grant to *Noyes?* This would have been an extremely hard bargain on the part of *Noyes*, had such intention been expressed; but certainly so unjust a provision ought not to depend upon slight implication.

The common maxims of law, applicable to the construction of instruments, will come in aid of the probable intent of the parties, in ascertaining the legal effect of this grant. Doubtful words and provisions are to be taken most strongly against the grantor, he being supposed to select the words which are used in the instrument. In this grant of the proprietors, they give three sides of the lot which they convey, and leave indefinite the fourth; it must be taken that they intended that the extent of the lot in the rear should be limited only by their claim. And the legal construction of their own words will not be thought to operate rigorously, if we carry our minds back to the year 1680, when from testimony in the case, we may reasonably infer that the channel ran so much nearer the upland, as to leave no flats between *Noyes'* shop and the channel worth the attention of the proprietors.

But in addition to all this it appears in the case that all those, who occupied under the grant to *Noyes*, claimed and used the flats, as they needed them, in the rear of the breast-work, upon which the shop was placed; and this too in the view of the proprietors and their agents, for nearly the space of a century after the grant was made; during all which time no complaint was made by the proprietors, and no act of ownership exercised by them. Here then was a practical construction by both parties, sufficient to remove all doubts as to the true extent of the grant. It is true that in 1750 the proprietors undertook by their deed to convey these flats to *Spencer Bennett*, but at this time *Perkins*, the demandant's ancestor, was in possession as tenant in common with *Bennett*, claiming derivatively under *Noyes* the first grantee, and immediately from *Bennett* himself, who in 1742 sold to him one moiety of these very flats. Now if any thing passed from the proprietors, it inured to the use of *Perkins* as well as *Bennett:* and on this ground the claim set up by the tenant, who claims under *Bennett*, is without foundation.

The *second* exception to the Judge's charge relates to his decision that the deed from *Bennett* to *Perkins* in 1742, created a tenancy in common between the grantor and grantee of the flats in question. Previous to the date of this deed, *Perkins* had conveyed to *Bennett* all the flats, as also an upland lot which the proprietors had granted to the same *William Noyes* in 1721, and by this deed *Bennett* conveyed back to *Perkins* one half of the upland or house-lot by metes and bounds, and one moiety of the flats behind the house *in quantity and quality*. Can it be doubted that this created an estate in common and undivided in those flats? We are at a loss to imagine any form of words more technically proper for this purpose.

But it is said, and this constitutes the *third* exception, that the parties *occupied* in severalty, and that this several occupancy was a partition in fact, which ought to have concluded against the demandant's action, which is brought for an undivided moiety. Whether there was a several occupancy or not, was matter of fact for the jury; and although the Judge intimated an opinion that there was not sufficient evidence to prove it, yet we do not find that he withheld any evidence on this point, nor do we find any evidence of the depositions submitted to us, from which the jury could have inferred that fact.

The *fourth* exception, relied upon by the counsel for the tenant, respects the opinion, delivered by the Judge, relative to so much of the flats, as may have gathered by *alluvion* since the death of the demandant's ancestor. To give this objection its full force, we must recur to some of the testimony used in the case, by which it appeared that the channel of the river *Merrimack*, towards its mouth, had considerably receded from the shore on the *Newbury* side: and some of the witnesses imputed this to the numerous improvements, which have been made on the bank of the river, and on the flats, by the erection of wharves, &c. It is contended that the ancestor could have been seized only of so much of the flats as existed in his life-time, and as the demandant has declared on the seizin of her ancestor, she cannot recover more than he was actually seized of.

But we do not think much of this objection. It has already been shewn, that the ancient statute, relative to the subject of flats, annexed them to the adjoining upland, to the distance of one hundred rods from the shore. Whatever increase, therefore, happened from natural causes, or from an union of natural and artificial causes, within that distance, must be to the benefit of the owner of the upland, or of him who owned the flats, to which the increase was attached. This increase is of necessity gradual and imperceptible. No man can fix a period when it began, no testimony can mark the exact margin of the channel on any given day or year. The ancestor being seized of the estate, of which all the flats now demanded are part, and having the right by law to all such additions as should be made by the gradual retiring of the waters, he must be supposed to have been seized of all which now exists, for no one can show any parcel of which he was not seized. We think the opinion delivered at the trial right on this point; and further we think this an instance in which we may safely apply the maxim, *de minimis non curat lex.*

The form of the verdict constitutes the *last* exception. It is said this is uncertain, and no judgment can be rendered upon it.

The verdict is conformable to the nature of the demand, and a judgment thereon will be sufficiently certain to enable the sheriff to execute it by an *habere facias.* We are therefore all of opinion that judgment must be entered according to the verdict.

NOTE. The *Chief Justice* was of counsel in this cause, while at the bar, and of course was not on the bench during the argument or decision of it.

1 ANSTRUTHER'S REP. 603.

THE ATTORNEY GENERAL *v.* RICHARDS.

THIS information stated, that, by the royal prerogative, the sea and sea-coasts, as far as the sea flows and reflows, between the high and low-water marks, and all the ports and havens of the kingdom, belong to his Majesty, and ought to be preserved for the use of his Majesty's vessels, and others, and that his Majesty has the right of superintendency over them, for their preservation.

It was then stated, that the defendants, in 1784 erected a wharf or key, two docks, and other buildings, between high and low-water mark, in *Portsmouth* harbour, adjoining to *Gosport*, so as both to prevent the boats and vessels from sailing over that spot, or mooring there; and also to endanger further damage to the harbour, by preventing the free current of the water to carry off the mud. The information therefore prayed, that the defendants might be restrained from making any further erections, that those made might be abated, and the harbour restored to its ancient situation.

The defendants claimed to hold the soil of the place in question, under letters-patent, 14th *July*, 4 *Ch.* I. These letters-patent recited, that a commission had issued to the sheriff of *Hampshire*, and other persons, to examine all the mud-banks and sea-marshes, within a certain district, on the coast; and, by a legal inquest, to inquire and report, whether any, and what part of them, might be recovered from the sea, without injury to any person. They made a return, certifying, that certain mud-lands, and lands covered with the sea, around the town of *Gosport*, might be recovered from the sea, to the great benefit of the nation, and without injury or damage to any person. The letters-patent, on the foot of this return, and in consideration of the services of the grantees, and of the money to be by them expended in recovering from the sea the lands granted; of the special favour, certain knowledge, and mere motion of the King, did grant to *Mary Wandesford* and *William Wandesford*, certain mud-lands, and lands overflown with the sea, among others, certain lands overflown with the sea, on each side of *Gosport* and there fully described, and also discharged the same from all claim of tithes from the Crown, during seven years from the date of the lands being recovered and embanked from the sea, rendering a rent of 4d. *per* acre for every acre recovered till the year 1630, and from that period, the rent of 1s.

Two of the defendants also pleaded possession of the place in question for more than sixty years.

It was much disputed, upon the evidence, whether the place in question was included within the grant, or not. The defendants did not produce the conveyances, and the deduction of title from the *Wandesfords*, to the persons from whom they derived immediately their claim. They only produced the conveyance of this parcel of mud-land to themselves, by persons stated in the conveyance to be entitled under the letters-patent.

It was admitted, that the defendants, or those under whom they claimed, had had possession of a piece of mud-land adjoining to the piece in question, for upwards of sixty years. The ground in question had never been recovered from the sea, till the erections complained of by the bill, and which were made after notice of the intention to dispute the right; but the defendants had had possession, by keeping floats of timber moored there, for some time before.

It was proved, that the embankment was highly prejudicial and dangerous to the harbour, and that it was peculiarly hurtful to the town of *Gosport*, by preventing boats from coming immediately up to the town, on that side, as formerly.

This case was argued during the term by

The *Attorney General* and *Solicitor General*, *Alexander*, *Campbell*, and *Percival*, for the Crown. The *prima facie* right of the Crown to all ports and arms of the sea, and to the soil thereof, is clearly established. The nature of that right is explained by Lord *Hale*, in his *De Jure Maris* and *De Portibus Maris*.* It is there shown, (p. 12) that the King has the soil of the sea-coast and havens, and is entitled to the profits thereof as a *jus privatum ;* and so far as it is considered in that light merely, he may grant it away. But he has also (p. 81, 83, 88, 89,) another right in the arms of the sea, the right of a free passage for all his subjects and others, and of having all havens, and branches of the sea, preserved from nuisances, for that purpose. This is a right similar to the King's property in highways, a mere *jus publicum* vested in the King for the use of the subjects. This, by its nature is unalienable, and shall prevail against any claim set up against it. Lord Hale, *De Jure Maris*, 12. *De Jure Portibus*, 85.

Where any invasion of the *jus privatum* of the Crown, in arms of the sea, or ports, takes place, by encroachment on the soil, it is a purpresture. Glanville, l. 9. c. 11. Spelm. Gloss. Purpresture. Where the *jus publicum* is violated it is a nuisance ; and it frequently happens, as in the present case, that a nuisance in a port is accompanied with a purpresture, or encroachment on the soil of the Crown.

All nuisances may be abated by the mere act of any individual; but in the case of the Crown, the more proper and decorous mode of proceeding, is by information in a court of justice, for ascertaining the right. This may be done by information in equity, as well as at law; and the nuisance may be decreed to be abated.

In the case of a purpresture, the same mode of proceeding has been held proper. In case of a decree for the Crown, an inquiry is directed, whether it be most beneficial for the Crown to abate the purpresture, or to suffer the erections to remain, and be arrented. Where the purpresture is also a nuisance,

* See Mr. *Hargrave's* Law Tracts.

the Crown has not this election; for it cannot sanction a nuisance.

In the case of the *Attorney General* v. *Philpot*, in this court, 8 *Ch.* I. the information stated the Crown to be seized of the river *Thames*, where navigable and an arm of the sea, for the use of the ships resorting there; and that the Crown was also seized of the soil between high and low-water mark: that the defendants had lately encroached upon the soil of the King, and had thereby stopped the course of the river, and rendered it less convenient for shipping, and for their mooring in the pool. The information therefore prayed, that the encroachment might be declared a purpresture, and be abated as such. The defendants set up a defence, that they had had the leave of the High Admiral, and that their encroachment was no damage to the shipping. The court declared, that purprestures on navigable rivers ought to be abated. They accordingly directed a commission to inquire, whether the fact complained of was a purpresture.—The Commissioners returned that it was, and the encroachment was abated.

So in the case of *the city of Bristol* v: *Morgan*, cited in Lord *Hale's* treatise *De Portibus Maris*, p. 81. The bill stated the benefit of navigable rivers for commerce, and the right to have all purprestures therein abated. It was proved that the defendants had erected houses on the banks of the *Avon*, so as to straighten the river, and to incommode the passage to and from the shipping to the shore: that these houses also intercepted the commerce to the town, and tended to defraud the revenue.—The encroachments were ordered to be abated, on the ground of the damage to the city; but were never destroyed, some composition having probably been entered into. A similar case is there cited to have been determined between *the Town of Newcastle* and *Johnson*, relative to the right of towage on the river *Tyne*.

In *Churchman* v. *Tunstal* Hardr. 62, the plaintiff sued by bill, as tenant of an ancient ferry under the Crown, to suppress a new ferry set up in the neighbourhood, to the damage of his ancient ferry, and to obtain an injunction against renewing it. The court there dismissed the bill, as seeking to establish a monopoly; but another bill being afterwards filed for the same matter, the court, on the 7th *April*, 14, *Ch.* II. (Lord *Hale* presiding in it,) decreed, that the new ferry should be suppressed and that the defendants should not have liberty to use any ferry boat, to the annoyance of the plaintiff's ancient ferry.*

So in the anonymous case. 3 Atk. 750, where it was moved to issue an injunction against building a small-pox hospital in *Cold Bath Fields*, Lord *Hardwicke* lays it down, that, in the case of a public nuisance, an information by the Attorney General is the proper remedy. He was then sitting in equity, and must be understood to mean an information in a court of equity. Besides, he refused the injunction in that case, upon the want of merits, not from any doubt of his jurisdiction. So *Coulson* v. *White*, 3 Atk. 21, establishes the authority of equity to abate nuisances. *Ryder* v. *Bentham*, 1 Vez. 543. Sir *Lister Holt's* case, 2 Vez. 193.

The grant is bad on another ground. The King, in his *jus publicum*, had possession of the soil covered with the sea, by the passage of his subjects in ships over it. But there was no possession of the soil under the *jus privatum;* and the right to enjoy it being then only a possibility, when it should be recovered from the sea, could not be granted to a subject. The *Attorney General* v. Sir *Ed. Fermer*, 2 Lev. 171. Sir T. Raym. 241. Much less could one subject transfer this right to another : for, between them, there is not even a colour of possession. It is within the rule against buying pretended titles.

The grant can at most give only a right of entry : but if I convey an estate, and die before entry by the purchaser, the right of entry is gone. So here, the right of entry could only be during the life of King *Charles* I.

The nature of the grant shews, that it was to be reduced

*See the Minute Book 1662 p. 131.

into possession within a reasonable time, if at all. The grant proceeds on a surmise of the public benefit to accrue from embanking the mud-lands. The tithes were not to be demandable for seven years after the embankment. The rent from 1630 was to be increased. Then the embanking within a reasonable time, was considered as a condition annexed to the grant, and has not been complied with during 150 years. The non-payment of the rent during that period proves, that there was no possession, actual or constructive.

But even if this passed by the grant, the grantee has since thrown it open for the public use, by allowing it to continue an open passage for ships during so long a period. The King has acquired a new right to it, by the possession of his subjects in passing and repassing over it for 150 years. A place thrown open to the public as a highway, cannot, after long enjoyment, be shut up.

The possession of another part, under the letters patent, during 60 years, cannot inure to give possession of the whole; nor can entry upon any part, under the grant, be considered as entry upon this land which remained overflowed. If there is a conveyance of *Blackacre* and *Whiteacre*, entry upon *Blackacre*, in the name of both, is good. But this supposes that the entry upon *Whiteacre* was also possible. But if *Whiteacre* was then held by a disseisor, so as that the feoffee could not enter, the entry upon *Blackacre* does not inure to both. Here the entry upon this parcel of land was impossible till recovered from the sea. Besides, the King, by the passage of his subjects, has had actual possession of it, so that the entry upon the other parts of the grant cannot be extended to this.

The defendants, in order to avail themselves of the letters-patent, must either deduce to themselves a regular title against the Crown, or must shew, that the subject was once severed from the Crown, and that they are in possession, which presumes all the mesne conveyances. The defendants do neither. The deduction of title, under the letters-patent, to the persons under whom the defendants immediately claim, is not shewn. It is clear these persons never had any possession, of this spot. Then there is no privity, either by title or by possession, between them and the grantees, and the defendants may be wholly strangers to the letters-patent.

Even if they claim under the letters-patent, yet these erections must be abated; for it is clear that the King cannot permit a public nuisance, as this is proved to be. *De Port. Mar.* 85.

Piggot and *Richards*, for the defendant.—It is clear, that as far as the *jus privatum* of the Crown is concerned, a grant of the soil of the sea-coast, or of a harbour, is good. But, if the argument be true, that no possession could ever be taken of the soil while overflown, no grant or feoffment of land covered with water could ever be good.

But, on the contrary, Lord *Hale* says (*De Port. Mar.* p. 85) that there are a thousand instances of license from the King to build new wharves or keys, in which license the right to the soil, within high and low-water mark, or beyond, is necessarily included.

It is agreed, that a great part of the lands granted have long ago been embanked; but possession of a part is possession of the whole; and we are therefore entitled to hold by length of possession, in corroboration of the grant.

This is a grant of lands to be afterwards recovered from the sea. It implies, throughout, that immediate embankment of the whole was not expected; and, as no time is limited, it is still open to us to take advantage of it. Our title is sufficiently made out; for the soil being once granted away from the Crown, mere possession is evidence of the right of the person entitled. To produce the whole conveyances is impossible; for this is a small parcel out of an extensive grant, and we are not entitled to the possession of the deeds, under which the whole lands granted are held. It appears that the land immediately adjoining has been embanked for more than sixty years, and floats of wood used to be moored over the place in question, long before the erections now complained of. This was a possession; for it prevented the free passage over that part of the harbour. Then the mode of trying the right to the land, when the possession was in the subject, is by suit at law. As to this point, it is in the nature of a mere ejectment bill.

Besides, the information does not pray that the soil may be declared to belong to the King, which would be the proper prayer, if the right to the soil were in question. It merely prays, that the erections may be abated, which is the proper prayer on a complaint of nuisance, if at all; and as a nuisance is charged in the bill, the only matter in issue must be that which relates to and supports the prayer of the bill. But as to the question of nuisance, the title to the lands is perfectly immaterial, and therefore our possession, not being properly put in issue, remains unimpeached.

As to the question of nuisance, that is a matter completely foreign to the jurisdiction of a Court of Equity. It is a breach of the general police of the kingdom, and as such is considered as a crime, and to be prosecuted in the criminal courts. But a Court of Equity cannot hold cognizance of any criminal matter. It never was attempted to prosecute a suit in equity, to remedy any other public mischiefs—as to prohibit rope-dancing, plays, &c. or to abate a nuisance or purpresture on the highway. That is exactly like the present case, and is every day prosecuted in the ordinary criminal courts. Questions of nuisance are particularly improper to be discussed in equity, because the remedy at law is complete.

It is true, that in the precedents cited, such informations have been allowed in the case of purprestures; but these were in the time of *Ch.* I. when the right to trial by jury was not so firmly established as it now is. Besides those were, in part at least, suits as to a civil right, and therefore gave a colour to the jurisdiction. Lord *Hale* expressly declares, (p. 85) that the question of nuisance is a question of fact, and not of law: that is, that it ought to be decided by a jury, not by the court. In the cases relied upon, on the other side, the court directed a commission to inquire into the fact. The mode now adopted in Courts of Equity is to direct an issue in such case, instead of granting a commission; and those authorities, therefore, entitle us to expect, that the court will not decide against us, without an issue.

MACDONALD, Chief Baron, this day delivered the opinion of the court (after stating the case) to this effect.

It is clear that the right to the soil between high and low-water mark, is *prima facie* in the Crown. Then the *onus* of proving an adverse title is thrown upon the defendants.

This they attempt to do, under the letters-patent; but upon the whole evidence, as far as we can now trace the meaning of the grant, this spot does not seem to have been included in it. The return of the inquisition finds that the embanking the lands granted would be of no detriment to any person. But that is not consistent with the evidence here, that the embanking this land would hurt the harbour, and prevent the passage of boats up to the town of *Gosport*: then the inquisition and grant must have related to other lands; and the grant, in describing the parcels, gives the mud lands on each side of *Gosport*, studiously passing by the town; so that it does not appear that this land was ever meant to be granted from the Crown.

But the grant appears also to have been made for the sake of the public interest, in having this land brought into cultivation. The exemption from tithes for seven years shews the intent to have been, that it should be put into a state capable of producing titheable matter. The rent also proves the embankment, and regaining from the sea, to have been the condition and spirit of the grant. That has not been complied with.

But the defendants do not deduce their title from the grantees; they shew a title under *A.* and *B.*, who, they aver, were entitled under the grant; but the *onus* of establishing their claim being upon them, they must shew how *A.* and *B.* derived that right. At present it appears to be the conveyance by mere strangers. The lease and release from them recites the releasers to be entitled under the grant; but that is no evidence of the fact.

They next went on the evidence of possession. But it appears, that instead of their having possession, the Crown has, by its subjects, had possession of the place in question; and its being open as a public passage from 1629, precludes any right now to question the title of the Crown. If the grantees ever had any title, it has been abandoned. It would be extremely inconvenient, if old dormant grants of the Crown could be enforced in this manner, when the evidence of their nature and extent is lost by lapse of time. Upon the whole, we are of opinion, that the defendants have not made out any title to the soil of the place in question.

But it is argued, that the prayer of the bill being to abate the erections as a nuisance, the court can only consider that question, as alone supporting the relief prayed; and it is contended, that this court cannot give such a decree, or at least not without the intervention of a jury, the question of nuisance being, as laid down by Lord *Hale*, a question of fact, and not of law. That may be, where the question is of nuisance only, and the evidence doubtful. But the cases cited, and those which Lord *Hale* has given us, in the treatise *De Portibus Maris*, clearly prove, that where the King claims and proves a right to the soil, where a purpresture and nuisance have been committed, he may have a decree to abate it. The case of *the river Thames*, and the *Bristol* and the *Newcastle* cases, cited by Lord *Hale*, are all authorities for this proposition. The case in Hardr. 162, was at first determined otherwise; but the reporter doubts its authority, as it was afterwards overturned. It is objected, that these cases were in the time of *Ch.* I.; but it must be remembered, that Lord *Hale* determined some of them, and approved the rest. Supported by such authority, we do not hesitate to declare, that the soil is the property of the Crown; and of course do decree, that these buildings be abated.

1 Mass. Rep. 231.

AUSTIN & *al.* *v.* CARTER & *al.*

TRESPASS for breaking and entering the close of the plaintiffs in *Charlestown*, on and adjoining to *Charles River* there, and cutting down piers, &c. by the plaintiffs therein erected.

Plea, (with a reservation to give any special matter in evidence) the general issue, which (consenting to the reservation) was joined—And there was also filed in the case an agreement of the parties, that either of the defendants might give in evidence any special matter which might have been pleaded in justification.

The plaintiffs proved their title and possession to a tract of land in *Charlestown*, adjoining to *Charles River* there, in which the tide ebbs and flows—and that the piers alleged in the declaration to have been destroyed by the defendants, were erected by the plaintiffs in the close aforesaid, between high and low-water marks, and were cut down by the defendants.

Ward, for the defendants, grounded his defence, on a right which the inhabitants of *Charlestown* had, as he contended, to the occupation of the waters of *Charles River* where the piers were erected, and which the defendants cut down and removed as obstructing them in the exercise of that right—and he stated that the defence would rest on three grounds—*first*, that one of the defendants being a surveyor of highways in and for the town of *Charlestown* entered, with the others as his assistants, and removed the piers as a nuisance on a public highway—*Secondly*, that the defendants were the Selectmen of the town, and entered in the right of the corporation and removed the piers—and *thirdly*, that every individual inhabitant, as such, of the town had a right to the use of the waters of *Charles River*, and that the defendants being inhabitants of *Charlestown* entered and removed the piers, as obstructing them in the free exercise of that right.

The *Attorney General*, (*Sullivan*) for the plaintiffs, insisted that the defence stated was irrelevant—because, *first*, surveyors of highways, as such, have no authority excepting as to highways and roads on land—such ways as they are obliged to keep in repair—*secondly*, because the town as a corporation had no such right as was claimed, the land to low-water mark belonging to the proprietor of the adjoining land—and *thirdly*, that although it is true that the individual inhabitants of *Charlestown*, and so also all the inhabitants of the Commonwealth, had a right to pass and repass on the waters so long as the owner of the adjoining land, leaving them open and unobstructed, yet the owner of the adjoing land may, whenever he pleases, enclose, build and obstruct to low-water mark, and exclude all mankind.

The Court were unanimously of opinion with the *Attorney General*, particularly on the two last points, which they said had been repeatedly *so* decided—and directed a verdict for the plaintiffs.

2 Bosanquet & Puller's Rep. 472.

BAGOTT *v.* ORR.

TRESPASS. The 1st count was for breaking and entering the plaintiff's closes, called the *Foot-Muscle-Skear*, the *Great-Out-Muscle-Skear*, and the *Sea Shore*, in the parish of

Keysham, and Plaintiff's shell-fish and shells there finding, catching, taking, and carrying away, and converting and disposing thereof to defendant's own use. The 2d count was for breaking and entering the same closes, and with defendant's feet, and the feet of his servants in walking, treading and trampling upon, subverting and spoiling plaintiff's soil, earth and sand, and with the feet of cattle, and with the wheels of carriages, and the keels of boats, treading up, trampling, &c. and plaintiff's shell-fish and shells, breaking, crushing and destroying, and with spades, shovels, mattocks, pickaxes, and other instruments, digging and making holes and pits, and turning up, &c. plaintiff's earth, soil, and sand, and digging up, raising up, and getting up divers large quantities of plaintiff's shell-fish and shells, and carrying away the same, and converting and disposing thereof to defendant's own use.—There were several other counts for breaking and entering plaintiff's several fishery and his free fishery, on which issues in fact were joined.

The defendant pleaded, 1st, the general issue. 2dly, As to the trespasses mentioned in the two first counts, that the closes therein severally mentioned were the same, and that the said closes in which, &c. at the said several times when, &c. were and still are, and from time immemorial have been, part and parcel of a certain arm of the sea, in which every subject of this realm, at the said several times, when, &c. of right had, and of right ought to have had, and now hath, and of right ought to have, the liberty and privilege of fishing and catching, digging for, raising, getting, taking and carrying away shell-fish and shells there; therefore defendant being a subject of this realm, at the said several times when, &c. entered into the said closes in which, &c. so being part and parcel of the said arm of the sea to fish therein, and to catch, dig for, raise, get, take, and carry away the shell fish and shells there, and did then and there fish, and caught, took and carried away the said shell-fish and shells in the first count mentioned, and also dug up, raised up, and got up, took and carried away the said other shell-fish and shells in the second count lastly mentioned, as it was lawful for him to do, and for the digging up and carrying away of the said shell-fish, he entered the said closes in which, &c. by himself and with other persons, and with the said cattle, carts, wagons and other carriages, and the said boats, lighters, and other vessels, the same being reasonable, proper, and necessary in that behalf, and in so doing he necessarily and unavoidably with his feet, and the feet of those other persons, in walking a little trod up, trampled upon, subverted and spoiled the soil, earth, and sand, in the second count mentioned, and with the feet of the said cattle, and with the wheels of said carts, wagons, and other carriages, and with the keels of the said boats, lighters, and other vessels a little trod up, trampled upon, tore up, and subverted and spoiled other the soil of plaintiff's last mentioned closes, and the said shell-fish and shells in the second count first mentioned necessarily and unavoidably a little broke, crushed, and destroyed, and with the said spades, shovels, mattocks, pickaxes, and other instruments, the same being useful, proper, and necessary in that behalf and in digging up, raising and getting the said shell-fish and shells in the second count lastly mentioned, necessarily and unavoidably dug and made the said holes and pits in plaintiff's said closes, and necessarily and unavoidably with the spades, shovels, mattocks, pickaxes and other instruments, dug up, turned up, subverted, and spoiled a little of the earth, soil, and sand in the said closes, doing as little damage on that occasion as he could, which are the same, &c. whereof, &c.— And this, &c. wherefore, &c.

Upon this the plaintiff new assigned, alleging that defendant on the days in the first count mentioned broke and entered plaintiff's closes in the first count mentioned, "being certain closes lying within the flux and reflux of the tides of the sea in the plaintiff's manor of *Keysham*. and the said shell-fish and shells there then found, caught, took, and carried away, and converted and disposed thereof to his own use when the same closes in which, &c. were left dry and not covered with water." And also, that defendant, on the days and in the manner in the second count mentioned, broke and entered plaintiff's closes "being certain closes lying within the flux and reflux of the tides of the sea within plaintiff's said manor of *Keysham*, and with his feet, &c. trod up, &c. the said earth, soil, and sand in the second count mentioned, and with the feet of the said cattle in that count mentioned, and with the wheels of said carts, &c. and with the keels of the said boats, &c. trod up the said other soil in the plaintiff's last mentioned closes in the said second count mentioned, and plaintiff's said other shell-fish and shells in the second count mentioned, broke, crushed, &c. and with spades, &c. dug and made holes, &c. and raised up and got up the said shell-fish and shells, &c. and took and carried away the same, and converted and disposed thereof, &c. when the last mentioned closes in which, &c. were left dry and were not covered with water, as plaintiff hath in the first and second counts of the said declaration complained against him, which several trespasses so above new assigned are other and different trespasses, &c. Wherefore, &c.

To the new assignment the defendant pleaded, 1st, the general issue; 2dly, "that the said closes first above newly assigned, and the several closes secondly above newly assigned are, and at the said several times, &c. were the same closes, and not other or different closes, and are, and at those times when, &c. were certain rocks and sands of the sea, lying within the flux and reflux of the tides of the sea; and that the said shell-fish and shells in the said closes in which, &c. were certain shell-fish and fish-shells, which at the said several times when, &c. were in and upon the said rocks and sands of the sea, and which but a little before the said times when, &c. were, by the ebbing of the tides of the sea, left there in and upon the said closes in which, &c.; and that in the said closes in the said declaration mentioned, every subject of this realm at the said several times, when, &c. of right had, and of right ought to have had, and now hath, and of right ought to have, the liberty and privilege of getting, taking and carrying away the shell-fish and fish-shells left by the said ebbing of the tides of the sea in and upon the said closes, in which, &c. wherefore the defendant being a subject of this realm at the said several times when, &c. entered into the said closes in which, &c. to get take and carry away the shell-fish and fish-shells left by the ebbing of the tides of the sea in and upon the said closes in which, &c. and then and there got, took, and carried away the said shell-fish and shells in the said first count mentioned, and also got, and for that purpose, with spades, shovels, mattocks, pickaxes and other instruments necessarily dug up and raised up, and took and carried away the other shell-fish and shells in the second count lastly mentioned; and for the getting, taking, and carrying away of the said shell-fish and shells, the defendant at the said times when, &c. entered the said closes in which, &c. as it was lawful for him to do by himself and with other persons, and with the said cattle, carts, wagons, and other carriages, and the said boats, lighters, and other vessels, the same being reasonable and proper and necessary in that behalf, and in so doing he necessarily and unavoidably with his feet, and the feet of those other persons in walking, a little trod up, trampled, subverted and spoiled the soil, earth, and sand, in the said second count mentioned, and with the feet of the cattle, and with the wheels of the said carts, wagons and other carriages, and with the keels of the said boats, lighters, and other vessels, a little trod up, trampled upon, tore up, subverted and spoiled other the said soil of the said last-mentioned closes of the plaintiff, and the shell-fish and shells in the second count first mentioned, necessarily and unavoidably a little broke, crushed and destroyed, and with the said spades, shovels, mattocks, pickaxes, and other instruments, the same being useful, proper and necessary in that behalf, in digging up, raising, and getting the said shell-fish and shells in the said second count lastly mentioned, necessarily and unavoidably with the said spades, shovels, mattocks, pick-axes, and other instruments dug up, turned up, subverted and spoiled a little of the said earth, soil and sand in the said closes, as it was lawful for him to do for the causes aforesaid, doing as little damage on that occasion as he could, which are the same, &c. whereof, &c. And this, &c. wherefore, &c."

To this plea there was a replication, traversing the right of every subject to take shell-fish and shells, and a special demurrer thereto, because it traversed matter of law: but the court seeming to think that the replication was clearly bad, it was abandoned by the Plaintiff's counsel, who relied upon objections to the plea.

Marshall, Serjt. in support of the plea. The question is, whether every subject of the realm has a right to take the shell-fish and shells which are left upon the sea-shore by the ebbing of the tides. The right of fishing in the sea is acknowledged by all nations; it is universal, and part of the law of nations. *Grotius de Jure Bel. ac. Pac. lib.* 2. *c.* 2. *s.* 3. And according to *Grotius*, no person can have any property either in the main sea, or in the principal arms of the sea; neither can a man have any property in the shores and sands of the sea: these are all incapable of improvement, and never can be exhausted by the only uses to which they can be applied, namely those of supplying fish and sand. *Bracton (lib.* 1. *c.* 12. *fo.* 7. *b.)* adopting the doctrine of the civil laws, says, "*Naturali vero jure communia sunt omnia hæc, aqua profluens, aer, et mare, et littora maris, quasi maris accessoria nemo enim ad littus maris accedere prohibetur dum tamen a villis et ædificiis abstineat: quia littora sunt de jure gentium communia sicut et mare.*" And he adds, "*Publica vero sunt omnia flumina et portus; ideoque jus piscandi omnibus commune est in portu et in fluminibus; riparum etiam usus publicus est de jure gentium sicut ipsius fluminis.*" So Sir *Matthew Hale* in his *Treatise de Jure Maris, part* 1. *cap.* 4. *Hargrave's Law Tracts, p.* 10, 11, observes, "In the sea the king of England hath a double right, namely a right of jurisdiction, which he ordinarily exerciseth by his admiral, and a right of propriety or ownership. The king's right of propriety or ownership in the sea is evidenced principally in these things that follow: 1st, The right of fishing in this sea, and the creeks and arms thereof, is originally lodged in the Crown, as the right of depasturing is originally lodged in the owner of the waste whereof he is lord, or as the right of fishing belongs to him that is the owner of a private or inland river. But though the king is the owner of this great waste, and as a consequent of his property, hath the primary right of fishing in the sea, and the creeks and arms thereof, yet the common people of *England* have regularly a liberty of fishing in the sea, or creeks or arms thereof, as a public common of piscary; and may not, without injury to their right, be restrained of it, unless in such places, creeks, or navigable rivers where either the king or some particular subject hath gained a propriety exclusive of that common liberty." In the same treatise, p. 12, it is said, "that *de jure communi* between the high-water and low-water mark, doth *prima facie* belong to the king: *Constable's* case, 5 *Co.* 107, and *Dyer*, 326. *b.*; although it is true, that such shore may be, and commonly is parcel of the manor adjacent; and so may belong to a subject, yet *prima facie* it is the king's." From *Constable's* case, 5 *Co.* 107. 2 *Rol. Abr.* 170, it appears, that the shore may belong to the subject, either in gross or as parcel of his manor: but merely being the manor of a particular person is not sufficient to exclude those who have a right to fish there. One may have a manor, and another the right of fishing in the water; but if a man would claim a right of fishing in the water of another, the proof of the right lies upon him. In *Warren* v. *Matthews* 6 *Mod.* 73. 1 Salk. 357. *S. C.* HOLT, Ch. J. says, "Every subject of common right may fish with lawful nets in a navigable river as well as in the sea: and the king's grant cannot bar him thereof." So in 1 *Mod.* 105, Lord *Fitzwalter's* case, HALE, Ch. J. says, "In case of a river that flows and reflows, and is an arm of the sea, there *prima facie* it is common to all: and if any one will appropriate a privilege to himself, the proof lieth on his side; for in case of an action of trespass for fishing there, it is a good justification to say, that the *locus in quo est brachium maris in quo unusquisque subjectus Domini Regis habet et habere debet liberam piscariam.* The soil of the river *Thames* is in the king, and the lord mayor is conservator of the river, but it is common to all fishermen, and therefore there is no contradiction in the soil being in one and the right of fishing in the river common to all fishermen."—Again, in *Ward* v. *Creswell, Willes' Rep.* 265, 16 *Vin. Abr.* 354, tit. *Piscary* B. *S. C.* the Court held, that all the subjects of *England* of common right might fish in the sea, it being for the good of the commonwealth, and for the sustenance of all the people of the realm; and that therefore a prescription for it as appertenant to a particular township was void, and as absurd as a prescription would be for travelling the king's highway, or for the use of the air, as appertenant to a particular estate. The statute 7 *Jac.* 1, *c.* 18, after stating in the preamble, that divers persons having lands adjoining to the sea-coast in the counties of *Devon* and *Cornwall*, had of late interrupted the bargemen and such others as had used at their free wills and pleasures to fetch sea sand and take the same under the full sea mark, as they had theretofore used to do, enacts that all persons in the said counties should be at liberty to take sea sand at all places under the full sea mark. That statute was in fact a full recognition of the right of the subject to use the shore of the sea in every way in which it could be serviceable to him. It proves that his right is not confined to the privilege of taking shell-fish left on shore by the ebbing of the tides, but that he may also take the fish shells and even the sand of the shore.

Best, Serjt. *contra*. Admitting the general right of the subject to take the fish of the sea, still in this case that general right is circumscribed by the circumstance of the place in which these shell-fish and fish-shells were taken, being part of the manor of *Keysham*. Unless, therefore, the defendant set up a right of common on the soil, he cannot support the casement which he claims. *Prima facie*, the shores of the sea belong to the king, and he may grant any part of them to a subject, either reserving or not, as he pleases, a general right of fishery to all his subjects. The plaintiff ought not to be called upon to prescribe for a right of fishery over that which is admitted to be his own; for when once it is established, that the *locus in quo* belongs to the plaintiff, it must be presumed to be exclusively his, unless some inconsistent right is set up by the defendant. The common law right of the subject to go upon the shores of the sea between high and low-water mark, only applies to cases where no exclusive right is vested in any individual. Now, it appears from the passage cited from *Hale's* Treatise, *Hargrave's* Tracts, p. 12, that an exclusive right to the shore may belong to a subject, though *prima facie* it is in the king. Indeed, in pages 26 and 27 of the same tract, Sir *Matthew Hale*, speaking of the sea-shore, says, "It may not only belong to a subject in gross, which possibly may suppose a grant before time of memory, but it may be parcel of a manor," and proceeds to mention the several ways by which such a right may be evidenced. To the same effect is *Com. Digest*, tit. *Navigation* A. and the case of the abbot of *Ramsay*, *Dyer* 326, b.; and the same is admitted by Lord MANSFIELD in the case of *Carter* v. *Murcot*, 4 *Burr.* 2164. Although, however, the common law right of the subject should be established to take sea-fish, yet it by no means follows, that the subject has a right to take the shells which are thrown upon the sea-shore. It is well known, that in many parts of *England* much of the various matter which is deposited upon the shore by the sea, belongs to the owners of the adjacent soil, and is disposed of by them to very great advantage. The statute *7 Jac.* 1, which has been cited in support of the right of the subject to take whatever is found between high and low-water mark, seems to afford a contrary inference; for it is to be observed, that it is an enacting and not a declaratory law, and that a peculiar privilege is thereby granted to the men of *Devon* and *Cornwall*, which peculiar privilege it would have been absurd to grant, if all the people of *England* had been entitled thereto by common law.

The Court were of opinion, that if the plaintiff had it in his power to abridge the common law right of the subject to take sea-fish, he should have replied that matter specially, and that not having done so, the plaintiff must succeed upon his plea as far as related to the taking of the fish; but observed, that as no authority had been cited to support his claim to take shells, they should pause before they established a general right of that kind. They, therefore, offered to allow the defendant to amend his plea without costs, by striking out his claim to the fish-shells, and shaping his justification in such way as he should be advised. Which offer was accordingly accepted.

14 Johnson's Rep. 255.

BRINK AND OTHERS *v.* RICHTMYER.

THIS was an action of trespass, which was tried at the *Ulster* circuit, for breaking and entering the close of the plaintiffs, covered with water, usually called the *Green Flats*, and fishing therein.

The plaintiffs were the lessees of *Alexander Cockburn*, who derived his title under a patent, dated the 5th of *January*, 1768, to *Hugh Patrick*, of "All those eight certain islands, and two flats of land, lying and being in *Hudson* river, &c.;" and the premises in question are thus described: "one other island directly opposite the mouth of the said *Saugerties* creek, commonly called and known by the name of the *Green Flats*, containing forty acres." *Alexander Cockburn*, by lease dated 4th of *May*, 1815, leased to the plaintiffs, "the exclusive privilege of fishing with their nets on the westerly side of the *Green Flats* in *Hudson's* river, beginning at the southernmost station of the *Ariantie*, and extending southerly down the westerly side of the said flats ten chains, eighty links, for the term of ten years next ensuing the date." It was proved that the *Green Flats* were usually covered with water, and were used for the purpose of drawing nets from the channel of the river. The trespasses alleged in the declaration were proved, and a verdict was found for the plaintiffs for 200 dollars damages, subject to the opinion of the court, on a case containing the facts above stated.

Thompson, Ch. J., delivered the opinion of the court. This is an action of trespass for breaking and entering the plaintiff's close, called the *Green Flats*, and fishing thereon. A title to the *locus in quo* is made under a patent to *Hugh Patrick*, bearing date the 5th day of *January*, in the year 1768, by which eight islands and two flats of land, lying and being in *Hudson's* river, are granted to the patentee. The *locus in quo* is claimed as an island, which is described, in the patent, as follows: "One other island, directly opposite the mouth of the said *Saugerties* creek, commonly called and known by the name of the *Green Flats*, containing forty acres." From the testimony it appears that the land claimed under this patent is usually covered with water, and could not, therefore, in strictness, be called an island. There does not, however, appear to be any island, or other land, in any way answering the description in the grant; and as it is called a flat, as well as an island, it may be considered as sufficiently descriptive, and as coming within the patent. There can be no doubt but this was the land intended to be granted. There are no words in the patent showing an intention in the government to grant any fishery. It would therefore seem to be a reasonable interpretation of this grant, to consider it an ordinary grant of land for agricultural or other purposes, to which land is usually applied; subject, however, to be used as a common highway and public fishery, until otherwise appropriated by the private owner.

In Lord *Fitzwalter's* case, (1 *Mod.* 105,) *Hale*, Ch. J., says, "a river which flows and reflows is, *prima facie*, common to all; and if any one will appropriate a privilege to himself, the proof lieth on his side; and there is no contradiction, in the soil being in one, and the right of fishing in the river common to all fishermen." If the injury complained of, in this case, was the taking fish in the waters covering this flat, or island, I should very strongly incline to think the action was not sustainable. The case is not very explicit on the subject, but it is very fairly to be collected from it, that this flat is only used for the purpose of drawing the nets from the channel of the river; if so, it is not the fishery that is claimed under the patent; that still remains common. And, although the want of the convenience of drawing nets upon this flat may virtually exclude others from the fishery, yet this will not give a right to use the flat, or island, adjoining the fishery, any more than it would the shore when the convenience of fishermen might require it.

Although the lease from *Cockburn* to the plaintiffs purports to grant the exclusive privilege of fishing with their nets on the westerly side of the *Green Flats*, within certain bounds therein mentioned, we are not to construe this as a lease of the fishery, but only of a certain part of the island, or flat, for the convenience of drawing nets; and thus far it was within the right and power of *Cockburn* to grant. In this point of view, the case comes within the rules and principles which governed the court in the case of *Jacobson* v. *Fountain*, (2 *Johns. Rep.* 176.) The right being established in the plaintiffs, and those under whom they claim, to the *flat*, or *island*, the trespass and measure of damages are not controverted. The plaintiff must, therefore, have judgment upon the verdict, as found by the jury.

Judgment for the plaintiffs.

14 Burrow's Rep. 2162.

CARTER AND ANOTHER *v.* MURCOT AND ANOTHER.

THIS was an action of trespass for breaking and entering the plaintiff's close called *The river*, or *The river Severn*. The defendant pleaded that it is a *navigable river*; and also, that it is an *arm of the sea*, wherein *every* subject has a *right to fish*. The plaintiff (without traversing these allegations) replied, that this was *part of the manor* of *Arlingham*; that Mrs. *Yates* was seized of that manor: and prescribes for a *several* fishery there. Issue being joined thereon; a verdict was found for the plaintiff.

On *Monday* 9th *November* last, Mr. *Ashhurst*, on behalf of the defendant, moved in arrest of judgment, and had a rule to shew cause.

He objected that though the *fact* was so found, yet the *law* is otherwise; *viz.* that *every one* has a *right* to fish in a *navigable river*, or in an *arm of the sea*. He cited 1 *Mod.* 105. anonymous. 6 *Mod.* 73. *Warren* v. *Matthews*. 1 *Salk*. 357. S. C. and *Ward* v. *Creswell*, C. B. 14 and 15 *G*. 2. which recognizes 1 *Mod.* 105.

Mr. Serjeant *Nares*, for the plaintiff, now shewed cause.

It is *not* an arm of the sea where the sea flows and reflows: but a *part of a manor*.

It is found to be IN *the manor of Arlingham*, in the county of *Gloucester*. And a place *may* be parcel of a manor, if between the high and low-water marks; though the sea flows and reflows upon it. So is Sir *Henry Constable's* case, 5 *Co.* 107, *a. Bracton*, *lib.* 2. c. 12.

Mr. *Ashhurst*, *contra*, for the rule.

An exclusive right cannot be maintained by the subject, in a river that is an arm of the sea: the *general* right of fishing in an arm of the sea is common to all.

The replication ought to have shewn that this was a separate pool: but the plaintiff cannot maintain a *general* right in the river, in exclusion of all other the king's subjects.

In Sir *Henry Constable's* case—The Admiral had jurisdiction between the high and the low-water mark. When the tide is in, the water cannot belong to a manor: and a fishing can only be exercised when the tide is in—when there is water.

In Sir *John Davy's* Reports, *p.* 55—the case of the fishery in the river *Banne* in *Ireland*—it is said that the King has a right as high as the sea flows and reflows. And an arm of the sea, where the tide flows and reflows, is the same as the sea itself. *Justinian Inst. lib.* 1. *c.* 1. *tit.* 1.

6 *Mod.* 73. *Warren* v. *Matthews*—Every subject of common right, may fish with lawful nets, &c. in a navigable river, as well as in the sea, and the king's grant cannot bar them thereof. 1 *Salk.* 357. 8. S. C. *Per Holt* Chief Justice—"the subject has a right to fish in all navigable rivers, as he has to fish in the sea."

1 *Mod.* 105. *Anon.* In case of a river that flows and reflows, and is an arm of the sea: *Hale* says, "The right of fishing, is, *prima facie, common to all.*"

Lord MANSFIELD—The rule of law is uniform.

In rivers *not* navigable, the *proprietors of the land* have the right of fishery on their respective sides: and it generally extends *ad filum medium aquæ.*

But in *navigable* rivers, the *proprietors of the land* on each side have it *not;* the *fishery is common:* it is, *prima facie,* in the *king,* and is *public.*

If any one claims it *exclusively,* he must *shew a right.* If he can shew a right by *prescription,* he may *then* exercise an exclusive right: though the *presumption is against him,* unless he can *prove* such a prescriptive right.

Here it is claimed, *and found.* It is therefore consistent with all the cases, "that he *may* have an exclusive privilege "of fishing, although it be an arm of the sea." Such a right shall not be *presumed;* but the contrary, *prima facie:* but it is *capable of being proved;* and must have been so in the present case.

Mr. Justice YATES—I was concerned in a case of this kind. Such a claim was made: but the claim failed, because it there happened that such a right could *not be proved:* therefore it was in *that* case determined that the right of fishing was *common.* But such a right *may* be proved. By the law of *England,* what is otherwise common may, by prescription, be appropriated. GROTIUS owns, that navigable rivers *may* be appropriated.

The cited cases prove only this distinction, "That navigable rivers or arms of the sea *belong to the* CROWN; and not (like private rivers) to the land-owners on each side:" and therefore the *presumption* lies the *contrary* way in the one case, from what it does in the other. Here, indeed, it lies, *prima facie,* on the side of the *king and the public:* but it *may* nevertheless be appropriated by prescription.

The case of the royal salmon-fishery in the river *Banne,* in Sir *John Davy's* Reports, is agreeable to this: and 'tis a very good case. It appears by it, that the Crown may grant a several fishery in a navigable river, where the sea flows and reflows, or in an arm of the sea: and in the case of *Abbotsbury* there mentioned—the court said, "it must be intended that the abbey had originally had a grant from the Crown." And in the case in 1 *Mod.* 105. *Hale* says truly—"If any one will *appropriate* a privilege to himself, the *proof lyeth on his side.*" Now if it may be granted, it may be prescribed for: a prescription implies a grant. But it can't be presumed: it must be *proved.*

Why then may not this plaintiff *prescribe* for an exclusive right of fishing in an arm of the sea, and PROVE this appropriation, though the *prima facie presumption* is contrary?

Mr. Justice ASTON concurred. This is the true distinction: and 1 *Mod.* 105. is in point.—Rule discharged.

DAVIES' REP. 149.

THE CASE OF THE ROYAL FISHERY OF THE BANNE.

IN the river *Banne* in *Ulster*, which divides the county of *Antrim* from the county of *Londonderry*, about two leagues from the sea, where the stream is navigable, there is a rich fishery of salmon, which was parcel of the ancient inheritance of the Crown, as appears by several pipe-rolls and surveys, where it is found in charge as a several fishery; but now it is granted by the king, to the city of *London*, in fee farm. The profit of this fishery for the space of 200 years past, was taken and shared amongst the *Irish* lords, who made incursion and intrusion on the possessions of the Crown in *Ulster*, and possessed by strong hand the territories adjoining the said river *Banne*, until the first year of the reign of our lord the king that now is.

In the first year of this reign, Sir *Randall Mac Donell* obtained a grant to him and his heirs, by letters patents. of the territory of *Rout*, which is parcel of the county of *Antrim*, and adjoining to the river *Banne*, in that part where the said fishery is, and hath all times been. By these letters patents the King grants to him, *omnia castra, messuagia, tofta, molendina, columbaria, gardina, hortos, pomaria, terras, prata, pascua, pasturas, boscos, subboscos, redditus, reversiones, et servitia, piscarias, piscationes, aquas, aquarum cursus, etc. ac omnia alia hæreditamenta in vel infra dictum territorium de* Rout *in comitatu* Antrim, *exceptis, et ex hac concessione nobis hæredibus et successoribus nostris reservatis, tribus partibus piscationis fluminis de* the Banne.

And upon this grant, Sir *Randall Mac Donell* made petition to the lord deputy, to be put in quiet possession of the fourth part of the said fishery, which then by special order of the council-table was put in sequestration. The lord deputy being informed by the king's attorney, that no part of the fishery passed to Sir *Randall Mac Donell* by this grant, required the resolution of the chief judges, being of the privy-council, in this matter; who upon view of several pipe-rolls, in which this fishery was found severally in charge, as part of the ancient inheritance of the Crown, and upon consideration of the said grant made to Sir *Randall Mac Donell*, certified their opinion and resolution, that no part of the said fishery passed to the said Sir *Randall Mac Donell*, by the letters patents aforesaid. And in this case divers points were considered and resolved.

First, Although the rule of the civil law be, that *Flumina et portus publica sunt, ideoque jus piscandi omnibus commune est in portu fluminibusque*, which rule is found in *Bracton, lib.* 2 *cap.* 12. yet by the common law of *England*, a man may have a proper and several interest, as well in a water or river, as in a fishery; and therefore a water may be granted,

11 *R.* 2. *Plow. Comm.* 154. *a.* If one grants to another *aquam suam*, the fishery in it shall pass, because it is included in the word *aqua;* and *F. N. B.* 123. *quod permittat* lies *de libera piscaria*, in this form; *Præcipe A. quod permittat B. habere liberam piscariam in aqua ipsius A.* in *N.* which shews that *A.* hath an interest in the water. Also a fishery lieth in grant and tenure, and by a grant of it, the soil passeth; for 40 *Ed.* 3. 45. *Monstraverunt* lyeth of a fishery, which implieth that it contains land and demesne, for otherwise distress could not be taken in it, as is observed, *Plow. Comm.* 154. *a.* see 34 *Ass. p.* 11. grant of fishery in the river of *Tese*, to the abbot of *Rivaux*, *salvo stagno molendini.* Also fishery is demandable by *præcipe*, *F. N. B.* 2. *c.* and assize lieth of fishery. *F. N. B.* 179. *l.* for a man may have an estate of freehold in a fishery, *Fitz. Ass.* 422. in the time of *Ed.* 1. in assize of nuisance, the plaintiff counts that he is disturbed in his fishery; exception was taken to the count, for that no freehold was assigned to which the fishery was appendant, and there it is said, that fishery is a freehold in itself, wherefore it is not necessary to shew to what freehold it is appendant. See also *Fitz. Ass.* 427 12. *Hen.* 3. *Ass. de lib. tenem.* plaint of a fishery, and recovery. Also a man may make a bailiff of his fishery, 11 *Hen.* 7. 20. *a.* 10. *Hen.* 7. 24. *b. F. N. B.* 88. *h.* see also 23 *Hen.* 3. *Brook Ass.* 450. and 34 *Ass. p.* 11. *Et. de proventu fluminum decimæ solvi debent; Linwood*, fol. 101. and it is noted by *Linwood, Supra, quod fluvius est perennis decursus aquarum, flumen vero proprie est ipsa aqua.* And the gloss on the rule of the civil law aforementioned is, *Flumen ipsum, nisi alveum mutet, semper in eodem loco manet, sed aqua profluens est communis, quia non manet, sed procul fugit extra ditionem ejus cujus flumen est, ut ad mare tandem perveniat.*

Secondly, There are two kinds of rivers; navigable and not navigable. Every navigable river, so high as the sea flows and ebbs in it, is a royal river, and the fishery of it is a royal fishery, and belongs to the king by his prerogative; but in every other river not navigable, and in the fishery of such river, the ter-tenants on each side have an interest of common right. The reason for which the king hath an interest in such navigable river, so high as the sea flows and ebbs in it, is, because such river participates of the nature of the sea, and is said to be a branch of the sea so far as it flows; 22 *Ass. p.* 93. 8 *Ed.* 2. *Fitz. Coron.* 399, and the sea is not only under the dominion of the king (as is said 6 *R.* 2. *Fitz. Protect.* 46. *The sea is of the ligeance of the king as of his Crown of* England;) but it is also his proper inheritance; and therefore the king shall have the land which is gained out of the sea, *Dyer* 15 *Eliz.* 226. *b.* 22 *Ass. p.* 93. Also the king shall have the grand fishes of the sea, whales and sturgeons, &c. which are royal fishes, and no subject can have them without the king's special grant, *Prær. reg. c.* 11. *Stamf.* 37, 38. *Bract. lib.* 3. *c.* 3. 39 *Ed.* 3. 35. *a.* and the king shall have wild swans, as royal fowls, on the sea and branches of it; the case of *swans*, 7 *Co.* So wreck of the sea is a royal perquisite, 5 *Co.* 107. Sir *Hen. Constable's* case. And for this reason before the statute of 18 *Ed.* 3. no subject could pass over the sea, without the king's special license: but there it is enacted, that the sea shall be open to all merchants. And all ports and havens, which are *ostia et januæ regni*, appertain to the king, because he is *custos totius regni;* and *F. N. B.* 113 *a.* the king ought of right to save and defend his realm, as well against the sea, as against his enemies. And that the king hath the same prerogative and interest in the branches of the sea and navigable rivers, so high as the sea flows and ebbs in them, which he hath *in alto mari*, is manifest by several authorities and records.

1. The king by his letters patents made to the high Admiral of *England*, grants to him not only jurisdiction and power to determine maritime causes, but *omnia bona waviata, Flotzon, Jetzon, et Lagan, ac omnia bona, mercimonia, et catalla in mari deperdita, seu extra mare projecta, ac omnia et singula casualia, tam in vel super mare, vel litora, crecas, vel costeras maris.*

quam in vel super aquas dulces, portus, flumina, rivos, aut alia loca superinundata quæcunque, infra fluxum et refluxum maris, seu aquæ ad plenitudinem, a quibuscunque primis pontibus versus mare, per totum regnum Angliæ aut Hiberniæ, etc. emergentia, contingentia, seu provenientia, etc.

2. The commission of *Sewers*, which was awarded by the king, by virtue of his prerogative royal, before any statute made in such case, extends not only to walls and banks of the sea, but also to navigable rivers and fresh waters; *Reg.* 127. *a. b. F. N. B.* 113. *a.* And it is recited in the statute of 25 *Hen.* 8. *c.* 10. that the king, by reason of his dignity and prerogative royal, ought to provide that navigable streams be made passable, &c.

3. The city of *London*, by a charter from the king, hath the river *Thames* granted to them; but because it was conceived that the soil and ground of the river did not pass by that grant, they purchased another charter, by which the king granted to them *solum et fundum* of the said river; by force of which grant, the city to this day receives rents of those, who fix posts, or make wharves or other edifices on the soil of the said river.

4. Amongst the pleas of the Crown, 40 *Ed.* 3. *in Archiv. castr. Dubl.* this entry is found, *Domini reges Angliæ et domini Hiberniæ de jure coronæ habent per totam aquam de Boine, a Villa de Droghedagh, usque ad Trim, filum aquæ vulgariter vocatum le Watershard, continens in latitudine 24, pedes in loco profundiore ejusdem aquæ, ita quod batellæ, maremium, et marchandizæ per hujusmodi filum, hinc atque illinc, ire et redire possint, per filum aquæ predictæ, absque impedimento, etc.* And there a judgment was entertained in the same roll, that a weir erected by the abbot of *Millefont* in the said river should be abated, and a fine imposed on the abbot, &c. And this agrees with *Glanville*, who saith, that a *purpresture* may be made as well *in aquis regiis quam in viis regiis.* See 19 *Ass. p.* 6. that the river *Lee* is found by inquisition, the king's high stream; and in the stat. of 28 *Hen.* 8. *c.* 22. enacted in this

kingdom, the rivers *Barrow*, *Noire* and *Suire*, are called the king's rivers, and the weirs erected in them are called *purprestures*. And although the king permit his people, for their ease and commodity, to have common passage over such navigable rivers, yet he hath a sole interest in the soil of such rivers, and also in the fishery, although the profit of it is not commonly taken and appropriated by the king, if it be not of extraordinary and certain value, as the fishery of the *Banne* hath at all times been. See in the case of *Swan 7 Co.* 16. *a.* king *Hen.* 8. granted to *Strangewaies totam illam liberam piscariam vocatam*, the fleet in *Abbotsbury*, which is a bay or creek of the sea: and although the abbot had a fishery there before the dissolution, it is to be understood, that the abbot at first had it by the king's grant, it being a several fishery on a branch of the sea, and by consequence a royal fishery. See *Plow. Comm.* 315. *b.*

Wherefore it was resolved, that the river *Banne*, so far as the sea flows and ebbs in it, is a royal river; and the fishery of salmon there is a royal fishery, which belongs to the king, as a several fishery, and not to those who have the soil on each side of the water. But on the other part it was agreed, that every inland river not navigable, appertains to the owners of the soil, where it hath its course. 28 *Ass. p.* 93. and if such river runneth between two manors and is the mear and boundary between them, the one moiety of the river and fishery belongeth to one lord, and the other moiety to the other; and this appears, *lib. Intrat.* 666. *b.* in trespass *quare piscatus fuit in seperali piscaria, et piscem inde, viz.* 2 *salmones, etc. cepit, etc.* the defendant saith that he was seized of the manor of *B. quod se extendit usque ad finem aquæ de W. quæ est eadem piscaria in qua supponitur piscationem prædictam fieri, ex australi parte*, and that the plaintiff *eodem tempore quo, etc. fuit seisitus de manerio de A. cum pertinentiis, quod se extendit ad medium fili aquæ prædictæ ex parte boreali ejusdem aquæ, maneriaque prædicta ab oriente æqua longitudine versus occidentem se extendunt, et quod ipse* the defendant, *et omnes illi quorum statum ipse habet in manerio de B. a tempore quo non extat memoria, seisiti fuerunt de parte australi prædictæ aquæ, ut de seperali piscaria sua, ut de parcella manerii sui prædicti. et similiter habuerunt communiam piscariæ in prædicta parte boreali ejusdem aquæ, dicto manerio de A. pertinentem.* The plaintiff replies, *quod aqua prædicta ex utraque parte est sua seperalis pisaria;* without this that the defendant had common of fishery *in boreali parte dictæ aquæ. Vid.* 2. *R.* 2. *fol.* 5. *a.* that a writ *de rationabilibus divisis* lieth of such fishery.

Thirdly, It was resolved, that no part of this royal fishery of the *Banne* could pass by the grant of the land adjoining, by the general grant of all fisheries; for this royal fishery is not appertenant to land, but is a fishery in gross, and parcel of the inheritance of the Crown by itself; and general words in the king's grant shall not pass such special royalty, which belongeth to the Crown by prerogative; as mines royal, amerciaments royal, escheats royal, shall not pass by general words of all mines, amerciaments and escheats; and to this purpose are many cases in point, in the case of mines; *Plow. Comm.* 333. *b.* 334. *a.* and 9 and 10 *Eliz.* 268, 269.

Lastly, It was agreed, that where the king granted to Sir *Randall Mac Donell* all the territory adjoining to this river, and all fisheries within this territory, *exceptis tribus partibus piscariæ de Banne,* that the fourth part of this fishery should not pass to him by this grant; for the king's grant shall pass nothing by implication, 2 *H.* 7. 13, &c.

These points were resolved in this case, by the rules and authorities of the common law. But besides, divers rules of the civil law, and customary law of *France,* agreeable to our law in this point, were cited out of *Renatus Choppinus,* a very good author, in his treatise *De domanio Franciæ, lib.* 1. *titul.* 16. *de fluminibus. Fluminum sunt duo genera,* he saith, *regalia quædam, alia bannalia, sive privata. Regalia dicunter, ex quibus princeps jure patrimoniali vectigal capit, et in quibus modum et tempus piscationis constituit.* *Vid. stat. W.* 2. c. 47. *Et non solum regalia flumina nuncupantur, quod regum dominio sunt attributa, sed etiam quod eorum curam sibi reges ac principes assumpserunt, nec non ex eo, quod piscarias, cæterosque publicorum fluminum redditus, qui ærarii publici fuere, in fiscum suum redigerunt. Sunt et lacus publici regales, fluviorum superiorum instar; nam lacus publicos locant, et vectigalia in fiscum suum referunt; ideoque publicano, qui lacum vel stagnum conduxit, si piscari prohibeatur, utile interdictum competit. Justissimum enim est ob vectigalis favorem, interdicto eum tueri.* And as to other rivers which run *per confinium prædiorum*, he saith, that by prescription or permission of the princes, *aut alio justo titulo, omnia talia flumina facta sunt privata, quæ natura publica erant; et quod piscatio in certa parte fluvii potest ex pacto constitui, vel continenti multorum annorum usu acquiri; et sic potentiores omnis accolæ, si pluribis annis soli piscati sunt, cæteros pari jure uti prohibent, quamvis mari, quod natura omnibus patet, servitus imponi privatorum cautione non potest.* And moreover he shews that the ancient kings of *France piscationi in fluminibus publicis modum præscripserunt, et piscarias, ac reliquos fluminum proventus, qui ærario publico olim ascribebantur, passim in fiscum suum retulerunt.* For the prerogative of the king within the sea, he cites a verse of *Juvenal.*

Quicquid conspicuum pulchrumque ex æquore toto est,
Res fisci est ubicuaque natat.

Et Cujatius de feodis f. 205. *a.* was also cited; where he saith, *regalia sunt viæ publicæ, flumina navigabilia et ex quibus fiunt navigabilia, portus, vectigalia, monetæ, etc.*

2 Brod. & Bing. 403—and 6 Serg. & Lowr. 171.

CHAD, Bart. v. TILSED.

TRESPASS *quare clausum fregit.* Pleas, first, general issue; second, leave and license; third, that the *locus in quo* was part of *Poole* harbour; fourth, that the *locus in quo* was an arm of the sea, and that the defendant entered there to fish, as he lawfully might. The replication traversed these pleas: the rejoinder took issue on the replication. At the trial before *Graham* B., *Dorchester* Summer assizes, 1820, the plaintiff, who was proprietor of *Brownsea*, an island of about 1000 acres lying within the ambit of *Poole* harbour, deduced title to the island, including the *locus in quo*, from the *Sturt* family and the abbot of *Cerne*. A grant of wreck from *Henry* the second, in the first year of his reign, 1154, to the abbot of *Cerne*, confirmed by *inspeximus* in the first year of *Henry* the eighth, was proved; also a grant from *Henry* the eighth, in the 36th year of his reign, to the earl of *Oxford*, of the island of *Brownsea*, and a grant of the same year from the earl of *Oxford*, to *Richard Duke* of the same island, with wreck of the sea. At one extremity of the island is a bay of about 60 acres, called *St. Andrew's Bay*, which at low water, becomes a great expanse of uncovered mud, intersected by a small inlet or gully, only a few feet wide, called, in the language of the country, a lake. In this lake there is about three or four feet water at low tide, and about the same depth over the adjacent mud at high tide. About forty years ago, Mr. *Sturt*, at a great expense, constructed an embankment all across the chord of *St. Andrew's Bay*, with a view to reclaim the mud and bring it into cultivation, and frequently made use of the sea-weed, and mud and gravel, which was within the bank. The bay is about a mile and a half from *Poole*, in full view of the town; and no opposition was ever made to Mr. *Sturt's* undertaking. The bank was afterwards forced by a storm, and the sea again entered the space within, at high tide. Mr. *Sturt*, however, always treated it as his exclusive property; and no fisherman or other person was permitted to remain in the gully or lake, until Mr. *Sturt's* consent had been obtained. Repeated assertion of property, on his part, was proved; and uniform acquiescence therein, as also collection of wreck in *St. Andrew's Bay*, and application of it to his own use. It was admitted that *St. Andrew's Bay* formed no part of the harbour of *Poole*, and that vessels of any burthen could never float there.

The case on the part of the defendant, who had insisted on fishing in the lake or gully, within the artificial embankment, consisted of two grants of the *locus in quo*: the first to the duke of *Richmond*, for 31 years, in the 13th year of Charles the second; the second to *Robert Gifford*, for 41 years, in the 17th year of the same reign, (wherein the spot in question was described as waste land, and ooze and ooze lands, the grantee having covenanted to endeavour to reclaim and bring it into cultivation within seven years,) and of an attempt to prove that the *locus in quo* had, previously to Mr. *Sturt's* time, been commonly fished on; as also afterwards, in defiance of his assertion of property. This, however, was not satisfactorily established; and it appearing that nothing had ever been done under the grants of *Charles* the second, the jury, without allowing the learned baron to conclude his summing up, found a verdict for the plaintiff.

Lens, Serjt. in the last term had obtained a rule *nisi* for a new trial, and cited *Vooght* v. *Winch*, 2 *B.* & *A.* 662.

Pell, Serjt., *contra*.

Lens having been heard in support of his rule, the court now gave judgment.

Dallas C. J. I agree that cases of this sort may rest on one or both of the two following grounds, that is to say, on grant or on usage which presupposes a grant: I agree, also, that in the case of a grant, no usage, however long, can countervail the clear words of the instrument, for what is done under usurpation cannot constitute a legal usage: but it is equally clear, that when a grant of remote antiquity contains general words, the best exposition of such a grant is long usage under it. Unless, therefore, the usage of forty years ago can be proved to have originated in usurpation, it is evidence, whence usage anterior to that time may be presumed: and such a length of modern usage, connected with the ancient usage, affords the strongest exposition of the meaning of the original grant. The rule laid down in a book of authority on this subject is, 'If the language of an ancient grant be obscure or doubtful, constant usage may be resorted to, to expound, though not to control the deed,' and the uniform course of modern authorities shows, that however general the grant, usage may afford a true construction of it, reducing this question to a question of fact, namely, what was the usage here? I agree that if the usage be only of forty years' duration, and be applied to establish an exclusive right over an arm of the sea, this could not destroy the right of the subject, but we must look to the way in which this modern usage arose, and that is as strong as possible to establish the plaintiff's claim; his predecessor raises a bank in the face of the whole town of *Poole*, and according to the pleas, in a place which was part of the harbour in which all the inhabitants of the town had an interest. This was done at considerable expense, and occupied a great length of time. After the bank had been broken down, there was no interruption of the plaintiff's assertion of his claim: permission to enter within the bank was constantly asked, and given or refused, as to the proprietor seemed fit. The usage was as strong as it possibly could be under such circumstances. But it was asked—if the corporation of *Poole* had been in confederacy with the then proprietor of the island, and did not choose to sue upon this usurpation, should a poor fisherman by such means be deprived of his right? Certainly not. However, if so general a right had existed, it may be presumed any usurpation on that right would have been resisted. And why are we to presume any such confederacy between the owner of the island and the corporation of *Poole*? I have said, that where the words of a grant are general, they must be explained by usage. The grant of *Henry* the second, conveys the island of *Brownsea* and its shores. What then are its shores?—what usage has pointed out. And if I find the usage such as existed here, how can I resist the evidence? It is urged that this is only a grant of wreck, but wreck must rest on the soil, usage must determine what has been deemed soil, and vessels of burthen could at no time float over the mud in question. The lakes which have been mentioned, were only such small inlets as every where intersect the shore. The grants of *Charles* the second confirm this usage, inasmuch as those grants were never acted on or acquiesced in by the owner of the island. I think, therefore, the question has been properly disposed of, and that a new trial cannot be granted.

Park J. If the grants in question contained any thing inconsistent with the usage established, the case might be different, but, the grant consisting of general words, we are driven to inquire what has been the usage under it. That is all one way, and it is reasonable to suppose it was the same in ancient times as at present. Nothing in the present decision will conflict with that of *Vooght* v. *Winch*, which only decided that, in a public river, twenty years' possession of the water at a given level is not conclusive as to the right.

Burrough J. The verdict in this case is not contrary to the legal effect of the evidence, but serves to confirm the construction put on the grants. The first contains a grant of wreck to the abbey of *Cerne*, throughout all their lands upon the sea which shows they had other lands besides the main-land of *Brownsea;* now what could these other lands be but the lands in question? As to the grants produced by the defendant, deeds produced by a party avail him nothing unless the possession has gone consistently with them: Here, the parties who received the first grant from *Charles* the second, did nothing under it; then other adventurers came forward, who also failed to make any attempt conformable to their grant. For what reason did both these parties, who thought it beneficial to take the grant, abstain from acting under it, but because they found a person in possession under a former grant? Then, the assertions of right on the part of the plaintiff are strong beyond all measure; and though the erection of the bank forty years ago would not of itself confer a title, yet, from such erection unopposed, and the subsequent uniform usage, prior usage to the same effect may be presumed, which, coupled with the general terms of the grant, establish the plaintiff's claim beyond dispute.

RICHARDSON J. The evidence of assertion of right on the part of the plaintiff and those under whom he claims, is indeed abundantly strong; however, I should agree that the legal effect of this evidence would not invest him with a title, and that the whole might amount to nothing more than usurpation, if it were quite clear that, prior to the construction of the embankment forty years ago, the public had any right over the *locus in quo*. But in this case, as in every other, modern usage of forty years' duration is evidence not only for that period, but evidence from which it may be presumed, that the same course was pursued in earlier times, if nothing is shown to the contrary. Here there was evidence that the usage had been the same almost time out of mind; that the land in question was *littus maris*, not indeed so dry as *terra firma*, but still shore of the sea, and not covered at low water, with the exception of a small lake or inlet: the place, therefore, falls within the description of land, about which there can be no doubt as to the law, that an individual may claim a right in it, either by grant or by usage independently of grant. Most of the evidences, which *Hale, De Jure Maris, pars* 1. *c.* 6. *p.* 27, enumerates as denoting such a right, exist here "constant and usual fetching gravel and sea-weed and sea-sand, between the high-water and low-water mark, and licensing others so to do; inclosing and embanking against the sea, and enjoyment of what is so inned; enjoyment of wrecks happening upon the sand." The grants of *Charles* the second call the spot in question ooze land, and, therefore, are evidence to show that even in those days, the place was considered as between high and low-water mark; and, as nothing was done under them, they rather make against the defendant than for him, as it should thereby seem that, when the grantees came to act under their grant, they found an obstacle in an earlier and better title.

1 Pickering's Rep. 180.

COMMONWEALTH *v.* THE INHABITANTS OF CHARLESTOWN.

THE defendants were indicted for a nuisance in not repairing two bridges leading from Medford to the Canal bridge. They pleaded not guilty.

On the trial before *Putnam* J. at November term, 1819, it appeared that the road was laid out by the court of sessions in 1810, in due form of law; but the defendants contended that it was laid out over water navigable from the sea, where the sea ebbs and flows, and that they were therefore not bound to repair the bridges, inasmuch as the bridges in themselves were nuisances.

The defendants proved that the channel of Miller's river.

over which the larger bridge was built, was 74 feet wide at the bridge, and that the water there was 9 1-2 feet deep at high tides; that the bridge was 196 feet long, and that the river was open to the sea. They produced evidence to show, that for more than fifty years before the road was laid out, vessels of various kinds of from 15 to 30 tons burden, and upwards, used to go above the place where the bridge is built, carrying up West India goods, wood, bark, rails and manure, to a *range way*, on which they were carted across the marshes. It appeared that there was a constant stream of fresh water entering the head of Miller's river, on which there is a mill above the tide water, but that there was no village at the head of Miller's river; and that the land on each side of the river was owned by individuals, and not by the public.

It was testified that the creek over which the smaller bridge was built, was 7 1-2 feet in depth in spring tides, and that the channel was more than a pole wide; that for many years past gondolas of 14 or 15 tons burden, and other vessels, have passed above where the bridge stands, carrying hay, sand, and manure, and that there is water enough for vessels of 40 or 50 tons burden. No evidence was produced on the part of the commonwealth to contradict this testimony.

The jury, by direction of the Judge, returned a verdict against the defendants, subject to the opinion of the whole court upon the law arising out of the case.

The cause was argued at a former term, by *Webster* and *Otis*, on behalf of the commonwealth, and *A. Ward* and *Parker*, for the defendants.

On the part of the *commonwealth* it was contended, that the streams over which these bridges are built are not navigable, according to the rules of the common law. The great principle, that, where the sea flows and reflows, the waters are *publici juris*, is to be restrained by a reference to public necessity or general utility. It would be absurd to say that all the little creeks in our salt marshes are navigable waters. A creek is said to be an inlet of the sea which gives no harbour to ships, nor is endowed with any privileges. *Com. Dig. Navigation, C; Hargr. L. Tr.* 47. To be navigable it must admit of vessels of burden sailing in and out of it in ordinary times, and must be a highway or common passage for the whole community, either from necessity founded on its local situation, or from long uninterrupted usage. The actual, not the possible, use of it is to be regarded.

These streams have none of the distinctive properties of a highway. *Hammond's N. P.* 175; 1 *Hawk. P. C. c.* 76, § 1; *Commonwealth* v. *Coombs*, 2 *Mass. Rep.* 492; *Co. Lit.* 56 *a*; *Thrower's case*, 1 *Vent.* 208; *Austin's case, ibid.* 189; 2 *Domat, b.* 1, *tit.* 8, § 2, *art.* 14; *Shaw* v. *Crawford*, 10 *Johns. Rep.* 237; *Hargr. L. Tr.* 8, 9, 22; *Cr. Circ. Comp.* 520.

Supposing however that the public had a right by the common law in such waters, the statute of 1641, (*Anc. Charters, &c.* 148,) gave the right to the proprietors of the land adjoining, reserving only a private way for boats or other vessels to other mens' houses or lands; so that to obstruct these streams would not be a common nuisance.

But whether the bridges are nuisances or not, they have not been found so. This is a question of fact for the jury. *Rex.* v. *White*, 1 *Burr.* 337; *Hargr. L. Tr.* 85; *Palmer* v. *Mulligan*, 3 *Caines' Rep.* 307. If they are nuisances, they ought to be abated; if not, the town is bound to keep them in repair. The court of sessions may have exceeded its authority in laying out the road, and still the town be obliged to repair it, since a way becomes public simply by use, or by the dedication of an individual. 11 *East*, 376; *Rex* v. *Lloyd*, 1 *Camp.* 260, 262 *in notis*.

For the *defendants*, it was contended, that these waters were so far navigable as to be the property of the public; that the court of sessions had no authority to lay out a road over them; and that the bridges being therefore nuisances, the town was not obliged to keep them in repair. The counsel cited *Common-*

wealth v. *Coombs*; *Arundel* v. *M'Culloch*, 10 *Mass. Rep.* 70; 1 *Bl. Comm.* 264; *Hargr. L. Tr.* 9, 12; *Rex* v. *Smith*, *Doug.* 441; *Young* v. ———, 1 *Ld. Raym.* 725; *Just. Inst. l.* 2, *tit.* 1, §§ 2, 4, 5; *Ball* v. *Herbert*, 3 *D. & E.* 253; *Bac. Abr. Nuisance*, *A*; *Coolidge* v. *Williams*, 4 *Mass. Rep.* 144; *Peck* v. *Lockwood*, 6 *Hall's Law Journ.* 278; *Carter* v. *Murcot*, 4 *Burr*, 2164; *Dav.* 56.

The opinion of the court was delivered at this term by

PARKER C. J. By the common law it is clear that all arms of the sea, coves, creeks, &c. where the tide ebbs and flows, are the property of the sovereign, unless appropriated by some subject, by virtue of a grant, or prescriptive right, which is founded on the supposition of a grant. *Hale de Jur. Mar. pt.* 1, c. 1, 2, 3. The right however of fishing in such places or sailing over them in boats is common to all the subjects, but liable to be restrained or regulated by the sovereign power. So that the proprietor of upland contiguous has no greater right to the use of such privileges, than other subjects who are not the owners of upland.

And this right of the sovereign extends to ordinary high-water mark, so that the shore, which is the space between high-water and low-water mark, belongs also to the sovereign; the property of the owner of the upland reaching only to that line which limits the waters in the ordinary course of the tides. *Storer* v. *Freeman*, 6 Mass. Rep. 435.

This right in the waters and shores of the sea passed from the Crown, by letters patent from James I., to the council established at Plymouth, in the county of Devon, for the planting, &c. of New-England, and from that council so much of their territory thus acquired, as was contained in the colony of Massachusetts Bay, was transferred to the company who undertook the settlement of that colony; and their grant was confirmed by the charter of King Charles I., which constituted the company a body corporate and politic, giving them absolute property in the land within the limits of the charter, the power of making laws for the government of the colony, and full dominion over all the ports, rivers, creeks, and havens, &c. in as full and ample a manner as they were before held by the crown of England. *Anc. Charters, &c.* 1.

The company to whom this charter was made, having assumed a political capacity and become a state, exercised dominion over all the land within the limits of the charter, and all the privileges, immunities and franchises connected with it, as public property, parcelling it out in townships or smaller divisions for the purpose of settlement; so that by virtue of the grant from the Plymouth company, the charter of King Charles, and actual possession and disposition of it, the people of the colony, in their politic capacity, succeeded to all the territorial rights, franchises and immunities, which had ever belonged to the sovereign power of the parent country.

Among the earliest acts of legislation, was an exercise of sovereignty with respect to the shore, or flats, of coves, creeks, &c. which abounded all over the sea coast. By the common law, it has been seen, he to whom a house lot was granted which was bounded upon the sea, would be the proprietor only as far as high-water mark. The desire and necessity of wharves, quays or piers was soon felt by individuals and the community, and the occupation of flats became indispensable. The government, then, to encourage these objects, and to prevent disputes and litigations, transferred its property in the shore of all creeks, coves, and other places upon the salt water, where the sea ebbs and flows, giving to the proprietor of the land adjoining, the property of the soil to low water mark, where the sea does not ebb above one hundred rods. This was a grant of so much of the shore as would be contained within the exterior lines of the upland lot extending from high-water to low-water mark, provided it did not extend more than one hundred rods.' *Anc. Charters, &c.* 148.

The exceptions and provisions in this ordinance show clearly, that the principles of the common law relating to this kind of property were well understood by the colonial legislature. Those who thus acquired the property of the shore were restricted from such a use of it as would impair the public right of passing over the water, in boats or other vessels, through any sea, creeks, or coves, to other mens' houses or lands; by which it was intended to reserve a free passage over the water in such places, in the same manner as it existed before the public property in the shore was transferred. The ordinance of 1641 has therefore made no alteration in the use of places therein described, while they are covered with water, and they remain free for all the citizens of the commonwealth; so that even the proprietor of the flats can lawfully erect nothing upon them, which will obstruct or hinder such passage, though he may build wharves extending towards the sea to the distance of one hundred rods, provided he do not thereby straiten or interrupt the passage over the water in such manner as to constitute a public nuisance.

To build a bridge therefore from shore to shore over a navigable cove or creek, whereby the usual passage of boats or other craft would be impeded, could not be justified even by the owner of the soil; for he has only a qualified property in it, under the ordinance of 1641. None but the sovereign power can authorize an interruption of such passages, because this power alone has the right to judge, whether the public convenience may be better served by suffering bridges to be thrown over the water, than by suffering the natural passages to remain free; and this power may exact such conditions as to the manner of building, as will sufficiently preserve the natural passage, at the same time that the public may be accommodated with an artificial one. Conformably to this principle, it has been usual when a bridge was wanted over any creek, cove, or other inlet from the sea, for application to be made to the General Court, although no toll was intended to be taken, and an act has passed pursuant to such application. Instances of the kind are frequent in our statute books; in some cases it has been required, that draws should be made in the bridge; in others, that it should be so constructed that boats or gondolas loaded with hay might pass, under without obstruction, according to the use which has been made of the water over which the bridge was to be erected. (See *st.* 1804, *c.* 11, 16, 51; *st.* 1805, *c.* 1: *st.* 1801, *c.* 33; *st.* 1802, *c.* 74.)

There can be no doubt, therefore, that by the principles of the common law as well as by the immemorial usage of this government, all navigable waters are public property for the use of all the citizens; and that there must be some act of the sovereign power, direct or derivative, to authorize any interruption of them. The legislature may, without doubt, by a general law, delegate to the magistrates of a county, or to any other body, the power of determining when public convenience requires that a bridge should be thrown over a creek or a cove, but until they have made such delegation in express terms, it is a branch of sovereign power, to be exercised by the legislature alone.

Upon this ground it was determined, in the case of *Commonwealth* v. *Coombs*, that the court of sessions, to which body was given by a general law the power of laying out public ways, had not power to lay out such a way over a navigable river, so that the river might be obstructed by a bridge.

The statute giving power to the court of sessions, it is there said, must have a reasonable construction. "A navigable river is of common right a public highway, and a general authority to lay out a new highway must not be so extended, as to give a power to obstruct an open highway already in the use of the public." And in the case of *The Inhabitants of Arundell* v. *M'Culloch*, the same principle is recognized. The court say "it is an unquestionable principle of the common law, that all navigable waters belong to the sovereign, or, in other words, to the public; and that no individual or corporation can appropriate them to their own use, or confine or obstruct them, so as to impair the passage over them, without authority from the legislative power. It is upon this principle that so many acts of our legislature have been passed, authorizing the building of bridges over various streams and rivers within the commonwealth."

I do not know that this doctrine has been contended against, in the argument of the case before us. The question has been rather a question of fact than of law, to wit, whether the streams over which the bridges stand, for not repairing which the defendants are indicted, are navigable streams, within a reasonable use of those terms, so as to be public property in the manner before stated.

It may be remarked, that by the common law, the property of the sovereign is said to extend to all places where the sea ebbs and flows, whether such places are navigable or not; but it is probable the usages of our country have given a reasonable limitation to this doctrine, confining the public right to what may be of public use; so that in many little creeks into which the salt water flows, but which are incapable of being navigated at all, private property may be maintained. This is undoubtedly the case with many of the creeks which run through our extensive marshes, over which small bridges are thrown for the convenience of removing the hay; and yet whenever these streams are large enough for the passage of boats, and gondolas, or lighters, and pass through the lands of several proprietors, no one can obstruct them, even in his own grounds, unless he has acquired a right by prescription; which probably is the case with many of them. The question then in the case before us, is, whether the streams over which the bridges are placed, are public highways; if they are, the order of the court of sessions laying a road over them is void. This question has been only formally decided by the jury, and comes before us upon a motion to set aside the verdict, because the facts proved show that the road was illegally laid out; so that the verdict returned against the defendants is contrary to the evidence. If it appear from the evidence in the case, that the streams in question are navigable to any useful purpose, as that in our opinion would make them public property, the verdict ought to be set aside.

The evidence reported abundantly proves the navigableness of Miller's river for boats, scows, and lighters, with heavy loads of manure, wood, &c. and several witnesses testified to the actual use of the stream, by such vessels, before and until the bridge was built.

The facts thus testified were not contradicted. The effect of them was attempted to be avoided by an argument, which probably would be successful with the legislature, on an application for license to build a bridge. It is said there could be but little use of this stream for boats or other vessels, that there is not, and probably never will be, any settlement or place of business at its head, or on its banks, that the public are vastly more accommodated by a bridge, than they would be by an unobstructed passage of the stream. All this is probably true, and yet does not affect the question before us; for if the stream is a navigable river, it is for common use, and none but the legislature can authorize the interruption of it. If the court were to undertake to decide these questions of expediency, it would not be declaring law, but would be legislating upon each particular case. The same arguments might have been used, if individuals or corporations, without authority from the legislature, had thrown bridges over Mystic river, where the Chelsea or Malden bridges now are. Probably the advantage of navigating that river would bear no comparison, in public estimation, with the utility of such bridges; yet none would suppose, that any thing short of legislative authority would have warranted the building them. The difference between Mystic and Miller's river is only in their magnitude; there is no difference in the law to be applied to them.

The principle upon which the public right to navigable streams rests having never been controverted, and the necessary inference being, that no subordinate power can authorize any use of them, inconsistent with that right, there could be no difficulty in settling this or any other question relating to them, were it not that the insignificance of some of the streams, and the little use made of them for purposes of transportation, render the application of the principle sometimes questionable, on the ground of expediency. But this difficulty is solved by referring all such cases to the legislature; which will always relinquish the public control over such waters, when the public interest shall require it. There is but one principle for judicial courts to be governed by, and that is, to consider as public property all those inlets of the sea, which are capable of sustaining vessels of any description, with their loading, for purposes really useful to trade or agriculture. It has been urged, that the *actual use* of them for such purposes is necessary, to give them the character of public property: but it is obvious, there can be no such qualification of the principle at common law; for it would go to allow the occupation by individuals or corporations of many of the most important public privileges, in the early settlement of the country, before ports and places of deposit should become valuable.

It was urged also in argument, that a stream, to be public, must be actually a highway, leading from county to county; but there is no authority for this position. Highways, according to the common law, are places in which all the subjects have a right to pass; and this is peculiarly the case with the sea and all its branches. It is by statute only, that those roads are denominated highways which lead from town to town, to distinguish them from those which are laid out for the use of one town only, or certain individuals in one town, with a view to the different tribunals which are to authorize the laying them out.

We have considered with much attention a position advanced by one of the counsel for the prosecution, *viz.* that a bridge being actually in existence, the defendants, by the general laws, are obliged to keep it in repair, without reference to the original lawfulness or unlawfulness of the establishment of it. This position may be true in regard to ancient ways, the origin of which cannot be traced, but which have immemorially been in use. A way may exist by prescription. But we think it cannot be true, that a bridge or road recently built or laid out without any authority, can impose any obligation on the inhabitants of the town where it may be. This would be to encourage individuals to act from their own authority in such cases, and to punish others for any imperfect execution of their work. A way may also be given to the public so as to prevent the owner of the land from maintaining trespass against those who pass over it; but until it is laid out and established by the lawful authority, it cannot become a charge to the inhabitants of the town through which it passes. But in the case before us, the bridge is supposed to be an obstruction to a highway *before existing;* a mere dedication or use of it, therefore, cannot purge the wrongful erection of it; and the town which is called upon to repair it, has a right to show that it has no legal existence. And so it was ruled in the case of *Coombs*, and in the case of *M'Culloch*, before cited. The orders of the court for laying out the roads in those cases were considered void; if void, the bridges over the streams are nuisances, and if nuisances, no town can be held to keep them in repair.

Though the reasoning, in the foregoing opinion, has been principally applied to one of the counts in the indictment, *viz.* that which charges the inhabitants with neglect to repair the bridge over Miller's river, it is equally applicable to the other count, with respect to which the evidence reported abundantly proves the navigableness of the stream therein described, and the former use of it for valuable purposes. The verdict therefore must be set aside, and a new trial granted.

4 Tyng's Rep. 140.

COOLIDGE *v.* WILLIAMS.

THIS was an action of the case brought in *Middlesex*, pursuant to the private statute of 1797, c. 75, to recover treble the value of certain shad and alewives alleged to have been taken by the defendant within the limits of *Watertown*.

The statute gives a power to the inhabitants of *Watertown*, *Weston*, and *Waltham*, to regulate, by their agents, the times, places, and manner of taking those fish, within the limits of the said towns, and to sell the right of taking them. The third section enacts that "if any person, other than those to whom the said right shall be sold as aforesaid, shall take any fish of the description aforesaid, such persons so offending shall forfeit and pay treble the value of such fish so taken, to be recovered in an action on the case, to the use of any person who may sue for the same.

Upon not guilty pleaded, the action was tried at *Cambridge*, October term, 1806, before the *Chief Justice*, and a verdict found for the plaintiff, by consent of the parties, subject to the opinion of the court upon the following facts, *viz.*

"That the defendant caught, with a seine, shad and alewives to the value of the sum mentioned in the verdict, in *Charles river*, within the times mentioned in the plaintiff's declaration: that the place in said river, where the said fish were caught, lies where the said town of *Watertown* is on the north shore, and the town of *Cambridge* on the south shore: that the defendant put the said seine into the said river on the *Cambridge* side, and extended it across the river over the flats on the *Watertown* side, and then drew the seine on shore on the *Cambridge* side, with the said fish in it: that one witness testified, that it was reputed, that the limits of *Watertown*, at the said place, extended into the said river towards said *Cambridge*, to the middle point between high-water mark on each shore: that the deepest water was on the side of the channel nearest the said *Watertown* shore, where the greater part of the fish swim: that further up the river, over against the said *Watertown* shore, lies *Newton*, adjoining on the said river, or on the channel thereof: that still further up said river, *Watertown* lies on both sides thereof, and extends across it, in which place is a fishery for shad and alewives, commonly called the *Watertown fishery;* and in no other place but the last mentioned, have the inhabitants of *Watertown* been accustomed to carry on the shad and alewife fishery: that higher up the said river, where the tide does not flow, lies the said town of *Waltham*, on each side thereof, and extending across the same, where is carried on the *Waltham* fishery: that still higher up, on the said town of *Weston*, on both sides of, and extending across the same, but the said town has no fishery within its limits: that the place where the said fish were caught as aforesaid, is the most convenient place in said town of *Cambridge*, for carrying on the shad and alewife fishery: that the seine fishery cannot be conveniently carried on in the same river, unless the seine be carried across the said river: and that the inhabitants of *Cambridge* have been accustomed to carry on the shad and alewife fishery at the place where the said *Williams* caught them, it being a convenient place for that purpose."

"If upon these facts the court shall be of opinion that the verdict ought to have been found for the plaintiff, judgment shall be rendered accordingly: but if otherwise, the said verdict shall be set aside, and a verdict shall be entered for the defendant, and judgment be rendered accordingly."

Tyler Bigelow, for the plaintiff.
Samuel P. P. Fay, for the defendant.

The action stood continued until the last October term at *Cambridge*, when it was briefly spoken to by the counsel, who signed the foregoing statement of facts.

The action being continued *nisi*, the opinion of the court was delivered at this term by

Parsons, *C. J.* who after shortly stating the nature of the action, the provisions of the statute on which it was brought, and the terms of the agreement on which the verdict was found, proceeded as follows.

The defence relied upon is, that the defendant took the fish in *Cambridge:* that he put in his seine from the *Cambridge* shore, and having extended it into the river, he drew it upon the same shore, and there took the fish: and that the fishery thus carried on in *Cambridge*, is an accustomed fishery for the inhabitants of that town, in this place, and carried on in the accustomed manner.

The plaintiff insists that this fishery by the defendant is prohibited by the act, because *Watertown* is situate on the other side of the river opposite to this place, and the defendant extended his seine across the channel, and over the flats on the *Watertown* side.

The decision of the question must depend upon the construction of the statute. It is stated, that higher up the river, *Watertown* is situated on both sides of the river, where there is a convenient place for the shad and alewive fishery, and which is called the *Watertown fishery:* and that the inhabitants of that town have been accustomed to fish there, and in no other place.

Towns adjoining, or extending across a navigable river, may own the soil of the flats, and even of the channel, if a grant has been obtained from the government; but the property in the fish, and also in all tide-waters, is in the public. But it seems to be a part of the common law of the State, that the town may appropriate the fish, if not appropriated by the legislature: but for taking the fish, no man could lawfully go on the soil of another, without his leave. The rule of our common law probably originated from a declaration of *common liberties*, made by the General Court of the colony of *Massachusetts Bay*, as early as in the year 1641, which was cited at the bar. If therefore no appropriation has been made of the fish, any citizen may take them, so that he does not trespass on the land of others. But any town adjoining any river may appropriate the fish taken within its limits, and that the town on the opposite side of the river may have the same right, the limits must not include the tide waters ebbing and flowing, but the shores on which the fish are drawn and placed, when they may be said to be taken according to the intent of this privilege. If the fish, when caught swimming in the public tide waters, are to be considered as taken within the limits of any town before they are hauled on shore, it will be difficult in many cases to define the interfering rights of towns situate on opposite banks: and when the channel is not granted, fish swimming there out of the limits of any town, would not be subject to appropriation.

The power of appropriation only not meeting the wishes of many towns, acts have been passed, authorizing them, not only to fix the times and manner of taking the fish, but also the places, and the disposition of them when taken; and to sell the exclusive right of fishing; and guarding this authority by pecuniary penalties. And the place of fishing is always understood to be that part of the shore used for employing seines and nets, or other engines, and for bringing the fish to land; and not any part of the tide-waters in which they were swimming.

Independently of the statute in question, the defendant, or any other, might have put his seine into the river from the *Cambridge* shore, and might have landed his fish, if he had committed no trespass on the land: and the inhabitants of that town might have appropriated the fish, and have secured to themselves a several fishery. But the plaintiff supposes that these privileges are restrained, or at least that the fish shall not be caught on the *Watertown* side of the river.

Private statutes, made for the accommodation of particular citizens or corporations, ought not be construed to affect the rights or privileges of others, unless such construction results from express words, or from necessary implication. But every part of this statute may have a reasonable effect without any such construction. The object of it was to enable the towns of *Watertown*, *Weston*, and *Waltham* to regulate their own rights then subsisting, and to secure to themselves the benefits arising from such regulation, and not to grant any new privileges. The two last towns lay on each side of the river, and a part of *Watertown* extended across it. *Watertown* had a fishery on its shores, where the people were accustomed to fish, and not at the place opposite to the *Cambridge* fishery. The defendant was fishing on the *Cambridge* shore, where the people were accustomed to fish, and in the accustomed manner extending his seine across the river towards, but not upon the *Watertown* shore, and taking his fish on the *Cambridge* shore. This privilege of the defendant, it was not the intention of the statute to infringe. He may enjoy it consistently with all the provisions of the statute, giving them a reasonable construction

It is therefore our opinion that the verdict be set aside, and a verdict of not guilty be entered, upon which the defendant must have judgment.

2 Johnson's Rep. 357.

CORTELYOU *v.* VAN BRUNDT.

THIS was an action of *trespass, quare clausum fregit,* for entering and digging up the soil, and erecting a hut on the plaintiff's *close*, in *New-Utrecht*, in *King's County*. The defendant pleaded not guilty, and gave notice, that he would offer in evidence, that the freeholders and inhabitants of *New-Utrecht* had, from time immemorial, used, at all proper seasons, the right of fishing in the bay or sea adjoining the *close* in question, and of using and occupying the shore or beach, adjoining the said bay, for the purpose and convenience of fishing in the bay or sea, and that the defendant was one of the freeholders and inhabitants of *New-Utrecht*; and that on that day, it being the proper season for fishing, he had entered and erected a temporary hut on the *close* in question, for the purpose and convenience of fishing, &c. *And further*, that the defendant would give in evidence two patents to the freeholders and inhabitants of the said town, the one dated the 15th *August*, 1668, and the other dated the 13th *May*, 1686. *And further*, that the citizens of this state had, from time immemorial, used, at all proper seasons, the right of fishing in the said bay, and of entering and occupying the shore or beach adjoining the same, for the purpose and convenience of fishing in the said bay, and that the defendant is one of the said citizens. *And further*, that the said *close* is a public highway or landing place, and that the defendant had a right to enter and use it for the purpose aforesaid.

Upon the trial, the plaintiff produced a patent, dated the 23d *February*, 1671, to *Jaques Cortelyou*, for the premises, described as *stretching along the bay*, &c. He then proved that the patentee devised his lands to his two sons, who made partition; that the son of one conveyed to *Jaques Cortelyou*, son of the other, and grandfather of the plaintiff, on the 1st *February*, 1732, a parcel of land beginning at a rock commonly called the *Great Rock*. That the said rock is now at a considerable distance below ordinary high-water mark, and is a very conspicuous object. That the plaintiff is grandson and heir at law to the said *Jaques Cortelyou*, and claims the *locus in quo* as part of the land described in the patent.—It was admitted, that if the patent on the S. W. or bay side, extended to ordinary high-water mark, the place where the hut was erected was within its limits; and the Judge directed the jury to consider the ordinary high-water mark, as the S. W. boundary of the patent.

The defendant offered, under the first and third branches of his notice, to prove the facts therein stated, but the evidence was overruled.

He then produced and read the patents mentioned in his notice, and contended that he had a right, under them, to use the shore, not only between high and low-water mark, but as far as the spring, or uncommon tides flowed, and to erect huts thereon, for the purpose of fishing in the bay adjoining; and also offered to prove that from the date of the patents to that time, the freeholders and inhabitants of *New-Utrecht*, had uninterruptedly enjoyed that right, but the evidence was overruled by the Judge. The defendant then offered to prove, that the *locus in quo* was a public landing place; and the clerk of the county produced an ancient book, as the only existing record of the roads in *King's County*, in which there was an entry of a *common highway*, along the river upon the bank, to the meadow of *Peter* and *Jaques Cortelyou*, and so along the S. W. side of the meadow over the beach, to the house of said *P.* and *J.*, and from thence to the road to the town of *New-Utrecht*. At the bottom of the entry was the following memorandum: "Out of the way leading to *J.* and *P. Cortelyou*, to low-water mark, on the north side of the dock of *Peter Cortelyou*, for a common landing place, in breadth 6 rods, to be and continue forever."

The defendant then showed, that the hut, the erection of which was the only trespass attempted to be proved, was at a place within the distance of six rods from the north side of the dock of *Peter Cortelyou*, between the road to *J.* and *P. Cortelyou*, and the ordinary high-water mark, but below the limits of spring tides.

The plaintiff then proved, that the sea had, as far back as the memory of witnesses reached, gradually washed away the points of land opposite to the S. W. boundary of the land granted to *Jaques Cortelyou*; but that the land within the coves had undergone little or no alteration; that the *locus in quo* was above the present usual high-water mark, and between the sea and the upland; that upon a drain being cut from the meadow to the sea, stumps of trees were found, and traces of the existence of the meadow nearer to the sea than where the trespass was committed; that no use had ever been made, within the memory of witnesses, of the place where the trespass was committed, as a public landing place, and that the plaintiff had a house, for about twenty-five years, nearly adjacent to the spot where the hut was erected.

The jury found a verdict for the plaintiff for six cents damages.

A motion for a new trial was made at the last term, and argued by *Baldwin*, for the defendant, and *Hoffman & Harrison*, for the plaintiff.

For the defendant, it was contended, 1. That the evidence, offered under the first and third branches of the notice, annexed to the plea, ought to have been admitted on the trial. That the notice contained all reasonable certainty, and would have been good as a special plea; but that the courts, under the statute allowing notices of special matters, instead of pleading, were liberal in the admission of evidence. 2. That the evidence offered in support of the defendant's constructions of the patents of *Nicoll* and *Dongan*, ought to have been received. 3. That the Judge ought to have directed the jury that the S. W. boundary of *Cortelyou's patent* extended to ordinary high-water mark. That the boundary was matter of fact, which the jury were to decide. That the highest point to which the spring-tide rises, is the true boundary of the patent. *(Justinian Institutes, lib.* 2. *tit.* 1. *cap.* 3.*)* That the rule of the civil law ought to be adopted here, because it was a grant under the *Dutch* government, and the civil law prevailed, at the time, in the *Seven United Provinces.* 4. That the *locus in quo* was a public highway or landing place, which was clearly made out by the evidence; and that as the "act to regulate highways in the counties of *Suffolk*, *Queens*, *Kings*, and *Richmond*," directs compensation to be made for highways, the land became vested in the people of the state, as public property;* and it was a right which could not be lost by *non-user*. (2 *vol. Laws N. Y.* 191, 192.) That the erecting of a hut might be a nuisance, but it could not be a trespass. It was also contended, that as all prescriptive rights are presumed to have originated in grants, the evidence of which is lost, any thing which could be granted might be prescribed for. That, admitting the right of fishing to exist as a common right in the freeholders and inhabitants of *New-Utrecht*, the right of erecting a hut for the purpose of fishing was appertenant thereto. The right of drawing seines and nets on the shore, and erecting huts for the purpose, was a natural and inseparable incident of the right of fishing.

For the plaintiff, it was argued, that the notice annexed to the defendant's plea was of a prescriptive right of fishing; but the evidence offered at the trial was of a prescriptive right to erect huts. The notice under the plea must contain all the certainty requisite to make a good special plea, and nothing can be received in evidence which is not contained in the notice. Prescriptive rights are not to be favoured; in *England* they are considered as rights, the origin of which cannot be traced; but in this country almost every right can be traced to its origin. The right of fishing, being common to every person, need not be established by prescription. The right of fishing gives no right of occupying the soil or shore. The right of erecting a hut, being an exclusive appropriation, can only be established by grant. Parol evidence cannot be admitted in the construction of grants. The letters patent gave only the right of fishing. By the common law, fishing and fowling were considered as

* The clause of the act is as follows: "Provided always, that it shall not be lawful for the said commissioners, or any of them, to lay out any road through any person's land, without either the consent of the owner thereof, or paying the true value of the land so laid out into a highway or road, with such damages as he shall sustain thereby."

royalties, and did not pass without special and express words. The defendant set up a title under the patents, and evidence of any usage to explain or extend the grants could not be received. The letters patent only give a right of fishing within the limits of the grant, which must be considered as extending to the ordinary high-water mark. Whether the hut was erected on a public highway or landing place, was a fact to be submitted to the decision of the jury. It did not appear that the land was ever used or enjoyed as a public highway and landing place. Besides, in laying out public highways, the right of way only passes to the public; the right of soil remains in the original owner. It appeared also, that the whole road had been washed away, and destroyed by the encroachment of the sea.

THOMPSON, J. The case states that the erection of the *hut* was the only trespass attempted to be proved. The first question is, whether the matters of fact, contained in the 1st and 3d branches of the notice, annexed to the plea, were relevant to the defence, and ought to have been admitted in evidence. These facts went only to support a custom in the inhabitants of *New-Utrecht*, and in the citizens of this state, to fish in the bay adjoining the *close*, and to use and occupy the shore for that purpose. I think this evidence was properly concluded, because, if admitted, the facts did not amount to a justification of the trespass in erecting the hut. A right to fish in any water gives no power over the land. (*Ipswich* v. *Brown*, *Saville*, 11. 3 Term, 256.) Nor will prescription, in any case, give a right to erect a building on another's land. This is a mark of title and of exclusive enjoyment, and it cannot be acquired by prescription. Title to land requires the higher evidence of corporeal seisin, and inheritance. Prescription applies only to incorporeal hereditaments, and whether the right claimed be considered as strictly a custom, or prescription, the principle is the same; the only material distinction between them is, that one is local and the other personal in its nature. (*Coke Litt.* 113. *b.* 2 *Black. Com.* 264.)

The patent under which the plaintiff claims is described as stretching along the bay, and the rule of the common law carries it down to ordinary high-water mark. This is the settled rule, as appears from Lord *Hale's Treatise de Jure Maris. (Hargrave's Law Tracts,* 12.) The doctrine of the civil law is, therefore, not our rule, and the direction to the jury, in this respect, was correct. The patents introduced by the defendant gave no right of fishing, except what was comprehended within the bounds of those patents. There cannot be any real pretence for an authority under them, to encroach on adjoining patents. The usage offered to be proved was inadmissible, as a rule for the construction of those patents, because, when the language of a deed admits of but one construction, and is clear and pertinent, it cannot be controlled by any different exposition to be derived from the practice under it. The defendant must derive the right he sets up, either from the patent itself, or from usage; and if from the latter, it must be specially pleaded, or stated as a ground of defence in the notice. The defence, in both these respects, totally failed, as the patents contained no colour for the right, and the usage to erect huts was not one of the matters of defence expressed in the notice which had been given.

The question as to the *locus in quo* being a public highway, was a matter of fact, depending on proof offered on each side, and the jury must have had it fairly submitted to them. Their verdict is against the existence of the highway, and it appears to me to be agreeable to the weight of evidence. Even admitting the existence of the highway, the general rule here is, that the fee of a highway belongs to the owner of the adjoining ground, and that the sovereign has only a right of passage. It is but a *servitude*, or easement and trespass will lie for any exclusive appropriation of the soil. (1 *Burr.* 143. 2 *Stra.* 1004. 1 *Wils.* 107. 6 *East,* 154.)

In every view, therefore, of this case, I am of opinion that the motion for a new trial ought to be denied.

KENT, Ch. J. was of the same opinion.

SPENCER, J. not having heard the argument, gave no opinion.

Rule refused.

1 CONN. REP. 382.

CHALKER AND OTHERS *v.* DICKINSON AND OTHERS.

IN an action of trespass, the plaintiffs declared that they, and those under whom they claimed, for more than twenty years past, had used, occupied, possessed and enjoyed the free, several and exclusive right and privilege of a certain valuable fishery for shad and other fish in *Connecticut* river, between *Fort-Point* and *Pipestave-Point*, in the town of *Saybrook;* which fishery had been thus occupied and enjoyed by the plaintiffs to the entire exclusion of all the citizens of this state, and all other persons; and that the defendants, well knowing these facts, and intending to injure the plaintiffs, and deprive them of the use and profit of their fishery, did, with force and arms, and without right, wilfully disturb, vex and hinder the plaintiffs in fishing at said place, and in the free and full enjoyment of their right and privilege of the fishery aforesaid, and did with like force enter upon said fishing-place within the plaintiffs' limits, and draw a seine over the same, and take and carry away a great quantity of fish, &c.; by means whereof the plaintiffs were greatly injured and disturbed in their said right and privilege, and prevented from taking with their own seine said fish so caught by the defendants, and their fishery was greatly injured in the value by the doings of the defendants, &c.

The cause was tried at *Middletown*, *December* term, 1814, before *Trumbull*, *Baldwin* and *Ingersoll*, Js.

On the trial, the plaintiffs claimed the free, several and exclusive right of fishery in *Connecticut* river, from a point near the fort in *Saybrook*, down to *Pipestave-Point*, extending in front to the channel, by an uninterrupted possession and use for more than fifteen years. The defendants contended, that the right claimed could not be gained by such possession and use. On this point the court instructed the jury, that an exclusive right in the fishery in question might be acquired by an uninterrupted possession and use during a period of more than fifteen years; and left the question of fact, whether the plaintiffs, and those under whom they claim, had enjoyed such an undisturbed possession and use, to the jury to determine from the evidence. A verdict being found for the plaintiffs, the defendants moved for a new trial, on the ground of a misdirection; and the question of law arising on such motion was reserved for the consideration and advice of the nine Judges.

N. Smith and *R. M. Sherman*, in support of the motion, contended that an exclusive right of fishery in a navigable river could be acquired by an individual in one of two modes only, *viz.* by an express grant from the public, or by prescription, which presumes a grant; and that no such right could be gained in analogy to the statute of limitations, by the uninterrupted enjoyment for fifteen years of a privilege which was common to him and all other citizens of the state.

Daggett and *Staples*, contra. They cited *Pitkin* v. *Olmstead*, 1 *Root*, 217. *Weld* v. *Hornby*, 7 *East* 195. *Bealy* v. *Shaw* *& al.* 6 *East* 215. *Peake's Ev.* 294. *Sherwood* v. *Burr*. 4 *Day's Ca.* 244.

SWIFT, Ch. J. In this case, the court directed the jury, that an exclusive right of fishery could be acquired in a navigable river by an uninterrupted possession and use for more than fifteen years.

The right of fishery by the common law, in the ocean, in arms of the sea, and navigable rivers below high-water mark, is common to all, and the state only can grant an exclusive right. In rivers not navigable, the adjoining proprietors own the fishery, and can grant a right of fishing. *Connecticut* river being navigable in the place where this right of fishery is claimed, it could be acquired only in such manner as a public right can be appropriated or transferred. By the common law, no right could be acquired by use, possession and occupation, unless it had been from time immemorial; and this is called a right by prescription. In *England*, by statute 21 *Jac.* 1. *c.* 16. *s.* 1. it was enacted, that no person that has any right or title of entry, shall enter but within twenty years next after his right or title shall accrue. Courts extended the principle of this statute to similar cases within the same reason. A like statute was at an early period enacted in this country, limiting the right of entry to fifteen years; and courts extended the principle to similar cases. Hence it has become an established rule of the common law, that easements may be acquired by uninterrupted possession for fifteen years; such as rights of way, flowing another's land, diverting water courses, fisheries and the like. But in every case of this description, the use and possession in the first instance are a usurpation of the rights of some other person; and an action would always lie till the fifteen years were elapsed. It is considered, that no man would permit another thus to occupy and possess his right, without a grant; and in all these cases, the law presumes there has been a grant; for the idea is not entertained, that a man by being a trespasser for fifteen years, can by the common law acquire a right. But as the grant depends upon a presumption of law, it is always competent to rebut it by proof of such circumstances as shew no grant could have been made. The general rule then, is, that certain rights may be acquired against individuals by fifteen years uninterrupted possession and use, unanswered and unexplained. 2 *Wms. Saund.* 175. n. (2.)

But the case under consideration is of a very different description. The fishery in *Connecticut* river below high-water mark is common to all the citizens; the use and possession of the plaintiffs was lawful; and the mere lawful exercise of a common right for fifteen years has never been considered as conferring an exclusive right. This case, therefore, does not compare with the cases where a right is acquired by uninterrupted use and possession.

Further, it does not appear that the plaintiffs were the *sole* possessors and occupiers of this fishery. They might have used it without interruption for the term of fifteen years; and so might others. At this rate, several persons might, at the same time, be acquiring an exclusive right to the same fishery; an absurdity that demonstrates the fallacy of the principle contended for.

The public may grant an exclusive right of fishery in a navigable river; and if it may be granted, it may be prescribed for. Such a right shall never be presumed, but the contrary. It is however capable of being proved. In this case, the plaintiffs relied on the presumption arising from uninterrupted use and possession for fifteen years. This would be presuming, not proving, the prescriptive right. If he claims such right, he is bound to *prove* it. *Carter & al.* v. *Murcot & al.* 4 *Burr.* 2162.

In this opinion the other Judges severally concurred, except HOSMER, J. who declined acting, having been of counsel in the cause.—New trial to be granted.

1 Conn. Rep. 510.

CHALKER AND OTHERS v. DICKINSON AND OTHERS.

A new trial having been granted, pursuant to the advice of the nine Judges (vide preceding case) the cause was accordingly tried again at *Haddam*, *December* term, 1815, before *Trumbull*, *Baldwin* and *Ingersoll*, Js.

On the trial it was admitted, that the fishery in question was a common fishery, used by all the citizens of the state, until *May*, 1783, when, by an act of the legislature, being the 13th section of the act for regulating fisheries, the use thereof was wholly prohibited from the 15th day of *March* to the 15th day of *June*, in every succeeding year. At that time, and long afterwards, one *Ambrose Kirkland* was the proprietor of a piece of land fronting the west side of *Connecticut* river, and extending on the river about twenty-five rods, the southern line being about fifty rods below *Fort-Point*, and about fifty-five rods above *Pipestave-Point*. In *October*, 1788, *Kirkland* preferred a memorial to the General Assembly, in which he stated, that he was seized in fee of said piece of land, and had for a long time enjoyed a right and privilege appertenant to his soil, of drawing seines and taking fish, in the season thereof, to his profit and advantage; that by force of said act, he was deprived of the principal advantage which the God of nature and the laws of the land attached to his freehold; that as a free citizen, and enjoying rights in common with his fellow-citizens, invested with a freehold purchased for a valuable consideration, he conceived, by the laws of the land, and by the laws of nature, he was justly entitled to take all the profits and advantages naturally arising therefrom; that it appeared from the preamble to said act, that the mischief to be remedied, was the obstruction to the passage of the fish up the river, occasioned by the drawing of a number of seines at the mouth; that the memorialist's land lies at the distance of about one mile and a quarter north of the mouth; that the channel of the river is half a mile wide against his said land; and that the drawing of one short seine of about twenty-five rods length, at this place, would not, under proper regulations, in the least impede or obstruct the course of the fish up the river, any more than what the seine would actually take, while the using of one seine there would be annually attended with public advantage. The memorialist, therefore, prayed the General Assembly to grant him an exclusive right of drawing and using one seine of twenty-five rods length, in the river adjoining his said land, under such regulations as should appear fit, or in some other way restore to him his just rights incident to his freehold. At an adjourned session of the General Assembly in *January*, 1789, the following resolve, or private act, was passed. "Upon the memorial of *Ambrose Kirkland* of *Saybrook* in the county of *Middlesex*, shewing to this Assembly, that he is seized in fee of a piece of land situate in *Saybrook*, about twenty-five rods south of *The Fort*, so called, adjoining the river on the east; and that he long enjoyed the privilege of drawing a seine for catching fish, in the season of fishing, at said place, until by an act of this Assembly passed in a late session, entitled *An Act for encouraging and regulating Fisheries*, all persons are prohibited from setting or drawing any seine for the purpose of catching fish between the 15th day of *March* and the 15th day of *June* in any year, south of the east and west line from *Saybrook-fort*, so called; and that he, by said act, is totally prevented from using his said privilege of fishing at his fishing-place, aforesaid; and that by his using his fishing-place none of the mischiefs will accrue to the community or individuals, which said statute was made to prevent; praying for relief, &c. as per memorial.

"*Resolved by this Assembly*, that said memorialist have liberty, and liberty and license are hereby granted to him, and his heirs and assigns, to use, occupy and improve the said fishing-place for the purpose of setting a net or seine, and for drawing a seine for the purpose of catching fish, in the season of fishing, at the times, and under the same restrictions and regulations that are in said act provided respecting the fishing-places at *Lynde's* cove and at *Griswold's* cove, any thing in said act notwithstanding, during the pleasure of the General Assembly." The plaintiffs contended, and produced evidence to shew, that *Kirkland*, at the time of obtaining this grant, was in the exclusive occupation of the whole ground from *Fort-Point* to *Pipe-stave-Point*, as a fishing-place; and that he, together with the plaintiffs, who claimed under him, had ever since continued in such occupation, and had the possession of and title to said fishing-place when the trespasses complained of were committed. It appeared, that the plaintiffs used a seine twenty-five rods long only, immediately after their grant; but continued gradually to lengthen it from year to year; and that in the year 1813, and occasionally for more than five years before, they had fished with two seines, each about sixty rods in length. The plaintiffs contended, that they had proved to the jury, that the defendants committed trespasses in all parts of said fishing-place; particularly, that they run their seine above the south line of the plaintiff's land, and up against the middle thereof, and obstructed the plaintiffs in their fishing, as alleged in the declaration. The plaintiffs also contended, that they had proved that the front of their land was not of sufficient extent to allow them a fishery of any use or advantage, without going both above and below their land, as the current or tide should require. They now waived all claim of title from the length of time during which they had possessed the fishery. The act of *May*, 1783 (*tit.* 70. c. 1. *s.* 13.) was repealed in *May*, 1808, (*tit.* 70. c. 9. *s.* 2.) previous to the alledged trespasses. The defendants contended, 1. That said private act of the General Assembly was void on the ground of misrepresentation in the memorial, and was forfeited by misuser: 2. That said act if valid, did not confer on *Kirkland* any right to the fishery, but merely *suspended* the penal law of *May*, 1783, *as to him;* and had no continuing effect at all after the repeal in *May*, 1808: 3. That, at any rate, said private act had no operation south of the front of *Kirkland's* land; and that in point of fact the defendants did not draw any part of their seine or tackle in front of said land, nor so as to interfere with or disturb the plaintiffs in the act of drawing their seine. And the defendants prayed the court to charge the jury on the points of law accordingly. The charge was as follows: "The court are of opinion, that the act of the General Assembly amounts to a grant of the fishery in question, during the pleasure of the Assembly, which, it is agreed, has never been revoked; that it is not void on the ground of any false representations on the face of it, or of the memorial on which it was granted; and that although you should find that the mode of fishing has been varied, and that a much longer seine has been used than the grant gave a right to use, this does not render the grant forfeited. The question then arises, what is the extent, and what are the limits of the fishing-place thus granted? This depends chiefly on the construction of the grant. And the court are of opinion, that the fishing-place granted is not confined merely to the front of the plaintiff's land, but will of course extend so far above and below in the river as may be necessary to sweep over the ground with a seine of twenty-five rods in length, in order to the fair beneficial enjoyment of the grant." The jury found a verdict for the plaintiffs; and the defendants moved for a new trial on the ground of a misdirection. The questions of law arising on this motion were reserved for the consideration and advice of the nine Judges.

N. Smith and *Sherman* in support of the motion.

Daggett and *Staples*, contra.

SWIFT, Ch. J. The question is as to the effect of the resolve of the General Assembly passed on the memorial of *Ambrose Kirkland.*

To determine the nature and effect of the grant, we must consider the object of the party, and the intent of the legislature. Though some words may be used which might be proper in the grant of exclusive rights, yet these may be explained by the allegations in the memorial; and we must take into view all that is said to ascertain the intent.

The memorial alleged a right of fishery in the memorialist, and complained that this right had been infringed and destroyed by a public act prohibiting him to exercise his right. His object was not to obtain a new right; he supposed that to be complete. It was to obtain a suspension of the general law as it respected himself, for the purpose of exercising an existing right. The legislature unquestionably supposed, according to the common opinion prevalent at that time, that the memorialist had a right to fish in front of his land adjoining *Connecticut* river. They could have had no idea of giving him a new right; their intent was to suspend the operation of the law of which he complained, so far as it respected the exercise of an existing right. For this purpose, they have made use of proper and appropriate words. They *grant liberty and license to him, and his heirs and assigns, to use and occupy the fishing-place, any thing in the act prohibiting it to the contrary notwithstanding.* These expressions are precisely proper; admitting it to be their intent to repeal that law so far as it respected the memorialist; but if they had intended to confer a new right, to have made a grant of an exclusive fishery, a very different language would have been proper.

The extension of the license to *heirs and assigns* does not vary the construction. It was considered that the right of fishery was appertenant to the adjoining land; and the intent was, that the privilege should descend to heirs and be transferred to assigns. This was proper, admitting nothing was intended but an exemption from the penalties of the law.

The reference to *Lynde's* cove and *Griswold's* cove was not to define the nature or extent of the grant, but merely the limitation of it. It authorizes him to fish at the same times, and under the same restrictions and regulations, as at these places. It no where says, that he shall have the same right; and it would be strange to say, that a *limitation* should *extend* a grant.

It appears to me, on a full view of the subject, that the resolve of the Assembly only repealed the operation of a general law so as to give the memorialist a license to fish in the same manner as though that law had never been made; and that when the general law was afterwards repealed, it placed all those who lived on this part of the river in the same situation as they were before the law was passed; and of course, that the charge to the jury that the resolve amounted to a grant of a right of fishery was incorrect.

I would advise to grant a new trial.

EDMOND, SMITH and BRAINARD, Js. concurred in the opinion delivered by the Chief Justice.

BALDWIN, J. The correctness of the charge given in this case depends principally on the validity of the grant to *Ambrose Kirkland.* It is claimed, that it is void, because the representation of facts on which it was grounded was fraudulent, and the legislature thereby deceived.

It is not necessary in this case to enquire how far the doctrine of misrepresentation may be carried to avoid a grant, by collateral attack; for it does not appear to me, that any fraudulent statement or misrepresentation of facts has been made. *Ambrose Kirkland* in his memorial states, that his land abutted on the river; that he had long enjoyed the right of drawing seines and taking fish upon it, till prohibited by an act of the legislature; that this act deprives him of the natural advantages appertaining to his freehold, and of course of much of its value; that the mischief intended to be prevented by that act, can be avoided by suitable regulations consistent with the enjoyment of his right; and he therefore prays the General Assembly to grant to him an exclusive right of fishing in the river adjoining his land, under such regulations as the legislature may prescribe. The memorialist no where states an exclusive right in himself to the fishery. He does indeed claim the right of fishing in the waters adjoining his own land as a right appertenant. This, though not acknowledged in the extent claimed by some, is undoubtedly correct, and is exclusive as to the right of the shore for drawing. If, then, the right of sweeping the river is common to all mankind, the memorialist having that right, and the exclusive right of the shore, might fairly make the representation he did.

Although the prohibiting act was the cause which led him to address the legislature, yet the scope of his memorial evidently goes further than a dispensation of the penalty. He prays for an exclusive grant; knowing that others so circumstanced had it. The language of the legislature is that of a grant: "License and liberty is hereby *granted to him, and his heirs and assigns,* to use, occupy and improve the said fishing-place, &c. for the purpose of catching fish in the season of fishing, at the times, and under the same restrictions and regulations that are in said act provided, respecting the fishing places at *Lynde's* cove and *Griswold's* cove, any thing in said act notwithstanding, *during the pleasure of the General Assembly.*" This language admits of no construction. It is not a mere dispensation of the penalties. It is a *grant,* under specified restrictions and regulations, during the pleasure of the General Assembly.

But it is further claimed, that if the resolve is considered as a grant, it has ceased by the repeal of the act to which it refers for its regulations. This principle, if correct, would introduce a limitation not contained in the grant. That is neither limited by the existence of that act, nor is that the basis of it. The reference to the act is merely for regulations, which, when adopted, do not depend at all on the continuance of that act. They continue the same, whether the act remains in force or is repealed.

The only limitation in the grant, is, the pleasure of the General Assembly. It may by them be revoked, but remains in force until, in express terms, they shall manifest their pleasure that it cease.

If the grant claimed exists, it is admitted it cannot be defeated collaterally, by third persons, on the ground of misuser. But,

It is claimed, the court erred in the construction they gave the grant; and that they ought to have limited its extent to the waters in front of the plaintiff's land. I am of opinion, that the subject matter of the grant ought to be taken into consideration, and that construction given which will ensure the beneficial effect intended. A fishing-place is necessarily undefinable by metes and bounds. The ebb and flow of the tides, the strength of the current, and other circumstances, will require, at different times, a different direction and extent of sweep to the same length of seine, and yet the fishing-place will remain the same. I think the court gave a reasonable and fair construction of the grant when they said, it was not confined to the front of the plaintiff's land, but will extend so far above and below in the river as may be necessary to sweep the ground with a seine twenty-five rods in length, in order to the fair and beneficial enjoyment of the grant.

As I cannot say that the grant is void from misrepresentation, or forfeited by misuser, and am persuaded the court gave a fair construction of its extent, I find no cause for a new trial.

Trumbull and Goddard, Js. were of the same opinion.

Gould, J. I am of opinion, that the direction to the jury, upon the construction of the resolve of the legislature, in 1789, was wrong. It is clear, according to a rule heretofore established, that the fishery in question did not belong to *A. Kirkland*, in severalty, *before* that resolve was passed; and the inquiry now is, whether the resolve conferred it upon him.

By the general prohibitory law of 1783, *all* persons were forbidden, under a penalty, to fish, with seines, at the place in question. The resolve of 1789, granted to *Kirkland*, his heirs, &c. permission to use a seine there, the general prohibition notwithstanding. The statute of 1808, has now repealed the prohibitory act, and thus extended or restored the same permission, (the fishery having been originally a *common* one,) to *all* persons, unless the resolve amounted to a grant of a several fishery to *Kirkland*, under whom the plaintiffs claim. Does the resolve, then, contain such a grant? Or is it a mere *exemption* to *Kirkland*, his heirs and assigns, from the operation of the prohibitory act?

In construing the resolve, we have, doubtless, a right to recur to the recital, which precedes it, and the memorial, upon which it is founded, precisely as we might, in any case, consult the preamble of a statute. Now *Kirkland* in his memorial does not even ask for the grant of an original right, or, one which he did not, *before* claim, as his *own*. He represents the fishery as *his*; complains of the impediment which the statute of 1783 had interposed to the exercise of *his* privilege; alleges, that "none of the mischiefs," intended to be prevented by that statute, would be occasioned by the limited exercise of his right; and concludes with praying for the "exclusive right," or—which he represented as the same thing—to be "restored" to his original right. The recital, introductory to the resolve, without finding any fact, merely recapitulates these several representations; and the resolve then grants to him, his heirs, &c. "liberty and license," to use a seine at the place described, under certain restrictions, during the pleasure of the legislature. It does not import to grant to him, what was not before his own,—as a several fishery clearly was not; or to establish a right already vested in him. It does not even contain the word, *right*, *title*, *interest*, *franchise*, or any term of similar import; but grants "*liberty* and *license*," (terms almost appropriate to denote a matter of mere *favour* or *indulgence*,) during the pleasure of the legislature. From this review of the proceedings, which terminated in the resolve of 1789, the result appears to be, that the utmost amount of *Kirkland's* claim, or request, was, that he might be restored to a supposed right, (which, however, never existed,) *by an exemption from the penalty of the statute* of 1783: and that the legislature granted the exemption, during its own pleasure, without deciding, or intending to decide, the question of right. This, I think, appears from the whole scope of the proceedings. If so, it follows, that, by the subsequent repeal of the statute of 1783, the rights of *Kirkland*, and of all others, in relation to this fishery, are left, precisely as they were, before that act was passed; upon which supposition *Kirkland* never owned the several fishery, now claimed by the plaintiffs; and the plaintiffs, of course, do not own it.

The words, in the resolve, "under the same restrictions and regulations," as are prescribed for "*Lynde's* cove and *Griswold's* cove," obviously relate only to the *mode of exercising* the right or privilege, intended to be granted; not to the *character*, or *nature*, of that right or privilege.

I am of opinion, that a new trial ought to be granted.

HOSMER, J. gave no opinion, having been of counsel in the cause.—New trial to be granted.

8 Brown's Parl. Rep. 18.

THE DEAN AND CHAPTER OF DURHAM, AND SAMUEL SHEPHEARD, their Lessee, } *Appellants.*

THE MEMBER AND BURGESSES OF NEWCASTLE UPON TYNE, } *Respondents.*

THE appellants stated, that the dean and chapter were seized of the manor of *Westow*, in the county of *Durham*, on the south side of the river *Tyne*, extending to the middle of that river, and of the east part of a certain waste ground called *Jarrowslake*, about 150 acres (parcel of the manor) with divers liberties in the said river, and demised to the appellant *Shepheard* the said east part of *Jarrowslake*, with power to convert it to his best advantage; and this *Jarrowslake* being useless by the water overflowing it at every tide, which was thereby hindered from flowing up the river; and the appellant *Shepheard* conceiving it a fit place for erecting salt-works, began to inclose it with a ballast wharf, for salt ships, according to the ancient usage at *South Shields* (within said manor) where they had, time out of mind, enjoyed such wharves, without paying any acknowledgment to respondents, and particularly at a place called *Mildam Key*, where they had constantly taken the ballast of salt ships, for above three score years, without interruption; and that this place was many years ago certified by commissioners of sewers, as most commodious for a ballast key, and its advantages were reported to King *Charles* the second, by the Trinity Masters of *London;* and this liberty was confirmed to appellants by several orders of the king and council, in the case of Sir *Robert Heath*, above three score years ago: Yet respondents have, for many years, endeavoured either to get this ground themselves, or render it useless to all others; and fear-ing that coal ships should prefer to unload ballast at the intended quay, rather than sail many miles up a dangerous river to the town quays, not only demolished the said wharf, but exhibited their bill in the exchequer, prescribing for the sole licensing all ballast wharves there; and praying a perpetual injunction to restrain appellants in the premises. Whereupon the court directed a trial upon these issues: 1. Whether the appellants could lawfully erect and use a ballast key at *Jarrowslake*, without the respondents' license. 2. Whether the erecting such quay would be a damage to the river or navigation thereof, or port of *Newcastle*. And upon a verdict by a jury of *Bedfordshire*, an inland county, strangers to navigation, who never had any view or knowledge of the place in question, the court, without granting appellants further time to make out their right at law, by a jury of the neighbourhood, which they assert they can do by evidence never yet heard (and some of it discovered since the last trial) decreed a perpetual injunction; from which the defendants appealed, and insisted before the lords, that the issues tried (supposing them proper) were not tried by a jury of the neighbourhood, before whom the law gives every man right to have his cause once tried at least, as having best knowledge of usage and fact, and that such trial ought the rather to have been granted in this case; because it concerns not only the inheritance of the church, and the private interest of their lessee fairly purchased, but the coal and salt trades throughout the kingdom; and that no damage was proved to have arisen to the said river or port, by the appellants' ballast wharf, wherein they proceeded above seven score yards, or by the old wharf, built formerly at the same place, which had stood fifty years without pretence of prejudice: which appellants conceived would have been the proper issue, rather than an issue to try whether it will in future be any damage, which no jury can well take cognizance of, it being impossible to prove how much or how the appellants would build, till the same should be completed; and insisted further, that appellants, by this decree, are not only restrained from erecting ballast wharves for coal ships, but for salt ships too, though it was fully proved that salt ships contantly cast their ballast at the dean and chapter's key, at *South Shields*, without any duty or acknowledgment to the town of *Newcastle:* to which, in particular, the appellants' right could not possibly be found, upon so general issue as was then tried. And that appellants are, by this decree, forever precluded from making any use of their own ground, and the church forever disabled to make leases of *Jarrowslake*, as they have done for many years, and incapable either of hindering the tides overflowing more of their ground, or preventing damages to the port and haven, by the waters overflowing *Jarrowslake*, which must be while it lies uninclosed, and this upon one single trial by a foreign jury: and though the respondents may insist upon another trial, had about twenty years since, yet the same was upon a different case, and between other persons, and appellants no parties, and by a *Buckingham* jury, wholly unacquainted with the place. And appellants further insisted, that this verdict would be an evidence, not only against the appellants' right to the erection and usage of ballast wharves for salt ships at any time hereafter, in any other part of their said manor, but also against the ancient undoubted right and present usage of *Mildam Key*, and other places already built within the manor; so that salt ships must either pay duty to the respondents, or sail many miles up the river to the town keys, to the great discouragements of the salt trade at *Shields*, and prejudice of the church's interest; and that appellants' right could not, nor ever can be, determined upon this bill and proceedings in the exchequer, and that this decree wholly deprives appellants from all possibility of recovering, and even from trying their right; and the corporation of *Newcastle* hath a very great revenue, and a sufficient recompense for preserving this port, by impositions and customs on goods and merchandises imported and exported.

The respondents made this case: That they are an ancient corporation, and have held the town of *Newcastle*, the port and haven there, from a place in the sea called *Sparrhawke*, to a place in the river *Tyne*, called *Hedwynstreams*, and have the conservatorship of the river; the sole power of erecting and licensing ballast shores and keys thereon, and holding a court of record for the conservation thereof, before the mayor and some of the aldermen, time out of mind; and that such privileges have been confirmed to the corporation by divers ancient grants from the Crown, under the yearly fee farm rent of 100*l.*

That never any ballast shore or key, though not prejudicial to the river, navigation and trade, was erected on the said river of *Tyne*, without the license of the said corporation.

That about thirty years ago, Sir *Charles Adderly* and *John Crooke*, Esq. tenants under the then dean and chapter of *Durham*, of a great piece of ground called *Jarrowslake*, (the place in question,) attempted to build a ballast sewer or key, but were obstructed by the corporation, as it would endanger the navigation of the said river, be mischievous to the bar of *Tinmouth*, dangerous to ships and men's lives, and destructive to trade; and thereupon *Adderley* and *Crooke*, as also the said corporation, petitioned his late Majesty, king *Charles the second*, in council; and after hearings at the council board, it was ordered in council that a trial should be had at the exchequer bar, by a special jury of the county of *Bucks*, upon this issue, *viz.* whether the dean and chapter of *Durham* could lawfully erect and use ballast keys, and wharves, at *Jarrowslake*, without the license of the mayor and burgesses of *Newcastle;* and in Easter term, 1669, a trial was accordingly had before the late Lord Chief Baron *Hale*, upon the said issue, wherein *William Blackett*, Esq. (on the behalf of the said corporation) was plaintiff, and the said *Crooke*, (on the part of the then dean and chapter) was defendant; and after a long trial and full evidence given on both sides, the jury gave a verdict, *viz.* that a ballast key could not lawfully be erected and used at *Jarrowslake*, without the license of the mayor and burgesses of *Newcastle*. Not satisfied with which trial, *Adderley* and *Crooke* again petitioned the king and council, that it might be referred to the lord mayor and court of aldermen of the city of *London*, to examine and report concerning the alleged public utility of such ballast wharf, which was accordingly ordered; and 27th *October*, 1670, the then lord mayor and court of aldermen made their report to his said Majesty in council, and certified that, having heard counsel and examined witnesses on both sides, they found that the erecting a ballast sewer at *Jarrowslake* aforesaid, would prove destructive to trade in general, dangerous both to shipping and men's lives, would enhance the price of sea coals, obstruct and choke the river *Tyne*, be exceedingly mischievous to the bar of *Tinmouth*, and manifestly tend to the decrease of the trade and damage of the town of *Newcastle;* under which trial and report all persons rested satisfied for above twenty years, until 1691, when the appellant *Shepheard* obtained a lease from the dean and chapter, of *Jarrowslake* aforesaid, for twenty-one years, at some very small rent, and soon after attempted to build a ballast sewer, or key, there; which was presented as a nuisance to the river, and ordered to be demolished and abated, and was accordingly done; and in Trinity term, 1694, respondents exhibited their bill in the exchequer, stating their right, and the necessary prejudice of any ballast sewer, or key to be erected upon the said river of *Tyne*, and therefore prayed an injunction, to prohibit the appellants, and all claiming under them, from erecting such ballast sewer, or key, at *Jarrowslake;* which bill the appellants answered; and several witnesses were examined on both sides by commission, and before a baron in *London;* and the appellants joined in the commission, and their commissioners were present when all respondents' witnesses were examined, and cross-examined them, and exhibited interrogatories before the commissioners, and examined several witnesses on their part; and appellants having discovered what respondents' witnesses had sworn, appellants about two months after exhibited other interrogatories before a baron in *London*, differing in many material points from their interrogatories exhibited before the commissioners; which appearing to the court, it was ordered, that oath should be made by the appellants, or some on their behalf, what witnesses examined before a baron in *London* were dead, and the court would consider, at the hearing of the cause, whether their deposition should be made use of or not: and that the depositions taken on any interrogatories varying from the interrogatories exhibited before the commissioners, should be suppressed: and 19th *February*, 1696, the cause was heard, and the prejudice of this ballast wharf appeared so plain to the court, that a perpetual injunction would have been at once decreed, but that the appellants importuned the court for a trial at law, with which (as they alleged) they would rest satisfied; and thereupon the court directed a trial at bar by a special jury of *Bedford*, upon the two issues, stated by appellants; and in Trinity term, 1697, a trial was accordingly had, which continued about sixteen hours; and upon a full evidence on both sides, a verdict was found for the respondents upon both the said issues; and on the 10th of *February* last, it was finally ordered and decreed by the said court of Exchequer, that the appellants, and every of them, should be restrained from making or erecting any ballast key or wharf at *Jarrowslake* aforesaid; and that a perpetual injunction should be awarded as prayed; and the appellants, as a ground for the present appeal, pretend that the depositions taken in *London* were suppressed, and that the witnesses who made those depositions were, before the said trial, unfortunately drowned, whereby the appellants could not make their defence: but the respondents insist, that if the appellants had been aggrieved by the said order for suppressing the said depositions, they should have appealed to the lords before the trial of the said cause; and that having omitted to do so, they ought not now to be heard against that order; which, however is just and reasonable, and according to the rules and practice of the courts of law and equity: wherefore, and in regard the said decree is only to quiet the respondents in the enjoyment of a right which they hold by custom, and to hinder the appellants from erecting a nuisance to the destruction of a navigable river; and that the said custom and nuisance had been tried by two solemn trials at the bar, the respondents insisted that the decree should be affirmed, and the said appeal dismissed with costs.

And (*Die Sabbati*, 7° *Maii*, 1698,) after hearing counsel on both sides, that it was ORDERED and ADJUDGED by the lords, that the petition and appeal should be dismissed, and the order and decree appealed from affirmed. *Lords Journ.* vol. xvi. p. 278.

2 JOHNSON'S REP. 313.

EMANS *v.* TURNBULL, DENTON AND VOORHIS.

THIS was an action of *trespass*, for assaulting the plaintiff, and stopping and detaining him and his horse and wagon, for the space of twenty minutes, at *Gravesend*, in *King's* county.

The defendants pleaded, 1. The general issue. 2. *Son assault demesne*, to which the plaintiff replied *de injuria propria, &c.* 3. That the defendant, *Turnbull*, before and at the time of the trespass, was possessed of a certain close in *Gravesend*, and of the sea-weed which laid on the ground in the close; and being so possessed, &c. the plaintiff, with force and arms entered the said close and took a large quantity of the sea-weed of the said defendant, and would have it carried away, whereupon the said defendant, as owner of the said close and sea-weed, and the other defendants, as his servants, and by his order, gently laid their hands upon the said sea-weed, in order to keep the same, and also gently laid their hands on the horses and wagon of the plaintiff, to lead them out of the said close, &c. The plaintiff replied to this plea, protesting that the defendant, *Turnbull*, was not possessed of the close, &c. nor owner, &c. and stating that the defendants did the wrong *de injuria sua, absque*, &c. To this, the defendants rejoined, that the defendant, *Turnbull*, was possessed, &c. and was owner of the sea-weed, and the plaintiff joined issue thereon.

The cause was tried before Mr. Justice *Tompkins*, at the *King's* county circuit, in *April*, 1806, when the jury found verdict for the defendants.

The evidence produced at the trial, was as follows: 1. An *Indian* deed, dated the 7th *May*, 1654, to the patentees and inhabitants of *Gravesend*, for the neck of land from *Antonie Johnson's* house, southward, and *Conyne* island, with all the meadow-land, and marsh-land thereto belonging. 2. A patent from the *Dutch* governor *Kieft*, dated the 27th *May*, 1643, to *Anthony Jansen Van Salee*, for one hundred *morgan* of land, lying in the bay, over against *Conyne* island, and stretching along the strand, &c. &c. 3. A patent from governor *Kieft*, dated the 19th *December*, 1645, for the town of *Gravesend* to the four persons therein named, their associates, heirs and successors, &c. of a certain quantity of land, &c. beginning at the mouth of a creek, adjacent to *Conyne* island, &c. &c. 4. A patent of confirmation from governor *Nicolls* to *Francis Brown*, dated the 11th *June*, 1667, for the one hundred morgan of land, originally patented to *Anthony Jansen Van Salee*, under whom *Brown* held by mesne assignment. 5. A report of referees to governor *Lovelace*, stating that *Francis Brown* had no meadow mentioned in his patent, and was short of his 100 morgan of land, and they report one third of the meadow lying before his door, to make up the 100 morgan, *one third* to the inhabitants of *Gravesend* for the ditching they had done, though it did not belong to *Gravesend*, and one third to be at the disposal of government. 6. An order of governor *Lovelace*, dated the 23d *August*, 1669, stating a controversy subsisting between the inhabitants of *Gravesend* and *Francis Brown*, concerning some meadow ground adjoining to 12 morgan of upland in the patent to *Brown*, but claimed by the innabitants of *Gravesend*, as within their patent, and the governor allows one third of the meadow to *Brown*, and two thirds to the inhabitants of *Gravesend*; and, as the *neck of land* had hitherto most usually been enjoyed *in common* between the town and *Brown's* farm, he orders it to continue so, with a right of appeal to either party to the next assizes. 7. The proceedings of a court of assize, held in *November*, 1669, in which the inhabitants of *Gravesend* were plaintiffs, and *Francis Brown* defendant, and on a trial by jury, a verdict was found for the defendant; but the court annulled the verdict, and ordered the division of the meadow, as divided by governor *Lovelace*, the 23d *August*, 1669, to stand good; and that the plaintiffs should have the benefit of those orders, if they took out their patent according to law, in twenty-eight days. 8. *An agreement*, dated the 29th *April*, 1670, between the inhabitants of *Gravesend* and *Brown*, in which it is agreed that the lands and limits lately in controversy, shall be held and owned to each party, their heirs, &c. &c. that *Brown* shall have the *neck of land with the timber and herbage* that lies from his house southward, bounded on one side by the bay to the west, and by a creek to the east, and the creek to be the boundary between *Brown* and *Gravesend*; but the inhabitants of *Gravesend* shall have *free egress and regress* over the said *neck* of land, and along by the water side, or strand on the west, with the *liberty of fishing and fowling, or any other needful occasion*, without any molestation from *Brown*, &c. 9. A patent of confirmation from governor *Lovelace* to *Gravesend*, dated 1st July, 1670, referring to and confirming the above articles of agreement. 10. An agreement dated the 12th *March*, 1734, between the trustees of *Gravesend* and *Albert Coerten*, (through whom the defendant claimed) in which it was agreed, that the inhabitants of *Gravesend* should have their way or road to their landing at the bay side, in a certain manner set forth in the agreement.

It was admitted that the *neck* was not within the boundaries of the patent to *Anthony Jansen*, or the patent to *Francis Brown*, but was within the limits of the patents for *Gravesend*. A deed from *Albert Coerten*, dated 9th *March* 1740, *to Van Voorhis*, and a deed from *Van Voorhis* to *B.* and *C. Van Voorhis*, dated the 5th *October*, 1756, were also read in evidence.

From the *parol* evidence, it appeared that the *neck* was a strip of poor sandy ground, uncultivated, but producing wild grass, and capable of maintaining cattle, &c. The defendant, *Turnbull*, and those under whom he claims, have used it for the purpose of pasturing cattle. A quantity of wood fit for fuel, was also growing on the neck; and as far back as the witness could remember, *Albert Coerten* and his assigns were considered as possessing the *neck*, and did exclusively pasture it, and take the wood; and that it was considered as possessed under the agreement of 1670: that the *neck* was used by the inhabitants of *Gravesend* for the purpose of passing and repassing, to fish, for a public landing, and for depositing manure, until it was convenient to remove it, and that it was so used under a belief of right; that previous to the war of 1775, the sea-weed was not known to be of any value, but since the war, it has been known as a manure; and from that time, the inhabitants of *Gravesend* have continually taken and carried away the sea-weed from the shore or beach of the *neck*, though continually warned not to take it, by the owners of the land under the patents to *Jansen* and *Brown*; that the plaintiff, being an inhabitant of *Gravesend*, collected a load of the sea-weed, on the shore or beach of the *neck*, and was about carrying it away, when the defendants forbid him, and the trespass complained of was committed. It appeared that if the sea-weed were left on the beach, it would, as driven up by the sea, form a row, and protect the bank from being washed, and the sand from being thrown upon the *neck*

A motion for a new trial was made at the last term, and argued by *Riggs* and *Benson*, for the plaintiff, and by *Harison* and *Hoffman*, for the defendants.

Kent, Ch. J. The first question arising upon this case is, who is seized in fee of the *locus in quo?* Does it reside in the inhabitants of *Gravesend*, or in *Turnbull*, the defendant? By the agreement of 1670 it was evidently intended to convey the fee of the *neck* to *Brown*. It is stated to be a final agreement or determination, concerning certain parcels of land lately in controversy between the parties, and the order of governor *Lovelace* of the preceding year stated that the title to the *neck* was one of the subjects of controversy. The agreement declares that the said parcels of land shall be *owned* and *held* by each party, as thereafter mentioned, and to their *heirs*, successors and assigns, as their proper right; and in the 7th and 8th articles it is declared to be agreed that *Brown* should have all the *neck* of land with the timber and herbage, and that the inhabitants of *Gravesend* should have free egress and regress over the same. The intention here is manifest, to vest the fee in *Brown*, and to reserve a right of way to the inhabitants. Considering the antiquity of the instrument, and that the defendant, *Turnbull*, and those under whom he claims by a regular deduction of title from *Brown*, for a period of time as remote as the memory of witnesses can reach, have exercised constant and exclusive ownership over the *neck* in question, the agreement ought at this day to be most liberally expounded, so as to give effect to the intention. The agreement purports to be signed by sundry persons, and the inhabitants of *Gravesend* cannot be permitted to say that those were not persons competent to convey the *neck;* for, afterwards, in the same year, 1670, they accepted from governor *Lovelace* a confirmation of their patent, which patent of confirmation expressly allows and confirms the agreement. The inhabitants of *Gravesend* are therefore to be considered as regular parties to the agreement; and as it was accompanied by a delivery of possession, (for so we are to intend, as the possession hath been uninterruptedly enjoyed and continued down,) the people of *Gravesend* are concluded from disputing the title of the opposite party. Admitting the writer to be deficient in the apt terms requisite to pass a fee, the agreement ought to bind the inhabitants, especially after such a lapse of time, accompanied by so long an acquiescence. An arbitration bond and award cannot have the operation of conveying land; but a party, by his agreement in that way, has been held to conclude himself from disputing the title, (*Doe* v. *Rosser*, 3 *East*, 15.) This is going much further than the present case requires. We need only say, that if one party agrees in writing with another that he shall *own* and *hold* a piece of land to him and his *heirs*, and he delivers him the possession, and that possession is held and enjoyed for a time beyond the memory of man, in such a case, we will not search curiously for technical terms, but will hold the party concluded, by his agreement and subsequent acts, from disputing the title.

The next point in the case is, whether the sea-weed thrown by the sea upon the shore or beach of the *neck*, did thereby vest in the owner of the soil, or belong to the first occupant? The plaintiff's right, if any, rested upon occupancy; for the liberty of egress and regress, and of fishing and fowling, reserved to the inhabitants of *Gravesend* by the agreement of 1670, gave them no other rights than those expressed. They could not take wood, grass, or any thing appertenant to the ownership of the soil. The plaintiff then had no right to the sea-weed, because he was an inhabitant of *Gravesend*. Any stranger would have had an equal right to take it.

The sea-weed thus thrown up by the sea, may be considered as one of those marine increases arising by slow degrees; and according to the rule of the common law, it belongs to the owner of the soil. The rule is, that if the marine increase be by small and almost imperceptible degrees, it goes to the owner of the land; but if it be sudden and considerable, it belongs to the sovereign. (2 *Blacks. Com.* 261. *Harg. Law Tracts*, 28.) The sea-weed must be supposed to have accumulated gradually. The slow increase, and its usefulness as a manure, and as a protection to the bank will, upon every just and equitable principle, vest the property of the weed in the owner of the land. It forms a reasonable compensation to him for the gradual encroachments of the sea, to which other parts of his estate may be exposed; this is one sound reason for vesting these maritime increments in the proprietor of the shore. The *jus alluvionis* ought, in this respect, to receive a liberal encouragement in favour of private right. I am of opinion, therefore, that the motion for a new trial ought to be denied.

THOMPSON, J. concurred.

SPENCER, J. not having heard the argument in the cause, gave no opinion.—Judgment for the defendants.

10 MASS. REP. 70.

THE INHABITANTS OF ARUNDEL *v.* M'CULLOCH.

THIS was an action of trespass for cutting down and tearing away a bridge within the town of *Arundel*, and alleged to be the property of the plaintiffs.

The action came under the consideration of the court upon certain facts agreed by the parties, from which it appeared that the bridge destroyed was built by the plaintiffs over *Kennebunk* river, connecting the towns of *Arundel* and *Wells*:—that this river, or rather arm of the sea, is navigable from the place where the bridge stood to the sea; and above the same bridge for light vessels of a large size to pass down, and for coasting vessels to pass up and down:—that the bridge was removed by the defendant, to facilitate the passage of a vessel belonging to him, built above said bridge: that as little damage was done to the bridge as possible to effect that purpose:—that a bridge has lain across said river in the same place upwards of fifty years:—and that in the year 1771 a county road was, by the court of sessions, located over said river in the direction of the said bridge.—And it was agreed that if the action was maintainable in the opinion of the court, the defendant should be defaulted, and the plaintiffs' damages assessed by a jury: otherwise they were to become nonsuit, and the defendant have judgment for his costs.

The cause was argued at the last May term in this county, by *Mellen* for the plaintiffs, and by *Dane* and *Holmes* for the defendant, and continued to this term for advisement.

Per curiam. It is an unquestionable principle of the common law, that all navigable waters belong to the sovereign, or in other words, to the public; and that no individual or corporation can appropriate them to their own use, or confine or obstruct them so as to impair the passage over them, without authority from the legislative power. It is upon this principle, that so many acts of our legislature have been passed, authorizing the building of bridges over various rivers and streams within the commonwealth.

In this case no such authority has been given; and the only claim of a right to continue the bridge rests upon the antiquity of the bridge, and the laying out of a road over the river in the year 1771.—But we think that neither of these facts sanctioned the obstruction of the river, so as to prevent those who had occasion to transport vessels up and down from removing it, if necessary, to a safe and convenient passage. Public rights cannot be destroyed by long continued encroachments: at least, the party, who claims the exercise of any right inconsistent with the free enjoyment of a public easement or privilege, must put himself upon the ground of prescription; unless he has a grant or some valid authority from the government: and a right by prescription does not exist in the present case.

With respect to the act of the sessions in 1771, laying out a road across the river, nothing can be inferred from it in favour of the plaintiffs, because it was an act without authority, and void in law; as was determined in the case of the *Commonwealth* vs. *Coombs.*

The only question remaining then is, whether the doings of the defendant, in cutting down and removing the bridge, were justifiable on his part.—And it is clear, that when any public way is unlawfully obstructed, any individual, who wants to use it in a lawful way, may remove the obstruction: and it is settled, that he may even enter upon the land of the party erecting or continuing the obstruction, for the purpose of removing it, doing as little damage as possible to the soil or buildings. Here nothing more was done, than was necessary to procure a safe passage for the defendant's vessel; and we are satisfied that no trespass was thereby committed by him.—Plaintiff's nonsuit.

1 Mod. Rep. 106.

LORD FITZWALTER'S CASE.

A trial at bar concerning the river of *Wall-fleet:* the question was, whether the defendant had not the right of fishing there. exclusive of all others?

Hale, Ch. J. In case of a private river, the lord's having the soil is good evidence to prove, that he hath the right of fishing; and it puts the proof upon them that claim *liberam pisca-*

riam. But in case of a river that flows and reflows, and is an arm of the sea, there, *prima facie*, it is common to all: and if any will appropriate a privilege to himself, the proof lieth on his side; for in case of an action of trespass brought for fishing there, it is, *prima facie*, a good justification to say, that the *locus in quo* is *brachium maris, in quo unusquisque subjectus dom. regis habet et habere debet liberam piscariam*. In the river *Severn* there are particular restraints, as *gurgites*, *&c.* but the soil doth belong to the lords on either side: and a special sort of fishing belongs to them likewise; but the common sort of fishing is common to all. The soil of the river of *Thames* is in the king; and the lord mayor is conservator of the river, and it is common to all fishermen: and therefore there is no such contradiction betwixt the soil being in one, and yet the river being common for all fishers, &c.

1 Caines' Rep. 543.

THE MAYOR, ALDERMEN AND COMMONALTY OF THE CITY OF NEW-YORK, *v.* RICHARD SCOTT.

THIS was an action commenced in the justices' court of the city of New-York, to recover eighteen dollars and fifty cents for wharfage. The suit being removed into the Supreme Court, a verdict was, by consent, entered for the plaintiff, subject to the opinion of the court, on a case, which was shortly this.

The lands which the corporation of New-York, under their charter hold, on Manhattan Island, and within the city, extend to low-water mark, and four hundred feet beyond that, into the east river. To these are annexed, "the right, benefit and advantage, of all docks, wharves, cranes and slips, or small docks within the city, with the wharfage, cranage and dockage, and all issues, rents, profits and advantages, arising, or to arise or accrue, by, or from, all, or any of them." By an act of the legislature, passed on the 7th of March, 1793, it is declared, that "all the right, title, interest, claim and demand, of the people of this State, of, in, and to all lands, at any time heretofore left for streets or highways, in the city of New-York, by any person or persons whomsoever, shall be, and hereby is vested in the mayor, aldermen and commonalty of the city of New-York, and their successors, for the use of streets and highways."

In the various grants by the corporation, of their water-lots on the north-easterly side of the coffee house slip, they had given in fee, the right of wharfage in front, and in consideration of erecting certain piers, given to their grantees for twenty years, the wharfage, &c. of the south-westerly sides of such piers, provided they should not grant away the water-lots on that side, which they reserved to themselves a right to do, in which case, the wharfage on the south-westerly side was to cease.

The corporation having granted away the whole of the land to which they were entitled, under their charter, applied in April, 1798, to the legislature, for an act to authorize them to run streets or wharves, of seventy feet width, in front of the water-lots already granted. This, by a law of that month and year, (re-enacted on the 3d of April, 1801,) the legislature was pleased to grant; and by the same act, the proprietors of lots, on the front of which, the streets or wharves might run, were to fill them up, and make piers, according to the directions of the corporation. On non-compliance, the corporation were to be at liberty so to do, and receive the wharfage to their own use. It was also further provided, that the corporation might grant to such proprietors in fee, a common interest in such piers, in proportion to the breadth of their respective lots, under such restrictions, and within such limits as the mayor, &c. might deem just and proper.

In pursuance of the authority, conferred by this act, the corporation laid out a street, called South-street, in front of the lots they had granted, joining the East river, and on the first day of *June*, 1801, made a by-law, or ordinance, by which they ordered the respective owners of lots, fronting and bounded on South-street, from the Wall-street slip to the Fly-market slip, to make a pier on the north-east side of Wall-street, and complete it according to the directions therein given, before the first day of *November*, 1802; on doing which, the corporation would grant the piers to the owners of the said lots, "reserving in the said grants, the exclusive right in the corporation of this city, of wharfage and slipage, on the side of each pier, adjoining a public slip, and that the said piers be, in all respects, considered as public streets or highways, and maintained and kept in repair, by the grantees, their heirs and assigns."

Previous to the passing the act of *April*, 1798, the corporation had laid out the plan of South-street, and had granted to the proprietors of lots, bounded by the East river, the vacant water-lots between them and South-street.

Among the grants thus made, there was one, the 10th of *May*, 1797, to *John Murray*, under whom the defendant claimed.

By this grant, *Murray* was to make a wharf or street, of seventy feet in width, along the whole front of the lot, granted to him, (which was to be South-street,) and another of at least twenty-five feet, along the whole west side of the same lot, and of the street, of seventy feet. The same to be and remain public streets; in consideration of upholding, maintaining, and keeping of which, in good and sufficient repair, he was to have all wharfage, &c. accruing or arising, by or from the same, fronting the East river, or by or from any part thereof.

Murray accordingly built the wharves and streets, specified in the grant, and also, under the direction of the corporation, a pier running in front of South-street, into the East river, the south-west sides of which, and of the wharves and streets he had erected, are bounded by, and in a line with Wall-street slip, which runs in front of Wall-street, and the wharf of twenty-five feet, built along the south-west sides of South-street, and the lot granted by the deed of 10th *May*, 1797, to *John Murray*. This pier, so erected, was not only opposite to the water-lots mentioned in the indenture of 1797, but ran about five feet more to the south-west, upon lands within the bounds of the city, as expressed in its charter, and opposite to the wharf, covenanted in the grant, to be built by *Murray*, which land however, was not granted to the corporation by their charter.

The pier, from the time of its being made, had been upheld by *Murray*, and no grant of a common interest in it had been made by the mayor, aldermen and commonalty, agreeable to the act of the legislature already recited.

The sole question was, whether the defendant, to whom by mesne assignments the rights of *Murray* had been conveyed, was entitled to the wharfage on the south-west side of the pier, which ran in front of the five feet of the city lands? If he was, then a non-suit to be entered.

Per curiam, delivered by *Livingston*, J. This is an action for money had and received by the defendant, as wharfage for vessels lying in what the plaintiffs call a slip, adjacent to that part of a pier which stands opposite *Murray's* wharf. From the form of action the plaintiffs must shew a title in them to demand this money. It is, therefore, unnecessary to inquire whether it belongs to the defendant or not. The corporation can have no such right, inasmuch as the land, on which the pier is erected, was never granted to them, nor was the soil under the water where the vessel lay, for which this wharfage was paid. No implied grant is contained in the act of the legislature. The corporation are only to grant as attornies of the public, in case piers are sunk. That this is to be done under certain restrictions and regulations means, not that they shall have a right to reserve the wharfage to themselves, which is to be theirs only in case of default in the owners of the lots in sinking piers, but they are to regulate in what manner the right to wharfage shall be enjoyed. Nor does the resolve of the common council of the first of *June*, 1801, make a difference. The reservation therein contained, if in an indenture, might have been binding on the defendant; but, the corporation having exceeded their powers in making this reservation in a resolve of this kind, it cannot be binding on him. They had no right, in this way, to impose any terms they pleased, or they might arbitrarily have deprived the owners of lots of the right, which the legislature intended they should have, of sinking these piers. It cannot, therefore, be regarded in the light of a contract; for the defendant had a right to make these piers and bridges without thereby sanctioning any terms which might thus be imposed on him. Nor can it be said that the corporation, not having executed the powers vested in them by the act, the individual has no right to receive the wharfage. This would be to take advantage of their own wrong and neglect; nor does it follow, as has already been observed, that the money belongs to the corporation, if it be admitted that the defendant was wrong in taking it.

This is no slip, which is an opening between two pieces of land or wharves. This pier extends into the East river and is twenty feet from the side of the slip. The grant to *John Murray* of *May*, 1797, is also important, for by this he is entitled to the wharfage of ninety-eight feet.

It is the opinion of the court, that the defendant have judgment.

COWPER'S REP. 86.

THE MAYOR OF LYNN *v.* TURNER.

ERROR from a judgment of the court of *Common Pleas* in an action upon the case against the corporation of *Lynn Regis* for not repairing and cleansing a certain creek or fleet called *Dowshill fleet*, into which the tide of the sea was accustomed to flow and reflow, as from *time immemorial they had been used*, whereby the sea was prevented from flowing therein, so that the said creek was rendered unnavigable, and the plaintiff obliged to carry his corn round about. The declaration consisted of nine counts: the *second count* stated *no special damage*, but only charged generally, that the plaintiff had lost the use of his navigation. Judgment by *nihil dicit* and damages upon a writ of enquiry.

Mr. BALDWIN for the plaintiff in error. If any one count is bad, the judgment may be set aside. Upon the face of this record it appears, that the *locus in quo* is a navigable river, where the tide flows and reflows, and the second count is general, without any special damage being stated. If so, the injury complained of is not the subject of an action, but of an indictment. For wherever a river flows and reflows, it is in the nature of a highway, and is common to all. *Davis* 56. *Sid.* 149. 1 *Mod.* 105. 1 *Salk.* 357, and where an injury is received by a nuisance or obstruction in a highway, it is incumbent on the party to shew a particular damage: otherwise an action does not lie. 1 *Inst.* 56 *Carth.* 191. *Cro. Eliz.* 664. 5 *Co.* 73.

Lord MANSFIELD. *Ex facto oritur jus.* How does it appear that this is a navigable river? The flowing and reflowing of the tide does not make it so; for there are many places into which the tide flows that are not navigable rivers; and the place in question may be a creek in their own private estate.

Mr. BALDWIN. Then it was incumbent on the plaintiff to shew a special reason or tenure why the corporation ought to repair, for they are not bound of common right. 2 Lord *Raym.* 1089. 1 *Salk.* 360. S. C.

Lord MANSFIELD. It is here alleged that the corporation have from time immemorial been used to repair. It states, therefore, that they are bound by prescription, and it might be the very condition and terms of their creation or charter.

The three other Judges concurred.—Let the judgment be affirmed.

4 DURNFORD & EAST'S REP. 437.

THE MAYOR AND COMMONALTY OF ORFORD v. RICHARDSON AND ANOTHER.

TRESPASS for fishing in the plaintiff's free fishery and also in their several fishery in *Orford Haven, Suffolk.* Plea, that *Orford Haven* from time immemorial hath been, and is an arm of the sea, in which every subject of this realm hath had and still ought to have the liberty of free fishing. Replication, that the corporation of *Orford* are a corporation by prescription, and also by charter granted by queen *Elizabeth;* and that the corporation have immemorially had and enjoyed, and still ought to have and enjoy, the exclusive liberty of dredging and fishing for oysters in the said place, &c. at all seasonable times of the year, traversing that in the said arm of the sea every subject has a right of free fishing, &c. Rejoinder, that the place in which, &c. hath been immemorially an arm of the sea, in which every subject has a right of free fishing, traversing the prescriptive right claimed by the plaintiffs in the replication. Demurrer, because the plaintiffs in their replication traversed a material and issuable point of the defendants' plea, and by that traverse tendered to the defendants a material issue, but the defendants in their rejoinder did not take issue upon that traverse, or join in issue with the plaintiffs thereupon, but passed by and took no notice thereof, and traversed another part of the plaintiffs' replication, and thereby attempted to put in issue another matter, and a matter alleged by the plaintiffs by way of inducement only to the traverse so made and taken by the plaintiffs; and thus attempted to introduce great uncertainty, confusion, and unnecessary length of pleading, &c.

Lord Kenyon, Ch. J. It seems clear from the cases cited that, where a traverse is tendered, which is not calculated to try the right in question, the other party need not take issue upon it, since it would be a nugatory issue. But it is admitted that there cannot be a traverse upon a traverse, when the first will decide the whole question. And this does not depend on any arbitrary or capricious rule, but is founded on good sense and reason; otherwise, pleading would answer no other purpose than that of lengthening the record. With regard to the question of law in this case, as to the right claimed by the plaintiffs, there can be no doubt but that there may be a prescriptive right in the subject to a several fishery in an arm of the sea. Here then after the defendants had pleaded that the place in question was an arm of the sea, in which every subject has a right of fishing, the plaintiffs replied a prescriptive right in themselves "without this, that in the said arm of the sea every subject has a right of free fishing," &c. That was saying in other terms, "The right of fishing in this place does not stand on the general public right, but on special grounds derogatory from the general law." That traverse necessarily involved in it the real question in dispute between the parties, and consequently the defendants should have taken issue upon it.

Ashhurst, J. It is clearly established that, wherever the point in question is traversed by one party, the other must take issue upon it, for they are not to go on in *infinitum*. The use of pleading is to bring the matter in litigation to one point. And there cannot be any doubt here but that the merits of this case might have been fairly tried on the first traverse. But it has been objected that this was a traverse of the law: that argument would have been well founded, if there could be no prescription against the general right: but, as it is clear that there may be a prescription to take away the general right of the public in an arm of the sea, the traverse tendered by the plaintiffs would put in issue the real question between these parties; for it is founded on an antecedent fact introduced into the replication, which, if true, would defeat the general right upon which the defendants relied.

BULLER, J. The defendants' counsel has endeavored to support the second traverse on two grounds; first because the traverse tendered by the plaintiffs is a matter of law; and secondly, because it is immaterial. The first is answered by saying that this is to be supported by evidence, and is not mere matter of law. And as to the other ground, the rule of pleading has been truly stated, that, if the first traverse tendered be immaterial, the adverse party may add another traverse. Then with regard to the materiality of the plaintiffs' traverse, the fair question might have been as well tried on the first, as on the second traverse. For one party is to prove that this is an arm of the sea, in which, *prima facie*, every subject has a right to fish; the other is to establish a prescriptive right, which destroys the general right. And if the point in litigation come directly to be tried on either of these issues, it must be tried on that traverse which is first tendered. It is like the case of a traverse where the life or death of another person is to be put in issue: if the first traverse tendered be that the party is dead, issue must be taken on that; or *vice versa;* because either of these traverses will bring the same question to trial. The case cited from *Hobart* is distinguishable from the present: there the defendant tendered an immaterial traverse: the *cutting down the trees* was the wrong, and it was immaterial to the merits of that case whether the tenant had or had not *sold them.*

GROSE, J. declared himself of the same opinion.—Judgment for the plaintiffs.

Note.—When this case was afterwards tried in the Exchequer Chamber (*vid.* 2. *H. Black.* 182.) Lord Chief Justice EYRE, said shortly in the name of the court, that they had sent this case to a second argument, rather from an unwillingness to adopt, without great deliberation, a decision contrary to that of the court from whence the record came, than from any difficulty they saw in the question. For, from the moment it appeared that upon the pleadings the plaintiffs might have recovered a verdict in an action of trespass, without having either possession or right, it seemed very difficult to support the judgment. That the first traverse was of the right of *all* the king's subjects to fish in the arm of the sea, stated by the defendants; now this was clearly a bad and immaterial traverse, for it was not only a traverse of an inference of law, but it was so taken, that if at the trial it had been proved that it was the separate right of others, and not of the plaintiffs, the issue must have been found for the plaintiffs, not only without their being obliged to prove either possession or right, but where in fact they had neither possession nor right. That an immaterial traverse might be passed over, and the matter of the inducement traversed; which had been properly done in this case by the defendants.

Judgment reversed.

1 SARG. & LOWB. 240 & 5 TAUNT. 705.

MILES v. ROSE AND ANOTHER.

THIS was an action upon the case for obstructing the plaintiff's barges in navigating a certain navigable river called *Rainham Creek:* and upon the trial of the cause by a common jury, at the last *Chelmsford* summer assizes, before *Le Blanc*, J. a verdict had passed for the plaintiff, which *Best*, Serjt. now moved to set aside. He stated that the plaintiff proved that the place was a creek running down from a bridge called *Red-Bridge*, in *Essex*, to the *Thames*, in which creek the tide flowed and reflowed as far as that bridge; and that boats and vessels came up the creek: but on cross examination it appeared that nearly all the vessels came to load or discharge cargoes at a wharf of the defendants, on the side of the creek near *Red-Bridge*; a few boats, however, had landed their cargoes at *Red-Bridge*, not at the defendant's wharf; that boats with parties of pleasure had been known to sail up the creek, and boats came with persons who cut reeds along the banks of the creek. That for the defendants, who claimed the soil of the creek, it was proved, that they purchased, for a large price, their premises, which were conveyed to them by the description of *Rainham* wharf and creek. That the creek was not navigable till the predecessors of the defendants had, at a considerable expense, made it so, and erected a wharf: that the defendants had, for many years, received from the owners of vessels which frequented their wharf, and amongst others from the plaintiff himself, not only wharfage, but also tolls for navigating the creek. He was not instructed to state that *Le Blanc*, J. was dissatisfied with the verdict. The question was of great importance to the defendants, and this verdict would bind their rights forever.

Gibbs, C. J. Upon the defendants' own showing, the case is extremely doubtful. The flowing of the tide, though not absolutely inconsistent with a right of private property in the creek, is strong *prima facie* evidence of its being a public navigable river, and the cutting of reeds is a very strong act indeed, and even as to the pleasure-boats, if a person wishes to protect his exclusive possession, he must keep up the evidence of his right by guarding it against intruders. The judgment in this case, though it is evidence, and strong evidence, in another action, is not conclusive evidence, as was determined in this court about thirty years since, in the case of a water-course. The court saw no ground for granting a rule. The defendants might provoke another action, if they thought that they could produce stronger evidence in support of their right.

Heath, J. The flux and reflux of the tide is strong *prima facie* evidence that this was a navigable river, and as for the circumstance of the defendant's scouring the channel, they might have done that for their own convenience.—Rule refused.

1 Southrad's Rep. 61.

POST *v.* MUNN.

MUNN owned a fishery and net on the *Passaick* river; had employed *N. Williams* and others to aid him in fishing, by giving them a certain portion of the fish caught. While his net was out in the river, *Post*, who was the owner of a vessel, was navigating in that part, and his vessel run through and injured the net, so as to deprive *Munn* of the use of it. *Post* himself was in the cabin when the injury was done; the vessel was hailed by the fishermen, and there was contradictory evidence, as to the manner of the injury, whether accidental or intentional. An additional return of the justice, certifies that there was strong evidence that it was by design or neglect. *Williams* was sworn as a witness; and the run of the shad in the river, at the time, was proved. Several objections to evidence, and a motion for nonsuit were made; all of which were overruled. There was verdict and judgment for twenty-five dollars.

The reasons relied on for reversal, were,

1. That it should have been an action on the case, and not in the trespass; and brought in the name of *Williams* and the other hands, as well as *Munn;* and against the sailors, and not the owner and captain of the vessel.

2. That *Williams* was interested; and the run of the shad, inadmissible evidence.

3. That the *Passaick* is a navigable river, and no suit can be supported for injuries resulting from the ordinary navigation of it.

Mr. *Halsey* and Mr. *R. Stockton*, for plaintiff in *certiorari*. *Attorney General*, for defendant.

The court unanimously affirmed this judgment, and the following opinions were delivered.

Kirkpatrick, Ch. J. This was an action of trespass brought by *Benjamin Munn*, jun. against *Henry F. Post*, for breaking and injuring a fishing net in the river *Passaick*. *Munn* was the owner of a fishery, and had a right to fish at a certain place in the said river. He kept a net for this purpose, and at this time, had employed men to fish, giving them for their compensation, a certain proportion of the fish which were caught. *Post* was the master of a boat in the same river, and was sailing the same, in the pursuit of his lawful business.

The plaintiff's hands had thrown out their net to make a haul, and whilst it was so thrown out, the defendant run his boat against it, and committed the injury complained of.

Several questions were raised before the justice, upon the trial, by the defendant's counsel, and being determined against him, are now brought up here for consideration.

1. It is said that the river *Passaick* is a navigable river, in which the tide ebbs and flows; that it is therefore a common highway, upon which all the citizens of the State have a right to pass and repass at pleasure; that the right of fishery is subordinate to the right of navigation, and must yield to it; and that therefore, the injury complained of, having happened in the legitimate exercise of this superior right, the defendant is not liable in damages.

Now it is certainly true, that the right of navigation in this river is superior to all other rights, and particularly to the right of fishery. The master of a vessel is not obliged to slacken his sail, or change his course, or yield the channel, to a fishing net. Yet if under the pretence of exercising this right, he shall turn out of his course to run upon a net, or if he shall lie in wait till the net be spread, and then crowd sail to reach it, or if he shall unnecessarily anchor on fishing ground, or otherwise loiter about it, to prevent its being used as such, in all these cases, and a hundred others of the like nature, which might easily be mentioned, he is answerable in damages. The right of navigation, though superior, does not take away the right of fishery; it only limits it, and limits only so far as it interferes with its own fair, useful, and legitimate exercise.

Whether a master of a vessel, therefore, be liable or not in any particular case, must depend upon the use he is making of this superior right. If he is using it fairly, for fair, useful, and legitimate purposes, he goes quit; but if, as a mere pretext, to suppress and destroy the subordinate rights of others, he must answer. And this is always a question of fact, which must be submitted to the jury. In this case, the justice certifies that there was *strong evidence* that the injury was done by design. He submitted the question to the jury upon this principle, and in so doing, he submitted it rightly.

2. The hands employed by *Munn* to fish, who were actually engaged in managing the net at this time, were objected to as witnesses, because they were to have for their wages a share of the fish caught, and not a sum certain in money, and therefore were interested.

This objection, certainly cannot be maintained. It is an action of trespass, for a direct injury to the property of *Munn*, the plaintiff. The judgment could in no way operate to the benefit of these hands, by direct and necessary consequence. What the plaintiff might think reasonable, and how he might think proper to distribute the money recovered, is nothing to the purpose. The whole sum recovered is his. They have no lawful claim against him for any part of it.

3. *Munn*, the plaintiff, offered to prove by these witnesses, at the trial, something concerning the run of the shad in the river, a day or two previous to this affair, and the number caught at a haul, and to this the defendant objected.

But in actions of trespass, the damages are not always to be measured by the actual costs of the thing injured or destroyed. The whole loss sustained, is to be taken into view; and this depends upon its uses, its profits, the particular season or time, or occasion of the injury done, and the benefits or advantages lost thereby. And if so, all these must necessarily be proved, and submitted to the consideration of the jury. The defendant seems to have entertained an erroneous idea too, with respect to the augmentation of damages, to arise from the proof of these facts. He urges before the justice, and now here, that this augmentation, at least, will go into the pockets of these very witnesses, they being paid in a share of the fish, and not in money. But there is nothing in this. As has been said before, they can take nothing by the judgment.

4. As to the action being brought in the name of the hands, and not of the owner of the net; and as to its being brought against the sailors, and not against the master of the vessel, because he was in the cabin; and as to its being an action on the

case, and not an action of trespass: objections like these cannot prevail. It is therefore the opinion of the court, that the judgment must be affirmed.

SOUTHARD, J. The injury complained of, in this action, is the destruction of a fishing net, in the *Passaick* river, by running a vessel through it, while extended for the purpose of taking shad. The defence rests upon the broad ground, that the *Passaick* is a navigable river; that the injury was done while in the regular and accustomed exercise of the right of navigation; and that this right is paramount to, and cannot be impeded or interrupted by, the right of fishing.

The positions assumed by the defendant, are supposed to be not only tenable, but such as cannot be overthrown. It is, however, unfortunate for him, that they do not go far enough to protect him in this action. The *Passaick* is a navigable river, and the right of navigation in it, is a paramount right (*Harg. Law Tracts*, 9—22. *Swift*, 341.) but it is not the only right. The right of fishing must yield to it, where they come in conflict: but is not swallowed up and obliterated by it. Where one only can be enjoyed, that of navigation must be the one; where both can be enjoyed freely and fairly; that of navigation has no authority to trespass upon, and injure the other.

The proper inquiry, in a case like the present, is; could both rights have been enjoyed? Did the defendant, in pursuit of his lawful and paramount right, intentionally and unnecessarily trespass upon the plaintiff, in the exercise of his lawful, but inferior right? If he did, no principle, either of law or justice, will prevent his being compelled to compensate in damages, for the injury he inflicted. The question of his liability, then, becomes one of intention; and must depend upon the evidence which the jury have before them, and which they will weigh, as in every other case.

It seems to me, therefore, that no possible objection can well be made, on this point, to the course taken by the court below.

The return states, that there was *strong* evidence that the injury was done by *design* or *neglect*, and that this evidence was left to the jury for their decision. Whether the jury decided correctly, it is not now in the power of this court to say: the presumption is in favor of their accuracy, and nothing appears to disprove the presumption.

The next objection taken to the proceedings below, is; that certain persons who were working with the net, and were to be paid by a share of the fish caught, were admitted as witnesses; whereas, they ought to have been parties.

In order to estimate correctly, the value of this objection, it is only necessary to recollect; that the net and the right of the fishery, belonged exclusively to the plaintiff; and that he had employed these men, agreeing to satisfy them for their labor, with a determined proportion of the fish caught. He was injured, as he alleged, not by an accidental or consequential effect of the plaintiff's action, but by a direct and designed trespass. He therefore sues for the injury, not to those in his employ, but to himself; for the injury to his net, and his loss of fish. Why then must *they* be joined in the action? Why precluded from giving testimony? He could in no possible shape recover what belongs to them. They can in no possible shape, claim the smallest portion of what he does recover. They can, in no way, be prevented from maintaining any suit, which they could have maintained before this was brought.

As little solidity does there seem in the objections, to the proof about the run of the shad, and the usual profits of the net. For what is the suit brought? Not alone for the mere tearing of the net. That is but a small portion of the damage sustained. The greatest part of the injury, arises from losing the use of the net; and the value of that use, depends upon the run of the shad. There is no other mode, in which the plaintiff could shew what really were the damages sustained by him.

I am something at a loss to contrive, by what mode of reasoning the counsel for the defendant could satisfy his own mind.

that the two remaining objections were even plausible. The defendant was still the master of the vessel, though he was sitting in the cabin; and the injury complained of, was direct, immediate, and intentional; not consequential or accidental.

Upon none of the objections is the defendant well founded. Judgment below ought to be affirmed.—Judgment affirmed.

5 DAYS' REP. 22.

PECK *v.* LOCKWOOD.

THIS was an action of trespass, *quare clausum fregit.*

The declaration stated, that the defendant entered upon the plaintiff's land, dug up the soil, and destroyed the sedge, herbage, &c. growing thereon, and took therefrom great quantities of oysters, clams, and other shell-fish.

The land described in the declaration, consisted of a tract of upland, and about seven acres of sedge flats contiguous thereto, which were overflowed at high water, but which were above low water mark, so as to be entirely overgrown with sedge.

On the trial of the cause, it appeared that the defendant, at the time mentioned in the declaration, entered upon such flats, at a place where clams are usually taken, for the purpose of digging clams, and dug and carried away about half a bushel; in doing which he necessarily dug up a part of the sedge there growing, after having been expressly forbidden by the plaintiff.

The plaintiff, in proof of his title to the land mentioned in the declaration, exhibited two deeds: one executed to him, in 1784, by *Jabez Ferris,* and the other in 1789, by *Titus* and *Charles Knapp.* The description of the land conveyed by the first deed, being a part only of the premises, is in the following words, viz.

"bounded east by *Timothy Knapp's* land, south by the water, west by said *Peck's* own land, north by *Joseph Sacket's* lands." The description in the second deed is in these words, viz. "bounded north by the *Reed's* meadow, so called, easterly and southerly by the cove, so called, and westerly by said *Peck's* land, in part, and partly by *Sacket's* land."

It was admitted that the grantors of the plaintiff owned all the land included in these deeds; but it was contended, on the part of the defendant, that the words "southerly by the water," in the first deed, and the words "easterly and southerly by the cove," in the second, could not legally be so construed as to include the sedge flats. The plaintiff also proved that he, and those under whom he claimed, had for more than forty years before the bringing of the suit, annually, and exclusively of all others, cut and taken off the sedge growing on such flats. To rebut the presumption arising from this fact, of a title in the plaintiff, by possession, and to establish the right of the defendant to take the clams in question, the defendant proved, that the inhabitants of the town of *Greenwich*, and other places, had, without molestation, from the first settlement of the country, at proper seasons, entered upon such sedge flats, and dug and carried away the shell-fish, and had also removed so much of the sedge as was necessary for the purpose of taking such shell-fish.

The plaintiff then offered to prove, that such persons, in going to the flats before mentioned, and other parts of the sea coast, for the purpose of taking shell-fish, proceeded either by water, or upon the land mentioned in the declaration, and other lands of the plaintiff, and of other persons. This evidence was rejected by the court as immaterial; it being agreed, that the defendant was not guilty of any other trespass than by digging the clams in question, in the manner above stated.

This case was reserved for the advice of the nine judges.

The question whether the evidence offered by the plaintiff was properly rejected, was also reserved.

Daggett and *Shearman*, in behalf of the plaintiff, contended,

1. That the possession of the plaintiff, and those under whom he claimed, vested in him an exclusive right to the use and occupation of the land, where the supposed trespass was committed.

2. That the deeds under which he also claimed conveyed to him the fee of all the land above low-water mark. 1 *Swift's Syst.* 343. *Adgate* v. *Stores*, 2 *Root*, 160. *Ward* v. *Creswell*, *Willes*, 265, 268. *Sir Henry Constable's case:* 5 *Co.* 107. 108.

N. Smith and *Denison*, for the defendant, contended,

1. That the plaintiff derived no exclusive title by deed to the place where the alleged trespass was committed.

2. That he had no right, by prescription, to the exclusive occupation of the soil.

3. That the public, at common law, possessed the right of fishery at the place in question. *Harg. Law Tracts*, 11, 12, 13. *Warren* v. *Matthews*, 6 *Mod.* 73. S. C. 1 *Salk.* 357. *Evans'* note. *Ward* v. *Creswell*, *Willes*, 265. Lord *Fitzwalter's* case, 1 *Mod.* 105, 106. *Carter et al.* v. *Murcot et al.* 4 *Burr* 2162. *King* v. *Smith, et al Doug.* 441. *The Mayor and Commonalty of Orford* v. *Richardson et al.* in the King's Bench. 4 *Term Rep.* 437, and in Error in the Exchequer Chamber, 2 *H. Blk.* 182. *Bagott* v. *Orr*, 2 *Bos.* and *Pul.* 472. *Carson* v. *Blazer et al.* 2 *Binn.* 475. *Ball* v. *Herbert*, 3 *Term Rep.* 253. 6 *Com. Dig.* 55. (D. 50.)

Reeve, J. This is an action of trespass for entering upon the plaintiff's land, and digging up his soil, destroying his sedge grass and taking away a quantity of clams, oysters, and other shell-fish.

The defendant claimed a right to enter on the said lands, to take clams; that it had been customary for the inhabitants of the town and other places adjacent, from the first settlement of the country, to take clams from this place without molestation, being sedge flats, which are covered at high water, but are above low-water mark. On these flats the defendant entered, and committed no other trespass than what arose from entering and digging up as much sedge as was necessary to take the clams, and no more. The defendant denies, indeed, that the place in question was covered by the plaintiff's deeds, as set forth in the case stated. I shall lay this question out of the case, by only observing, that I entertain no doubt but that the said flats are included in the plaintiff's deed, so as to convey to him the right of soil. But, however that is, by the state of the case it appears that it has been, for more than forty years, in the exclusive possession of the plaintiff, and those under whom he claims, except so far as that possession may be supposed to be interrupted, by the entry of people thereon, to take shell-fish, as before stated. This entry is not adverse to the plaintiff's title to the soil. It is not made with a view to affect such title. It is made only under a claim to fish, and not to occupy for any other purpose. It is a claim in perfect consistency with the plaintiff's title to the soil; and by forty years' possession, unmolested, by the laws of this State, he must have acquired a title, equally valid with a conveyance from the owner by deed. The flats, therefore, are the plaintiff's estate in fee, and the question is this, *viz.* has the defendant a right to enter thereon, for the purpose of taking clams?

It appears, from the state of the case reserved, that the plaintiff offered to prove that, in going to the said flats, for the purpose of taking clams, persons went either by water, or on or over the lands in the declaration mentioned, and other inclosures of the plaintiff, and of other persons. But such evidence was rejected by the court. I am of opinion that it was properly rejected; for it is not stated in the declaration that any trespass was committed by the defendant, except entering on the land described in the declaration. Whether the defendant might go across other inclosures of the plaintiff, for the purpose of getting to the flats, is not a question before the court. It is not even stated that the defendant was one of those people who went upon other inclosures of the plaintiff.

The only question which remains is this: is the right of fishing for shell-fish, where the ground must be dug to take them, on land which is covered with water at high-water mark, but which is above low-water mark, or, in other words, on lands over which the tide flows, and from which it ebbs, a public right, which may be exercised by every citizen, or is it a right which belongs exclusively to the proprietor of such land? If the former, judgment must be for the defendant; if the latter, judgment must be for the plaintiff. To settle this question, we are not to resort to any train of reasoning as to what is most or least reasonable. We are not, as in many cases of doubt, to infer what the law is, from the probable good or ill consequences which may follow from establishing one or the other system. It is a question which it is peculiarly the province of the maxim *ita lex scripta est* to determine.

I would here observe, that I do not contend that the proprietor of such land cannot acquire an exclusive right to fish thereon. I admit it. I think this is clearly established by authorities.

As it respects the various methods in which such a right may be acquired, in *England* and in this country, I have nothing to observe. The only question stated on the record is, does such a right result to the proprietor, by virtue of his ownership of the soil? If no such right results to him by the common law, as I shall attempt to prove from the authorities, it behooves him to show that he has gained such right. The presumption is against him; and he must remove this out of the way before he can avail himself of such exclusive right.

The law of *England*, in this case, must with great propriety be deemed our law; for our ancestors came from that country, bringing with them the legal notions which there prevailed: which have ever been considered the common law of this country, unless altered by our own legislative acts, or so manifestly improper to be received, arising from widely differing local circumstances, that our courts have been obliged to reject them, to attain the ends of justice, for which all laws are made. But in a case where the reason is the same, and as strong in this country as that, and of equal applicability to our circumstances as theirs, the law is the same. In relation to the present subject, there is no statute altering the common law, there is no reason for the existence of such a law in that country, which does not apply with equal force in this; and nothing in our local circumstances which militates against the adoption of it by us. The usage stated in the case I make no use of, except that it furnishes evidence that our ancestors always supposed that they had a right to fish and take clams on such lands as these, the subject of this controversy. Such notions by them adopted, I think, will appear to have been uniformly the law of that country from which they came.

In lord *Fitzwalter's* case, reported in 1 *Mod.* 105, and in 3 *Keb.* 242, we find it laid down by chief justice *Hale*, that in case of a river which flows and reflows, and is an arm of the sea, the right of fishing is common to all, and that, in an action of trespass brought for fishing there, it is a good justification to say, that the *locus in quo* is an arm of the sea. It is clear that by this is meant, *when the proprietor of the soil brings the action of trespass*; for no other person could bring trespass but the proprietor, or some person having a possession under him; and that the case before the court was by the proprietor, is manifest from the observation of lord *Hale*, who says there is no contradiction between the soil being in one, and yet the river common for all fishers. From this case we learn, that the right of fishing in such place where there is a flux and reflux of the sea, is a right common to every citizen, although the soil be the estate of a particular person.

The doctrine here laid down is every where recognized to be correct. We find the general rule established in *Warren* v. *Matthews*, reported in 1 *Salk.* 357, and in 6 *Mod.* 73, and in

Carter et al. v. *Murcot et al.* 4 *Burr.* 2162. In the last case, it was laid down by lord *Mansfield*, that a man may have an exclusive privilege of fishing in an arm of the sea; but such right is not to be presumed; it must be proved: and Mr. Justice *Yates* observes, that he knew a case to fail, wherein this claim was made, because such prescriptive right could not be proved: and in that case it was determined, that a right of fishing in such place was common to all.

The case of *The Mayor and Commonalty of Orford* v. *Richardson et al.* in the king's bench, 4 *Term Rep.* 437, and in error in the exchequer chamber, 2 *H. Black.* 182, was determined wholly upon the ground, that every subject, *prima facie*, has a right to fish in an arm of the sea; yet an appropriate right may be proved in another, which will give him the exclusive privilege of fishing there. No person can read and understand the pleadings in that case, without perceiving that the before-mentioned doctrine was admitted by the whole court, and all the counsel, to be correct. We have an authority to this point, in *Com. Dig.* 55. His words are, "Every one may fish in the sea, of common right, though it flows on the soil of another." He cites the case of *Warren* v. *Matthews*, 6 *Mod.* 73.

The foregoing authorities abundantly prove the general proposition, that the right of fishing on the soil of another, when overflowed with the tide from the sea, or arm of the sea, is a common right. The only doubt that can arise, in cases of this kind, is, whether there is a common right of fishing for shell-fish, after the reflux of the tide.

Although this right is nowhere denied by any authority, and as the principle is certainly included in the general proposition, that on such lands the right of fishing is common to every subject; yet, I think, some reasonable doubt might have been entertained on this subject, if no further authority could have been produced. The case of *Bagott* v. *Orr*, 2 *Bos.* and *Pul.* 472, is, I apprehend, a case in point. It was the very case of entering upon land of the plaintiff, and taking shell-fish, by digging up the earth betwixt high and low-water mark; which could be done only after the reflux of the sea. This case was determined in favor of the defendant, on the ground that such fishery, in such a place, which is the very case before the court, was a matter of common right. The court, in delivering their opinion, say, that if the plaintiff had it in his power to abridge the common law right of the subject to take sea-fish, (meaning in that case shell-fish, for that was the case before the court,) he should have replied that matter specially; and, that not having done so, the defendant must succeed upon his plea for taking the fish.

Here the court most expressly recognize the doctrine, that it is a right common to every subject, to enter upon the lands of the plaintiff, betwixt high and low-water mark, and to take from thence shell-fish, by digging up the soil.

In this opinion the other judges concurred, excepting

BRAINARD, J. who was absent from indisposition, and

INGERSOLL, J. who had been of counsel in the cause.

Judgment to be rendered for the defendant.

6 JOHNSON'S REP. 133.

PALMER v. HICKS.

IN error, on *certiorari*. *Hicks*, as supervisor of the town of *Flushing*, in *Queen's* county, brought an action of debt, against *Palmer*, the plaintiff in error, and two others, for the penalty of ten dollars, for an offence against the rules and regulations of the town of *Flushing*, made by the freeholders and inhabitants of the town, assembled in town meeting pursuant to the act. (*vol.* 1. *p.* 338. 24 *sess. c.* 78. *s.* 11.) The regulation in question was made in *April*, 1808, by which it was ordered, that no person should be allowed to rake clams within the boundary line of *Flushing*, running from *Wicke's* point to *Wilkin's*, after the 20th *April*, 1808, under the penalty of ten dollars for each offence; one half to the poor of the town, and the other half to the informer. The plaintiff below averred, that the place where the raking of clams was thus prohibited, was in the town of *Flushing*, and called *Little Neck Bay*; and was the common property of the freeholders and inhabitants of the town; and that *Palmer*, the plaintiff in error, on the 25th *June*, 1808, did rake clams, within the bounds above mentioned, whereby an action had accrued, &c.

The plaintiff below produced an authenticated copy of the rule or regulation, and proved that *Palmer* raked clams in *Little Neck Bay*, within the boundary line of *Flushing*, after the 1st *June*, 1809, and within the place above decided.

The defendant below admitted that he had raked clams in the place mentioned, but denied the right and power of the town of *Flushing* to prohibit any person from catching clams below the ordinary low-water mark. He did not plead any title, or demand any proof of the authority of the town: and the justice, thereupon, gave judgment for the plaintiff.

It was admitted, that the place where the clams were raked by the plaintiff in error, was within the limits of the town of *Flushing*, and below the ordinary low water mark, in *Little Neck Bay*, which communicates with the *East* river or *Sound*.

R. Riker, for the plaintiff in error, stated two objections.

1. That the town of *Flushing* had no right to pass a law to regulate the raking of clams.

2. That if it had such right, it could not be exercised below the ordinary low-water mark.

He cited *Act* 24 *sess. c.* 78. *s.* 11. (*Rev. Laws*, vol. 1. p.

331.) and *c.* 123. *s.* 2. (*Laws*, vol. 2. p. 2.) as to the bounds of *Queen's* county; *Harg. Law Tracts*, 11, 12. 5 *Bac. Abr. Prerog.* 498. (*B.* 3.) 6 *Mod.* 73. 4 *Burr.* 2162. *Davie's Rep.* 149.

Baldwin, contra, cited 5 *Bac. Abr.* 498. the *note*, as to a several fishery in an arm of the sea.

Per curiam. The town of *Flushing* must show a right of property to the lands below low-water mark, in the bay, on the *Sound*, in order to entitle them to make rules to regulate the use of those lands. We will not presume a grant of lands under navigable waters, to the owners of the adjacent soil, without evidence of long exclusive possession and use, to warrant such presumption. No grant has been shown, nor was any fact proved, from which a grant was to be presumed.

The act, extending the bounds of the town over the bay, and into the *Sound* or *East* river, so as to include the islands southward to the main channel, was merely for the purpose of jurisdiction, and is no evidence of a grant of property in the soil covered by the water. All the ground under the navigable waters of the *Hudson* river, is within the boundaries of some town, for the purposes of civil and criminal jurisdiction; but it does not follow that the lands under the water, belong to the towns situated on the river. The judgment below must be reversed.—Judgment reversed.

1 DALLAS' REP. 150.

RESPUBLICA *v.* CALDWELL.

THIS was an indictment for a *nuisance*, in erecting a wharf on the public property. The defendant offered witnesses to prove that the erection of the wharf has been beneficial to the public, and therefore, not to be regarded as a nuisance.

But M'KEAN, Ch. J. delivered the opinion of the Court, that the evidence was inadmissible, for two reasons : *First*, because it would only amount to matter of opinion, whereas it is on facts the court must proceed ; and the necessary facts are already in proof. *Secondly*, because it would be no justification ; for, on the same principle that the defendant might carry his wharf 12 feet, he could justify extending it further ; or any other man might excuse a similar intrusion. Suppose, for instance, a street were sixty feet wide, 12 feet might be taken off it, without doing any material injury to the public property, or creating any great obstruction to passengers ; yet, surely this will not justify any man's actually building upon, and assuming the property of the 12 feet that could be thus spared.

2 STARK. 510 & 3 SERGT. & LOWB. 455.

REX *v.* LORD GROSVENOR AND OTHERS.

THIS was an indictment against the defendants for a nuisance in erecting a wharf on the river *Thames*, to the injury of the navigation of the river.

It appeared that the corporation of the city of *London*, who were conservators of the river, were entitled to the soil of the river, and that they had let a space of ground at *Millbank* to Lord *Grosvenor*, for the purpose of erecting a wharf there, for a fine of 400*l.* and a rent of four guineas *per annum*. The wharf in question had been erected between high and low-water mark, and extended for a considerable space along the river. There had formerly been a recess there between two projections. Evidence was given on the part of the prosecution, to show that in the former state of the river, the recess afforded a place of refuge in time of storm, and that the eddy water which it produced afforded great convenience for the passage of watermen.

On the part of the defendants, it was contended, in the first place, that the defendants, claiming a right of soil from the corporation of *London*, who were the conservators of the river, had a right to make such an erection between high and low-water mark; and that by the st. 14 *Geo.* 3, they were entitled to build wharves and let them, provided this did not interfere with the navigation of the river.

ABBOTT, Ld. C. J. Will you contend that you have a right to narrow the river *Thames*, so long as you leave a space sufficient for the purposes of navigation? It is impossible that you should derive any protection from the corporation of the city of

London, as the conservators of the river. Although they have a right to the soil, they have no right to take a fine from a person who makes an erection for the benefit of the public. A great corporation professing to take a fine for that which is an advantage to the public, is a thing unheard of. If the erection be a nuisance, no protection can be conferred by a body which receives a pecuniary remuneration for permitting the erection.

It was then contended on the part of the defendants, and evidence was given tending to support that defence, that the erection of the wharf in question had been productive of advantage rather than of detriment to the navigation of the river. That the projection which had existed previously, had occasioned an eddy which had caused a deposit of mud in the river, and a diversion of the stream, and that the embankment would tend to remove it, and thereby be of material benefit to the navigation; by removing any collection of mud. Evidence was also adduced for the purpose of proving that the recess which had formerly existed was a nuisance, and that it was not covered with water for eighteen hours out of the twenty-four, and that it could not be used as a place of refuge for large vessels, except at spring tides, and that it was made a place of resort by boys for the purpose of bathing.

Abbott, Ld. C. J. This is an indictment against Lord *Grosvenor* and others, for making an erection in the river *Thames*, between high and low-water mark. It is proper to premise, that if any person meditate an alteration in a public highway, or in any other subject matter which is of public right, the legitimate course of proceeding is by means of an inquiry before the sheriff, in order to ascertain whether the change will operate to the prejudice of the public; and if any one undertakes to make a change without resorting in the first instance to this mode of inquiry, he incurs the burthen of proving, that what he does is not a nuisance to the public. The question here is, whether a public right has not been infringed. An embankment of con siderable extent has been constructed for the purpose of building a wharf. Much evidence has been adduced on the part of the defendant, for the purpose of showing that the alteration affords greater facility and convenience for loading and unloading; but the question is, not whether any private advantage has resulted from the alteration to any particular individuals, but whether the convenience of the public at large, or of that portion of it which is interested in the navigation of the river *Thames*, has been affected or diminished by this alteration.

It appears that at each end of this embankment there is a projection towards the river, and it has been said, that this affords great convenience to the navigation, by producing an eddy. The public have a right to all the convenience which the former state of the river afforded, unless by the change some greater degree of convenience is rendered. Again, it is said, that in stormy weather, vessels might have entered the recess and found shelter between the two projections at spring tides for some time, at neap tides for a shorter space of time; now, although they were not able to enjoy this benefit at all times, yet if they could derive benefit from it for the space of two hours each tide, they are entitled to that advantage, unless the want of it be compensated by some superior advantage resulting from the alteration. Another convenience afforded by the former state of the river has been proved, that is, that in the winter, vessels have been able to avoid large masses of ice floating down the river, by entering the recess.

The frequency of boys' bathing in the river is an inconvenience which the conservators would do well to remove; but this, at all events, is not a nuisance at all seasons. The question is, whether if this wharf be suffered to remain, the public convenience will suffer. The witnesses for the prosecution speak from facts, those for the defendants from opinion. Although the benefits which were enjoyed before the erection were limited to particular times, and seasons of the weather, and were enjoyed but occasionally, yet the public is not to be deprived of them by the erection of a wharf for mere private convenience.

The jury acquitted lord *Grosvenor*, and found the rest of the defendants guilty.

Gurney and *Chitty* for the plaintiffs.

Scarlet, *Knowlys*. C. S. and *Delany* for the defendants.

2 Doug. Rep. 441.

REX *v*. SMITH AND OTHERS.

THIS was an indictment against the defendants, for obstructing the mayor and commonalty of the city of *London*, in making a horse-towing path on the soil of the river *Thames*, under powers vested in them by the statutes of 14 *Geo.* 3. *c.* 91. and 17 *Geo.* 3. *c.* 18. The *first* count recited the act, and charged, that a horse-towing path was begun to be made from *Water-Lane* at *Richmond* bridge, and certain wooden piles fixed, by order of the common council, on the soil and bed of the river, between high-water mark and low-water mark, and that the defendants, intending to obstruct the mayor, &c. cut down one of the said piles, &c. The *second* count laid the piles to have been driven upon the soil and bed of the river, being the king's ancient common high-way for all the liege subjects to navigate. The *third* count laid the towing path to have been between the city of *London* and the city-stone at *Staines* bridge, between high-water mark and low-water mark. The *fourth* count stated, that a towing path was begun, &c. by the *committee*, (naming them,) appointed by the common council to execute the act, on the soil, &c. being the king's ancient and common highway, between high-water mark and low-water mark, &c. The *fifth* count set forth, that a towing path had been begun by order of the common council, &c. (but without mentioning the act of parliament.) The *sixth* and last count resembled the *fifth*, only stating, that the towing path had been begun by order of the committee. The trial came on before Ashhurst, *justice*, at the last *Lent* assizes for the county of *Surry*, when a verdict was found for the king, subject to the opinion of the court on the following case:

"The city of *London*, under the powers supposed to be delegated to them under the act of parliament of 14 *Geo.* 3. *c.* 91. and by the 17th of the same king, intituled, &c. (c. 18.) erected piles on the bed of the river, near *Richmond*, within the high-water mark, about the distance of twenty-nine feet from the shore, for the purpose of making a towing path for horses, adjoining and contiguous to a *wharf* in the possession, and the property of the defendants, or of those under whom they claim. The defendants cut down one of those piles, which is the subject of the present indictment, and which was proved to have been erected between the high and low-water mark, opposite to the said wharf. No acts of ownership were proved, *on either side*, in the spot in question; but it was proved, that the *Ait* in the middle of the river was Mr. *Price's*. It was proved, that, immemorially, at the time of low-water, persons used to pass on foot between the high and low-water mark, for the purpose of towing barges and other vessels.

"The question submitted to the court is, 'Whether, (this being a navigable river,) the right to the soil in the bed of the river, *usque ad filum aquæ*, is in the owners of the ground adjoining to the river?"

The case was argued, last term, on *Wednesday*, the 3d of *May*, by *Erskine* for the prosecution, and *B. Hunter* for the defendants.

Erskine contended, that the only question brought before the court was, whether the soil of the spot in question was, or was not the property of the defendants, or of those under whom they claimed? Its being the property of third persons would not be a justification on this indictment; for the defendants were not entitled by law to abate the piles driven on another person's ground, for a consequential injury to theirs. The defendants, therefore, must shew that the soil was theirs; and as they gave no proof of any actual exercise of ownership, it was incumbent upon them to maintain it was theirs by inference of law, because the property in the adjoining ground belonged to them.

Hunter, insisted, 1. That the statutes did not mean to vest in the city the power of making towing paths by *embankment*; 2. That the soil belonged to the defendants, and they were therefore protected by the 16th section of the statute, by which it is provided, "That the powers granted to the city should not extend to authorize them to make any *new* towing path, over, upon, or through, any garden, orchard, *yard*, park, paddock, inclosed lawn, or planted avenue, to any house, without the consent of the owner thereof." 3. That supposing it uncertain to whom the soil belongs, the city had not complied with the terms prescribed by the statutes to entitle them to make a horse-towing path.—1. On the first point, he said, that there was no express power given to make *embankments*, and the court would not raise a power, liable to great inconvenience and abuse, by implication. If such embankments could be made at the pleasure of the city, they would tend to diminish the value of the adjoining lands, and might alter the course of the river, besides exposing the villas and private property of individuals to the disorders and trespasses which bargemen might commit in passing through them.—2. On the second head, he said, that, if the soil was in the defendants, the case was clearly within the provision of the 16th section of 14 *Geo.* 3. *cap.* 91; for though *wharves* are not expressly mentioned, they might be fairly construed to be comprehended under the word "*yard*." That this was a *new* towing path was clear, because the case only stated, that persons *formerly* used to pass on foot *at the time of low-water;* but this would make a passage *at all times.* As to the property, the legal presumption was certainly in favor of the defendants, and there being no evidence on either side, the presumption ought to prevail. The soil must have some owner; the city had no claim to it; they did not pretend any right of ownership at the trial; and, as to the right of the Crown, a distinction was to be made: that right was only in navigable rivers, as far as the sea ebbs and flows. It did not depend alone on the circumstance of the river being navigable. Some rivers were so immemorially, by nature, and from the flux and reflux of the sea; others were kept in a navigable state by the effects of art. The *Thames* might be considered as falling under the first description up to *London* bridge. From thence upwards, it was preserved in a navigable state by art. The authorities concerning the right of the Crown to the soil extended only to navigable rivers of the first sort. The sea did not properly flow above *London* bridge. The tide, beyond that limit, was occasioned by the pressure and accumulation backwards of the *river water.* Therefore the soil there did not belong to the Crown. This distinction seemed to be adopted in several cases; 1 *Mod.* 105. *Anon;* 2 *Roll. Abr.* 170. *pl.* 14, 15.; *Davies' Rep.* 55. 57.; *Carter* v. *Murcot.* He also stated the pleadings in a case of *Cheshyre* v. *Dunball,* where the same idea was adopted, and which had been settled, on great consideration, by Sir *Joseph Yates,* and *Wynne,* afterwards baron of the exchequer in *Scotland.*

Lord MANSFIELD told *Erskine,* it was unnecessary for him to reply. His lordship said, the distinction between rivers navigable, and not navigable, and those where the sea does or does not ebb and flow, was very ancient; but that what *Hunter* contended for, *viz.* a distinction between the case of the tide occasioned by the *flux* of *sea water,* or by the *pressure backwards* of the *fresh water of a river,* seemed to be entirely new, and that there were no facts set forth in the case which let in the consideration of that distinction. That the case did not state, whether the water, when the tide rises at *Richmond*, is fresh or salt, but that it rather took it for granted that it is salt, describing the *Thames* generally as a navigable river. That as to the *first* and *third* objections, there was no question made by the case, on the authority of the city to embank, or whether they had pursued the directions prescribed by the legislature.

The verdict of *guilty* was ordered to be entered.

Afterwards, in this term, on *Monday*, the 5th of *June*, *Rous* having moved for judgment against the defendants, *Peckham* obtained a rule to shew cause, why the judgment should not be arrested. He applied for this rule on three grounds: 1. That the offence, (if at all indictable,) was for obstructing the execution of the statute, and, therefore, the indictment ought to have concluded, (which it did not,) that the defendants had acted "*against the form of the statute*." 2. That the prosecutors ought to have stated, that they have purchased the soil, according to the provision for that purpose in the statute. 3. That, as there are a great variety of powers given by the act, and adapted to a multiplicity of different cases, the indictment was too general and uncertain, not setting forth under what particular clause or power the city had acted.

On his first point, he cited *Hawkins' Pleas of the Crown*, *B.* 2. c. 25. § 116. where it is laid down, "That if an indictment do not conclude *contra formam statuti*, and the offence indicted be *only* prohibited by statute, and not by common law, it is wholly insufficient, and no judgment at all can be given upon it." But Ashhurst, *Justice*, observing, that it was an offence at common law to obstruct the execution of an act of parliament, this objection was abandoned.

This day, cause was shewn, by *Dunning*, *Davenport*, *Sylvester*, *Rous*, *Rose* and *Erskine*.—They insisted, that the directions in the act for *purchasing* the soil, only related to the case of private owners. If the soil belonged to the Crown, the act itself contained the king's consent, and if to the city, (which they said was most probable,) it would be absurd to apply the provisions for purchasing to such a case. But if the case had even stated the property to belong to some private owner, but to none of the defendants, it would not be competent to *them* to question what had been done. Let the *owner* complain of the supposed injury, which he might in an action or indictment for the trespass. *He* might not think it an injury, but a benefit. As to the method pursued by the city, in the execution of the statute, and the particular clauses under which they had acted, their authority was sufficiently shewn in the indictment, which set forth the statute; and none but the actual owners of the ground where they had made the path could question what they had done.

Peckham, *Mingay*, and *B. Hunter*, for the defendants.

Lord MANSFIELD absent.

WILLES, J.—Only two of the powers in the act, which are various, are necessary to be observed upon here, *viz.* the power to improve the navigation, and the power to compel a purchase. Now, if *they* are considered together, it will appear, that the improvements are to be carried on without purchasing, where there is no occasion to purchase, and nothing is stated here to shew, that this was a case where purchase was necessary. The indictment sets forth, that the prosecutors were interrupted in the due execution of the act, and *that* is found by the verdict. I see no foundation for arresting the judgment.

ASHHURST, J. of the same opinion. He said, there was no sort of doubt on the first point.

BULLER, J.—As to the first point, it was very properly given up; the indictment would have been wrong, if it had concluded *contra formam statuti.* I think, on the face of the indictment, we must take the soil of the spot in question to be in the Crown, for, though not necessarily, yet, *prima facie*, the soil of a navigable river belongs to the king. The fact of the obstruction is sufficiently averred.—The rule discharged.

CAMP. REP. 309.

ROGERS AND OTHERS *v.* ALLEN.

TRESPASS for breaking and entering the several oyster fishery of the plaintiffs in a certain river called *Burnham* river; and in divers parts of the said fishery, to wit, &c. [naming four places in *Burnham* river,] fishing and dredging for oysters, &c. A second count charged the defendant with fishing and dredging for oysters in divers parts of the fishery, between a certain place in the river called *Clayclods*, and a certain other place in said river called *Raysand*. The last count was general, stating that the defendant broke and entered a certain other several oyster fishery, and also a certain free fishery of the plaintiffs. Plea, 1. The general issue; 2. After averring the different fisheries mentioned in the declaration to be the same, that the *place in which*, &c. is a navigable river, and arm of the sea, in which all the king's subjects have a right to fish and dredge for oysters. The plaintiffs in their replication to the last plea prescribed under the persons seized in fee of the manor of *Burnham*, for "the sole, several, and exclusive liberty and privilege of fishing for, taking, and carrying away all oysters and oyster spats *in and upon the said several parts of the said fishery, in which, &c. in the said declaration particularly men-*

tioned, as to the said manor belonging and appertaining." Rejoinder, traversing this prescription; and issue thereupon.

An *Inquisitio post mortem*, and several other documents from the Tower of *London* being put in, to shew that in very early times there had been a fishery at the mouth of the *Burnham* river held by the *Fitzwalters*, the ancestors of the family now in possession, as parcel of the manor of *Burnham*; and three judgments being proved, which had been obtained in the reigns of *Charles* I. and *Charles* II. by the lords of the manor of *Burnham*, in actions for breaking and entering their several fishery in the *Burnham* river; in further support of the prescriptive right, certain licenses were offered in evidence, which appeared on the court rolls of the manor, and bore date from the year 1661, downwards, to the end of the 17th century; whereby the lords of the manor, in consideration of certain rents, had granted the liberty of fishing and dredging for oysters in their several fishery in the *Burnham* river, reserving to themselves the exclusive right to all floating fish therein.

The defendant's counsel objected to the admissibility of the licenses as evidence, unless it should appear by bailiff's accounts, or otherwise, that rent had actually been paid under them; urging, that if they could be received without this, it would be easy to manufacture evidence which now, or at some future time, might establish an unfounded claim, to the injury of some other individual, or to the exclusion of the public.

Heath, J. said he could not distinguish these licenses from old leases; which were always received in evidence in favour of those claiming under the lessors. Nor did he think it necessary to prove payment under the licenses, as they were of such an ancient date that it could not reasonably be supposed that evidence of such payments was still preserved. However, to give any weight to these licenses, it must be shewn that in later times, payments had been made under licenses of the same kind.

or that the lords of the manor had exercised other acts of ownership over the fishery, which had been acquiesced in.

After the licenses, a regular set of leases, or agreements for leases, of the oyster fishery during the whole of the last century, were produced, and it appeared that for the last forty years rent had regularly been paid under them. It was likewise proved, that as far back as could be remembered by the oldest witnesses, when strangers came to dredge for oysters within the limits of the fishery, they had constantly been driven off by a watchman kept for that purpose. The plaintiff's case being closed—

Several grounds of defence were opposed to it. In the first place, it was strenuously contended that a grant from the Crown ought to have been produced, and that a several fishery in a navigable river could not pass as appertenant to a manor. But

HEATH, J. said, there was no authority for this supposition, and that the fishery might well pass as an appertenance of the manor.

The defendant afterwards gave in evidence, that all who chose had been accustomed to fish in the *Burnham* river for all sorts of floating fish, without any interruption. It was therefore contended, on his part, that this completely disproved the exclusive right claimed by the lord of the manor of *Burnham*. A fishery must be entire; and it appeared from the licenses and leases, that the lords of the manor set up exactly the same pretensions to the floating fish as they did to the ground fish. Now as it had been clearly proved that it was lawful for all the king's subjects to catch the former, so might they lawfully dredge for the latter. This was like the right of free warren. If that were claimed in a particular place; and it appeared that hares and partridges (though not pheasants) had always been killed there in the same manner as over the rest of the country, it was impossible that the claim could be sustained.

HEATH, J. A right of fishery and a right of free warren are not at all like each other. The one is divisible and the other is not. Part of a fishery may be abandoned and another part of more value may be preserved. The public may be entitled to catch floating fish in the river *Burnham*: but it by no means follows that they are justified in dredging for oysters, which may still remain private property.

It was next contended, that the plaintiffs must be nonsuited on account of the variance between the evidence and the pleadings. It appeared that for certain oysters laying on one of the places mentioned in the declaration, the plaintiffs paid rent to the Earl of *Winchelsea*, and there was evidence of oysters being taken under a claim of right from another of these places by the occupier of the adjoining lands. On the supposition, therefore, that the exclusive right of the lords of the manor of *Burnham* to the oysters in the two places last alluded to was negatived, it was insisted that the prescription, on which issue was joined, had not been made out as laid. The replication prescribed for "the sole and exclusive liberty and privilege of fishing for, taking and carrying away all oysters in and upon the said several parts of the said fishery in the said declaration particularly mentioned." But the part for which rent was paid to lord *Winchelsea*, and the part from which oysters had been taken by the occupier of the adjoining ground, were particularly named in the first count of the declaration, and were comprehended within the limits mentioned in the second. As to these the lord of the manor had no exclusive right, and therefore the prescription failed. The plaintiffs had prescribed too largely: and if they were still to have a verdict and judgment, the consequence would be, that this record would afterwards be evidence of a right which had been expressly disproved in the course of the trial.

HEATH, J. was of opinion, that although the prescription was more extensive than the evidence would establish, this was immaterial, unless the trespasses had been committed in the expected places; and the plaintiffs had a verdict: but the court of king's bench being afterwards moved to set aside the verdict, on account of a misdirection of the judge upon this point, held that the prescription laid in the replication was negatived by the evidence, and ordered a new trial.

Shepherd, *Best*, *Onslow*, Serjeants, and *Trower*, for the plaintiffs.

Garrow, *Marryat*, and *Pooley*, for the defendant.

5 Coke's Rep. 107.

SIR HENRY CONSTABLE'S CASE.

SIR *Henry Constable* brought an action of trespass against *Gamble*, and declared, that King *Philip* and Queen *Mary* were seized of the manor and fee of *Holderness*, in the county of *York*, in their demesne as of fee; and by their letters patents granted the said manor and fee, with wreck of the sea within the said manor and fee, to *Henry* earl of *Westmoreland* in fee, who conveyed them to Sir *John Constable*, father of the plaintiff, whose heir he is in fee: And further declared, that certain goods; *scil.* twelve shirts and five cloaks were wrecked and cast upon the land within the manor of *Barneston*, which is within the said fee of *Holderness*, and that the defendant took the said goods, &c. The defendant pleaded to issue, and thereupon a special verdict was found to this effect; *scil.* That the conveyance to the plaintiff of the manor and fee aforesaid was true as he hath declared; and that the said manor of *Barneston* was within the said fee: and further, that parcel of the said goods were wrecked and cast *super arenas aqua salsa minime coopertas Manerii de* Barneston *infra fluxum et refluxum maris in Manei-ro de Barneston*, and for other parcels of the goods, that they were floating *super aquas maris refluentes ex arenas ejusdem Manerii de Barneston infra fluxum et refluxum maris.* &c. And that the defendant took all the said goods and seized them to the use of the lord admiral, &c. And damages assessed entirely for all: And *si super totam materiam, &c.* And this case was often well argued at bar and bench, and, at the last, judgment was given against the plaintiff. And in this case five points were resolved:

1. That nothing shall be said *wreccum maris*, but such goods only which are cast and left upon the land by the sea; for *wreccum maris significat illa bona, quæ naufragio ad terram appelluntur: Flotsam* is when a ship is sunk, or otherwise perished, and the goods float upon the sea; *Jetsam*, is when the ship is in danger to be sunk, and for lightening of the ship the goods are cast into the sea, and afterwards notwithstanding the ship perisheth. *Lagan*, or rather *Ligan*, is when the goods which are so cast into the sea, and afterwards the ship perisheth, and such goods so cast are so heavy that they sink to the bottom, and the mariners to the intent to have them again, tie to them a buoy, or cork, or such other thing which will not sink, so that they may find them again, and it is called *Ligan a ligando;* and none of these goods which are called *Jetsam, Flotsam*, and *Ligan* are called wreck so long as they remain in or upon the sea, but if any of them by the sea be put upon the land, then they shall be said wreck. So *Flotsam, Jetsam*, and *Lagan*, being cast upon the land shall pass by the grant of wreck: And where it is provided by the statute of 15 *R.* 2. *cap.* 3. that the court of admiralty shall not have jurisdiction of wreck of the sea, yet he shall have conusans and jurisdiction of *Flotsam, Jetsam*, and *Lagan;* for wreck of sea is, when the goods are by the sea cast

upon the land, and so *infra Comitat'*, whereof the common law taketh conusans, but the other three are all upon the sea, and therefore of them the admiral hath jurisdiction. *Bracton, lib.* 3. *cap.* 3. *fol.* 120. *Item magis proprie dici poterit wreccum si navis frangatur, et ex qua nullus vivus evaserit, et maxime si domin' rerum submersus fuerit, et quicquid inde ad terram* (note these words) *venit, erit Domini Regis.* And that also appeareth by the book of entries, *fol.* 611, 612. *Trespass in wreck.* Always when wreck is claimed by prescription, (as by law it may be, the pleading is *bona wreccata super mare, et ad terram projecti'.* And another prescription is there, *babere omnimod' wreccum maris infra præcinctum Manerii, sive Domini prædicti' project', et flootsam maris infra eundem præcinct' devenient':* by which the difference between wreck and *Flotsam* appeareth. See 9 *E.* 4. 22. wreck is when it is cast upon the land, 11 *H.* 4. 16. 5 *E.* 3. 3. *et* 29. 21 *H.* 6 *Prescription,* 14 *E.* 2. *in trepass* 236. 5 *H.* 7. 36. 39 *H.* 6. 37. *and* 9 *H.* 7. 20. *acc'. Vide Register* 102. *b.* the writ saith, *ostentasurus quare cum idem* Tho. *Dominus Mancrii de Estombavent existat et ibidem habere debeat, ipseque et antecessores sai Domini Manerii præd' a tempore quo, etc. non existat memoria, hucusque habere consueverunt wreccum maris infra præcinct' Manerii præd'* Johannes & Robertus, *bona et catella ad valenc' cent' solid' apud* S. *infra præcinct. ejusdem Manerii ad terram project', et quæ ad ipsum* Tho. *tanquam wreccum pertinere deberant, vi et armis ceperunt et asportaverunt.* Also the statute of 15 *R.* 2. *cap.* 3. proveth it also. And it is enacted and declared, that wreck of the sea shall be tried and determined by the laws of the land, which cannot be extended to *Flotsam, Jetsam,* and *Lagan,* for they are in or upon the sea, and therefore cannot be tried and determined by the common law, for it wanteth trial, but are to be determined before the admiral.

2. In this case it was resolved by the whole court, that the soil upon which the sea floweth and ebbeth; *scil.* between high-water mark and low-water mark may be parcel of the manor of

a subject, 16 *Eliz.* *Dier.* 316. *acc*'. And so it was adjudged in *Lacie's* case, *Trin.* 25 *Eliz.* in this court. And yet it was resolved, That when the sea floweth and hath *plenitudinem maris*, the admiral shall have jurisdiction of every thing done upon the water, between the high-water mark and low-water mark, by the ordinary and natural course of the sea: and so it was adjudged in the said case of *Lacy*, that the felony done upon the sea *ad plenitudinem maris*, between the high-water mark and the low-water mark, by the ordinary and natural course of the sea, the admiral shall have jurisdiction; and yet when the sea doth ebb, the land may belong to a subject, and every thing done upon the land when the land is ebbed shall be tried at the common law, for the same is then parcel of the county, and *infra corpus Comitat*', and therewith agreeth 8 *E.* 4. 19. So note, that below the low mark the admiral hath the sole and absolute jurisdiction, and between the high-water mark and low-water mark, the common law and the admiral have *divisum Imperium*, interchangeably as is aforesaid, *scil.* one upon the water, and the other upon the land. And Sir *John Popham*, chief justice, said, that in trial of a *nisi prius* between the city of *Bristow* and the lord *Berkley*, it was holden by the justices of assize, that where the lord *Berkley* had a manor adjoining to the *Severn*, and prescribed to have wreck within his manor, and certain goods floated between the high-water and low-water mark, and the city of *Bristol* had *Flotsam* there; and it was holden that the said goods were not wreck as long as they were floating upon the water between high-water and low water mark. See the book in 5 *E.* 3. 2. in a replevin brought by *William de Newport* of *London*, against Sir *Henry Nevil*, and counted that the defendant took three lasts of herrings and a ship; and the defendant pleaded that he was lord of the manor of *Warling*, and prescribed to have wreck within his manor, and that the herring and ship were wreck within his manor: To which the plaintiff said that they were our goods in the keeping of the mariners, which arrived by the sea, and that he took them out of their custody: Judgment if he can claim as wreck? To which the defendant said, we took them as wreck, *Hors de chescun gard*; upon which book I observe three things: 1. That wreck may be claimed by prescription: 2. That forasmuch as a ship cannot be wreck, *scil.* cast upon the land, but between the high and low-water mark, that there it followeth, that that was parcel of the manor: 3. That if the ship perish, yet if any of the servants escape, the law saith that they have the custody of the goods, and that they are not wreck, 39 E. 3. 5. One prescribed to have royal fishes, as porpoises, &c. found within his manor, that it seemeth to be between the high and low-water mark.

3. It was resolved, that the king shall have *Flotsam*, *Jetsam* and *Lagan*, when the ship perisheth, or when the owners of the goods are known, as in 46 E. 3. 15. appeareth, that goods cast into the sea for fear of tempest, are not forfeit. *Vide F. N. B.* 112. c. 5. *E.* 3. 3. 9. *E.* 4. 22. that the ship ought to perish, which is called shipwreck: And that is also proved by the act of *West.* 1. *cap.* 4. where it is said, if a man, dog, or cat escape alive, (which is to be intended when the ship perisheth) and therewith agreeth *Bracton, lib.* 2. *cap.* 18. *fol.* 41. *Item sine traditione res habita pro derelict', ubi Dominus statim definit esse Dominus, si autem causa navis alleviandæ, non sic, quia non ea volantate ejecit quis, ut desinat esse Dominus.* And a man may have *Flotsam* and *Jetsam* by the king's grant, and may have *Flotsam* within the high and low-water marks by prescription, as it appeareth before. And those of the west country prescribe to have wreck in the sea so far as they may see a *Humber* barrel.

4. It was resolved, that the statute of *West.* 2. *cap.* 4. by which it is enacted, that of wreck of the sea it is agreed, that there where a man, dog, or cat, escape alive out of the ship or vessel, not anything within them shall be adjudged wreck, but the goods shall be saved and kept by the view of the sheriff, coroner, or king's bailiff, &c. so that if any sue for those goods.

and can prove that they belonged to him, or that they perished in his keeping within a year and a day, they shall be restored to him without delay, &c. was but a declaration of the common law; and therefore all that which is provided as to wreck, extendeth also to *Flotsam*, *Jetsam*, and *Lagan*. *Bracton*, who wrote in the time of *H.* 3. before the making of the said act, speaking of wreck, saith, *Et quod hujusmodi dici debet wreccum verum est, nisi sit, quod verus Dominus aliunde veniens, et certa judicia et signa donaverit res esse suas, ut si canis vivus inveniat', et constare poterit, quod talis sit Dominus illius canis præsumptive, ex hoc illum esse Dominum illius canis et illarum rerum: eodem modo si certa signa imposita fuerint mercibus:* By which it appeareth, that the statute of *West.* 1. which is made 3 *E.* 1. was but a declaratory of the common law, against the opinion in *Doctor* and *Student* 118, that if the owner dieth, his executors or administrators may make their proofs. And in many cases concerning time, the common law giveth a year and a day for convenient time; as in the case of stray, if the owner (Proclamations being made) doth claim the same within a year and a day, the same is forfeited. So a year and a day is given in case of appeal, and in case of descent after entry or claim; of nonclaim upon fine, or writ of right at the common law; of a villain dwelling in ancient demesne; of the death of a man who hath blow or wound; of protections, essoins of the king's service, and in many other cases: and the year and day in case of wreck, shall be accounted from the taking or seizure of them as wreck; for although that the property is in law vested in the lord before seizure, yet until the lord seizeth, and taketh it into his actual possession, it is not notorious who claimeth the wreck, nor to whom the owner shall repair to make his claim, and to shew to him his proofs. And if the wreck doth belong to the king, the party may have a commission to hear and determine the truth of it, and that by verdict of twelve honest men, for no proof is allowable by law, but the verdict of twelve men: and if it doth belong to another than to the king, then if the owner cannot satisfy him who claimeth the wreck by his mark or cocket, or by book of customs, or by testimony of honest men, then the owner may have such commission, or may bring his action at the common law, and prove the same by the verdict of a jury; and if the commission be awarded, or the action be brought within the year and day, although the verdict be given for him afterwards, it is sufficient. See *Register* and *F. N. B.* 12. For the commission, *vide Statutes West.* 1. *cap.* 4. 4 *E.* 1. *de Offic. Coronat.* 15 *R.* 2. *cap.* 3. 27 *E.* 3. *cap.* 13. *Britton, cap.* 17. *and* 33 *Stramf. Prærogat. Regis.* And note that the act of *Prærogativa Regis* made in 17 *E.* 2. *cap.* 11. enacted *Quod Rex habebit wreccum maris per totum regnum, etc.* is but a declaration and an affirmance of the common law. For notwithstanding that the statute being made within time of memory, a man may prescribe to have wreck, as it appeareth in 11 *H.* 4. 16. *Stramf.* 38. *F. N. B.* 91. *a.* 5 *H.* 7. 36. 5 *E.* 3. 3. *and* 59. 9 *E.* 4. 12, &c.

5. It was resolved in the case at bar, that part of the goods passed by the name of wreck, and part of the goods were *Flotsam*, and did not pass by the grant of wreck, and damages were entirely assessed for all. And in trespass the plaintiff shall recover damages only for the value of the goods, and for this cause judgment was given against the plaintiff. And the book in 21 *H.* 7. 43. was cited, where the case is, that in trespass, the defendant justifieth as to one thing, and pleadeth not guilty of another, and they are at issue, and the jury enquired of one thing only, and taxed the damages for both entirely. *Fineux* held the verdict good for the thing found, and that he should have a writ of enquiry of damages, *Quad fuit negatum per totam Curiam Dier* 22 *Eliz.* 269. *in Ejectione custodiæ* agreeth with this judgment. And it was adjudged *M.* 14 and 15 *Eliz.* in this court in trespass by *Pooly* against *Osburn* of breaking his close and beating his servant, and doth not say, *per quod servertium amisit*, the defendant pleaded not guilty, and the jurors found him guilty and assessed damages entirely; and because the plaintiff had not cause of action for beating of his

servant, because he hath not averred that he lost his service, for this cause the plaintiff took nothing by his bill. And *Catline* then Chief Justice, caused the reason and cause of the judgment to be at large set down in the margin of the record, 9 *H.* 7. 3. in *Rescous acc'.* And it was adjudged accordingly, *M.* 30 *and* 31 *Eliz.* between *More* and *Bedell,* in an action upon the case upon *assumpsit,* which began in the *king's bench, M.* 28 *and* 29 *Eliz. Rot.* 476. where the defendant promised to do divers things, and the plaintiff alleged two breaches, whereof one was insufficient, the defendant pleaded *non assumpsit,* the jury gave damage generally. It was resolved, 1. That it shall be intended that they give damages for both: 2. That for as much as the plaintiff had no cause of damages for the one, for this cause the judgment given for the plaintiff in the *king's bench* was reversed by a writ of error brought in the exchequer chamber.

Note reader, at the first, the common law gave as well *Wreck*, *Jetsam, Flotsam,* and *Lagan* upon the sea, as estray (which *Bracton* calleth *animalia vagantia,*) or as others call them *animalia vacantia, quia Domino vacari debent,* treasure trove, and the like to the king, because that by the rule of the common law, when no man can claim property in any goods, the king shall have them by his prerogative. And therefore *Bracton, lib.* 3. *cap.* 3. saith, *Suntalia quædam quæ in nullius bonis esse discunt', sicut wreccum maris, grossus piscis, sicut sturgio, et balena, et aliæ res quæ Dominum non habent, sicut animalia vagantia, quæ sunt Domini Regis propter privilegium.* So that it appeareth by *Bracton* that the king shall have wreck, as he shall have great fishes, &c. because they are *nullius in bonis,* or as he shall have *animalia vagantia, sive vacantia, scil.* estrays because none claimeth the property. And note, that wreck is estray upon the sea coming to land, as estray of beasts is upon the land coming within any privileged place; and the law giveth in both cases a year and a day to claim them. And *Bracton* in the same book, *lib.* 3. *cap.* 33. *fol.* 135. saith, *Navis, nec batellus, nec alia catalla de his qui submersi sunt mari, nec in salvo nec in dulci aqua, wreccum erit, cum sit qui catalla illa advocet. et hoc docere poterit;* and so he fitly before resembleth it to an estray: and if the goods of an infant, feme covert executrix, a man in prison, or beyond sea, estray and be proclaimed according to the law, if none claim them within the year and the day, they all shall be bounden. The same law is of wreck of sea, for the law is strict and binding in both cases; but it appeareth by the opinion of *Bracton* and *Britton* also, that *Flotsam, Jetsam,* and *Lagan,* so long as they are in or upon the sea, do not appertain to the king, *sed occupanti concedunt', quia non est aliquis qui inde privilegium habere possit, Rex non magis quam privata persona propter incertum rei eventum (et paulo ante reddit inde rationem,) eo quod constare non possit ad quam regionem essent applicanda.* And *Britton, lib.* 1. *cap.* 17. Treasure hid in the ground, we will that it be ours, and if it be found in the sea, be it to the finder. But as it appeareth before by the resolution of the whole court, the king shall have *Flotsam, Jetsam,* and *Lagan,* as is aforesaid, by his prerogative, although they be in or upon the sea: and the sea is of the king's allegiance, and parcel of his Crown of *England,* as it is holden in 6 *R.* 2. *Protection* 46. and *Britton, cap.* 33. well agreeth with the opinion of *Bracton, scil.* that wreck is a thing *in nullius bonis;* for there he saith, there is also purchase by franchise granted, by name of a thing found in no man's goods, as a wreck of sea, and cattle estraying, conies, hares, partridges, and other savage beasts, by franchise to have wreck found in his soil, and waif and stray found in fee, warrens, and his demesne lands.

6 MASS. REP. 435.

STORER *v.* FREEMAN.

THIS was an action of trespass for breaking and entering the plaintiff's close, situate on *Gamaliel's Neck*, in the town of *Cape Elizabeth*, in this county, including a parcel of flats between high-water mark and low-water mark, over which the sea ebbs and flows.

The defendant pleaded two pleas; the general issue, and soil and freehold in himself. On these pleas issues were joined to the country, which were tried before *Sedgwick*, J. at the last *October* term in this county; and on both issues a verdict was taken for the plaintiff, subject to the opinion of the court upon two questions, *viz.*

1. Whether the deeds hereafter mentioned, one of which was from *Abigail Dyer*, as administratrix of the estate of *Benjamin Dyer*, to *Caleb Dyer*, bearing date *December* 9th, 1790, and the other from the said *Abigail*, administratrix as aforesaid, to *Joshua Dyer*, bearing date *December* 10th, 1790, did convey the land there lying between high and low-water mark.

It was agreed that those deeds legally conveyed the estate as therein expressed to the respective grantees; that the title to the same estate was in the plaintiff; and that the shore therein mentioned adjoins water of the sea, which ebbs and flows, but less than one hundred rods.

The first of said deeds purports to convey twelve and an half acres of land, within certain boundaries, two of which boundaries are "running from a certain stake there described, N. 28° W. *to the shore* of the neck, *thence by the shore* to other land of the said *Caleb.*"—The deed to *Joshua Dyer*, purports also to be a conveyance of twelve and an half acres of land adjoining on one side to the land described in the first deed. Among the boundaries, one line runs from a heap of stones there mentioned northwestwardly seven rods, to a heap of stones, *at the shore* of the neck at *William Elwell's corner*, so called, thence *by the shore* to the land conveyed in the first deed.

2. Whether by law the defendant might, by oral testimony, explain the intent of the grants made by the said deeds.

And now at this term, it was agreed by *Mellen*, for the plaintiff, that the signification of the word sea-shore, as universally understood in this country, was the line or margin of the water for the time being; and the true construction of these deeds must be, that they conveyed the land to such line; but as the boundary must be a fixed and certain line, as distinguished from a variable or changing one, and as every deed is to be construed most strictly against the grantor, the farthest boundary or low-water mark must be here intended by the shore.

But without the aid of construction, and supposing the grant to extend only to the edge of the upland; the ordinance of 1641, although perhaps repealed by the vacating of the first charter, still forms the common law of the country, and gives to the owner of upland adjoining the sea "the propriety to low-water mark, where" as the case finds here, "the sea doth not ebb above one hundred rods."

Longfellow, for the defendant, observed that the rule of construction mentioned by the plaintiff ought not to be applied here, where the grantor was merely executing a naked authority, and could pass no more than she was authorized to sell: and especially could the defendant resist such construction, since he claimed as heir to the intestate.

The *shore* is technically that parcel of land which lies between high-water and low-water mark, being alternately covered with water and bare. In common languages it has perhaps two meanings, in one of which it is applied to the edge of the upland, or top of the bank, distinctly marked upon the sea coast generally, where rocks do not constitute it, as the line to which storms occasionally push the water. The other and the only remaining use of the term in common parlance, is the high-water mark, to which the water rises in common and ordinary tides. In neither of these senses, does it include the land in question.

The ordinance of 1641, which has been referred to, annexed the flats to the upland, as an appertenance, rather than as an extension of the limits of the land conveyed; but it is observable that in these deeds appertenances are not mentioned.

As to the second question saved at the trial, it was competent to the defendant to explain a latent ambiguity by oral testimony: and the ambiguity in this case was a latent one in fact, although the judge has omitted so to describe it: the defendant wished to shew the boundary intended by the parties to the deeds, by shewing how the lines were actually run and measured by the surveyor at the time of the sales.

The opinion of the court was afterwards delivered by

Parsons, Ch. J. The first question referred to our consideration in this case arises upon the construction of the two deeds, whether the flats did or did not pass by them. The plaintiff's construction of the first deed is, that running *to* the shore is running to low-water mark, and running *by* the shore is running by low-water mark: and to support this construction he relies on a maxim of our common law, that the proprietor of land adjoining on the sea or salt water, where the sea ebbs and flows, shall hold to low-water mark, where the sea does not ebb more than one hundred rods, which it is agreed by the parties in this case, it does not. The origin of this maxim, and the true construction of it first require our consideration.

By the common law of *England*, which our ancestors brought with them, claiming it as their birthright, the owner of land bounded on a fresh water river owned the land to the centre of the channel of the river, as of common right; but if his land was bounded on the sea, or on any arm of the sea, where the tide ebbed and flowed, he could not, by such boundary hold any land below the ordinary low-water mark: for all the land below belonged of common right to the king. But the subject might claim the land below high-water mark against the king, either by grant, or by prescription, which presupposed a grant.

When our ancestors emigrated to this country, their first settlements were on harbors or arms of the sea; and commerce was among the earliest objects of their attention. For the purposes of commerce, wharves erected below high-water mark were necessary. But the colony was not able to build them at the public expense. To induce persons to erect them, the common law of *England* was altered by an ordinance, providing that the proprietor of land adjoining on the sea or salt water, shall hold to low-water mark, where the tide does not ebb more than one hundred rods, but not more where the tide ebbs to a greater distance.

This ordinance was annulled with the charter by the authority of which it was made: but from that time to the present an usage has prevailed, which now has force as our common law, that the owner of lands bounded on the sea or salt water shall hold to low-water mark, so that he does not hold more than one hundred rods below high-water mark; but the rights of others to convenient ways are saved, agreeably to a provision in the ordinance.

This rule applies only in cases, where the grantor, seized of the upland and flats, in conveying his land, bounds the land sold on the sea or salt water, or describes other boundaries of equivalent meaning, without any reservation of the flats. But the owner may sell his upland without the flats, or the flats or any part thereof, without the upland.

The present question is therefore a question upon the construction of the deeds of conveyance. The lands are not expressly bounded on the sea or salt water; but they extend to the sea shore and are bounded by it: which, as the plaintiff has argued, are expressions of the same import.

What is the sea shore, must first be defined. The sea shore must be understood to be the margin of the sea, in its usual and ordinary state. Thus when the tide is out, low-water mark is the margin of the sea; and when the sea is full, the margin is high-water mark. The sea shore is therefore all the ground between the ordinary high-water mark and low-water mark. It cannot be considered as including any ground always covered by the sea; for then it would have no definite limit on the sea board. Neither can it include any part of the upland, for the same reason. This definition of the shore seems to result necessarily from its nature and situation.

But we are not left without any authority. This question is largely considered by lord *Hale*, in his treatise *De jure maris et brachiorum ejusdem.* And his definition of the sea shore is "that ground that is between the ordinary high-water mark and low-water mark."

We must now return to the first deed: and as it appears from the report of the judge, that the shore mentioned in the deed is not covered with rock, but forms a beach or flats, we shall for *shore* substitute *flats.* The land described will then extend to the flats, and be bounded by the flats. On this substitution, the construction is manifest. The land conveyed extends *to* the flats, but not *over* them: and the flats being a bound of the land conveyed, are not a part of it. Thus by a strict and technical construction of the description of the land conveyed, we are satisfied that no part of the flats passed by the first deed.

The description in the second deed varies in one respect from the description in the former deed. In the first deed, the course runs to the shore, and thence by the shore. In the second deed, let us substitute flats for shore, and the course will run to a heap of stones by the flats at *Elwell's corner,* and thence by the flats to the land described in the first deed. *Elwell's corner* not being located by any evidence or admission, we cannot presume that the first course extended over the flats to that corner; for, especially when, being satisfied that by the technical construction of the first deed the flats were not conveyed, we observe that the boundary line from *Elwell's corner* runs by the flats to land which passed by that deed. For we cannot presume that this boundary line crossed the flats in its course. Adhering therefore to a technical construction of the two deeds, unassisted by any parole testimony to explain latent ambiguities, we are satisfied that the plaintiff has no title to the flats, derived under the two deeds of *Abigail Dyer*, or under either of them.

Another question reserved was, whether the defendant could, by oral testimony, explain the extent of the grants made in said deeds. In what manner he proposed to explain them is not stated. Unquestionably he could give no parole evidence, either to contradict the deeds, or to explain any latent ambiguities. These ambiguities must be removed by a sound construction of the words of the deed. But we might give parole evidence to explain any latent ambiguities. Thus he might locate all the land and monuments referred to as boundaries. But upon our construction of the deeds, he had no occasion for any parole explanation.

There is one latent ambiguity, which might possibly be so explained by parole evidence, as would change our opinions upon the construction of the deeds. And we mention it, that the plaintiff, if he should again try this cause, may be prepared for the explanation, if the facts are with him.

In the second deed, a boundary line is described to run to a heap of stones by the shore at *Elwell's corner*. The shore has two sides, high-water mark and low-water mark. *Elwell's corner* is described as a known monument. If it is at low-water mark, it is by the shore, as well as if it was at high-water mark. Now if it be a fact, that this corner was a known monument at low-water mark, the plaintiff might be admitted to prove it by oral testimony. Then the boundary line, running to *Elwell's corner*, would cross the flats to low-water mark: and the next boundary line running by the flats must run by the same side of the flats, on which *Elwell's corner* stands; and thus the flats would be included by the boundaries of the land conveyed by the second deed.—And further, from this fact the first deed would receive a different consideration, as it was executed by the same grantor. For as the boundary line running from *Elwell's corner* runs to the land conveyed by the first deed, if that line run by the low-water mark, then the land conveyed by the first deed must also extend to low-water mark: and we should presume that the word *shore* was used untechnically and without legal accuracy, as importing low-water mark.

As the case is now presented to us, the verdict must be set aside, and a new trial be granted.

WILLES' REP. 265.

WARD *v.* CRESWELL.

TO replevin for taking six boat oars at *Creswell Haven*, otherwise *Creswell Boat Landing*, in the parish of *Woodhorn*.

There was an avowry that the *locus in quo* was the soil and freehold of the defendant, and that the goods were doing damage there, &c.

The plaintiff pleaded in bar, first, that *E. Cook* was seized in fee of one moiety of the place in which, &c. and that he gave the plaintiff license to lay and place the goods there, traversing that the *locus in quo* was the soil and freehold of the defendant: on which issue was taken and found for the defendant.

Secondly, That the *locus in quo* for time immemorial hath been a certain piece of waste ground in the township of *Cres-*

well and parish of *Woodhorn*, containing three acres, lying contiguous to the sea, and that *E. Cook* was seized in fee of "certain ancient tenements consisting of divers messuages and several, to wit, two hundred acres of land, with the appertenances," and that he and all those whose estate he has in the said tenements with the appertenances, have from time immemorial had and been accustomed to have for themselves and their farmers and servants, common of fishery with *two boats* in the sea there, every year, at all seasonable times of fishing in the year, as belonging and appertaining to the said tenements, with the appertenances, and to have for themselves, their farmers and servants, the liberty of landing and putting on shore their said fishing-boats on the place in which, &c. for the necessary use of the said common or fishery; that the plaintiff, as the servant of *E. Cook*, and by his command, at the time of taking, &c. being a seasonable time of fishing, with a boat fished in the sea there, using the said common or fishery there, and on that occasion at the same time of taking, &c. landed and put on shore the said fishing boat in and upon the place in which, &c. the said six boat oars then being in the said boat and part of the tackle and furniture there, &c. whereupon the defendant of his own wrong took the said boat oars, &c.

There was a third plea in bar, similar to the second, except that instead of claiming the right of fishery with *two boats*, the right was claimed generally, "with their boats."

To the two last pleas there were general demurrers.

After two arguments at the bar, the first by *Draper*, sergt. for the defendant, and *Bootle*, sergt. for the plaintiff, on the 21st of *November*, 1738, and the other by *Burnett*, sergt. for the former and *Prime*, king's sergt. for the latter, on the 16th of *June*, 1740, the judgment of the court was delivered, as follows, by

Willes, Lord C. J. "It was said by the counsel for the defendant, and not contradicted by the counsel for the plaintiff.

that there has been a verdict for the defendant on the first plea; so it comes before the court only upon the demurrer to the second and third pleas.

To the second plea it was objected,

First, That the prescription was too general and uncertain, being laid to be appertenant to "certain ancient tenements consisting of divers messuages and several, to wit, two hundred acres of land."

Secondly, That the prescription was void, because the plaintiff insists on his right as a particular right of common appertenant to certain tenements, whereas it is a general right for every subject of *England* to fish in the sea of common right.

Thirdly, That the plaintiff had not brought his case within the prescription; he not having averred that the boat in question was necessary for the enjoyment of his common of fishery, or that it was necessary for that purpose to land it on the place in question.

To the third plea the same objections were taken and two more.

First, That the prescription was not laid for any certain number of boats, and therefore void.

Secondly, That the prescription is to fish *with their boats*, and that the plaintiff has not said whose the boat in question was.

We think that there is something in most of these objections: but as we are all clearly of opinion that the second objection, which goes to both pleas, is unanswerable, I shall say the less upon the rest.

The first objection likewise goes to both pleas. It consists of two parts; it is objected 1st, that "tenements" is too general a word; and 2dly, that the prescription is only claimed in respect of *certain* ancient tenements, &c. without saying how many, or whether it be claimed for all or for each of them, and it cannot be claimed jointly for several. It is said that the word "tenements" is too uncertain, unless ascertained by other words, as the messuage or tenement called *The Black Swan, &c.* : but we do not rely upon that. The other part of this objection seems to be fatal. In *Basket* v. Lord *Mordant*, *Dyer* 164. *a.* and *Bendl.* 74. it was ruled that if a man, having common in a waste for one hundred sheep as appertenant to a house and certain acres of land, purchase another messuage, with certain lands which also has common in the same waste for other one hundred sheep as appertenant, he cannot make title in pleading by prescription in the entire for common appertenant to both houses and lands together for two hundred sheep, but must make two several titles and prescriptions for the two hundred sheep. The same doctrine is laid down in *Palmer* 362.

The third objection which also applies to both the pleas, seems to be fatal. We think it is sufficiently set forth that the boat was necessary for fishing, but it is not sufficiently shewn that it was necessary to land it on the defendant's land.*

The first objection to the third plea appears to have but little weight ; for if a man have a right to fish, he may fish with as many boats as he pleases.

But the second objection to the third plea seems to be of weight, that the plaintiff should have shown that it was a boat of *E. Cook* or his farmer or servant; the prescription confining it to *their boats* in this plea.

But we are all clearly of opinion on the second objection, which equally applies to both pleas, that the prescription is void, because the right claimed as annexed to certain tenements is a general right for all the subjects of the kingdom.† In *Pell* v. *Towers*, *Noy* 20, it was agreed "That a man shall not prescribe in that which the law of common right gives." So in *Bro. Abr. title* "prescription" *pl.* 71. Now "every man may fish in the sea of common right;" 8 *Edw.* 4. 19. *a.* In *Warren*

* See *Peppin* v. *Shakspeare*, 6 *Durnf. & East* 643.

† See *Carter* v. *Murcot*, 4 *Burr.* 2163; and the Mayor, &c. of *Lynn* v. *Turner*, 3 *D. and E.* 437, and 2 *H. Bl. Rep.* 182

v. *Mathews*, 6 *Mod.* 63, and *Salk.* 357, it was holden that "every subject of common right may fish with lawful nets in a navigable river as well as in the sea." So is 1 *Mod.* 155. And this is not merely the law of this country, but is also the law of nations. *Grot. de Jure Belli et Pacis, b.* 2. *c.* 3. *f.* 9. And *Bracton, l.* 1. *c.* 12. *f.* 6. says *publica vero sunt omnia flumina et portus: Ideoque jus piscandi omnibus commune est in portu et in fluminibus.* This prescription therefore for a right common to all the subjects of the realm cannot be supported. A man might as well prescribe that he, and all those whose estate he has, have a right to travel on the king's highway as appertenant to his estate.

For these reasons, as the defendant has had a verdict for him on the first plea, and as we are of opinion that the plaintiff's second and third pleas in bar are both bad, judgment must be for the defendant.

6 Mod. Rep. 73.

WARREN *v.* MATHEWS.

PER Curiam. Every subject of common right may fish with lawful nets, &c. in a *navigable river* as well as in the *sea*, and the king's grant cannot bar them thereof; but the Crown only has a right to royal fish, and that the king only may grant.

1 Sarg. & Lowb. 268. and 5 Barn. & Ald. 91.

BLUNDELL *v.* CATTERALL.

[The following case, which was decided by the present court of king's bench, and which involves much legal learning, was not at hand in time to be inserted in the alphabetical order of the Appendix.]

TRESPASS, for breaking and entering the plaintiff's close, (describing it, first, as a close called the *Sea Shore*, within the manor of *Great Crosby*; secondly, as a close between the high-water mark and the low-water mark of the river *Mersey*, in *Great Crosby*, in the county of *Lancaster*;) and with feet in walking, and with the feet of horses, and with the wheels of bathing machines, carts, and other carriages, passing over, tearing up, damaging the sand, gravel, and soil of the said close. The defendant pleaded, as to the trespasses committed on the close called the *Sea Shore*, and on that between the high and low-water mark, a public right of way on foot, and with cattle, carts, and carriages; and, secondly, as to the same trespasses, that all the liege subjects of our lord the king, had been used and accustomed to have and enjoy, and of right ought to have had and enjoyed, and still of right ought to have and enjoy the right and liberty of bathing in the sea, from time to time, being over and upon the whole or any part of, or adjoining to, the said close, in which, &c., at all seasonable and convenient times, for their health and recreation, and for that purpose, of going and returning, passing, and repassing, into, through, over, and along the said close, in which, &c. on foot, and with their servants, and with carriages and bathing machines, and horses drawing the same to the sea and back again; and of staying in and upon the close a necessary and convenient time for the purposes of bathing as aforesaid: And, thirdly, as to part of those trespasses, a right of bathing and of passing on foot only. The plaintiff took issue on these pleas; and also newly assigned that the defendant committed the trespasses on other occasions, and for other purposes than those in the pleas mentioned, and out of the highway in the first set of pleas mentioned. Issue thereon. At the trial, at the last *Lancaster* assizes, before *Bayley*, J., a verdict was found for the defendant on the first set of pleas; and for the plaintiff on the new assignment, and on all the other pleas, subject to the opinion of the Court on a special case. The plaintiff was the lord of the manor of *Great Crosby*, which is bounded on the west by the river *Mersey*, an arm of the sea. As lord of the manor, he was the owner of the shore, and had the exclusive right of fishing thereon with stake nets. The defendant was the servant at a hotel, erected in 1815, upon land in *Great Crosby*, fronting the shore, and bounded by the high-water mark of the river *Mersey*, the proprietors of which kept bathing machines for the use of persons resorting thither, who were driven by the defendant, in machines, across the shore into the sea, for the purpose of bathing, and the defendant received a sum of money from the individuals so bathing, for the use of the machines, and for his service and assistance. No bathing machines were ever used upon the shore in *Great Crosby*, before the establishment of this hotel, but it had been the custom for the public to cross it on foot, for the purpose of bathing. There was a common highway for carriages along the shore, and it was proved, that various articles for market were occasionally carted across the shore, although the more common mode of conveyance for such things was by a canal made about forty years ago. The defendant contended for a common law right for all the king's subjects to bathe on the sea shore, and to pass over it for that purpose, on foot, and with horses and carriages. The case was argued in last *Easter* term.

Gregson, for the plaintiff, cited lord *Hale's* treatise *De Jure Maris*, and *De Portibus Maris*, chapters 5 and 6.—*Ibid.* pp. 73 and 76—*Morgan's* case, *Ibid.* p. 51.—*Bracton*, *lib.* i. *c.* 12. *s.*

6.—*Ball* v. *Herbert*, 3 *T. R.* 261.—Sir *Henry Constable's* case, 5 *Rep.* 107.—*Hammond* v. *Digges*, *Dyer*, 326.—*The Attorney-General* v. *Roll and Others*, cited *Hale*, p. 27.—*Stockwell* v. *Terry*, 1 *Ves. sen.* 115., and *Warwick* v. *Collins*, 2 *M.* & *S.* 361.*—*Vooght* v. *Winch*, 2 *Barn.* & *Ald.* 662.—*Rex* v. *Cross*. 3 *Compb.* 224.

Joy, *contra*, referred to lord *Hale*, pp. 6 and 7. pp. 11. 19. 20.—*Bagot* v. *Orr*, 2 *Bos.* & *Pull.* 472.—*Weld* v. *Hornby*, 7 *East*, 195.—*Bracton*, *ubi supra*.—*Ball* v. *Herbert*.—Lord *Hale* in his treatise, *De Portibus Maris*, c. 7. p. 83.—*Callis on Sewers*, p. 54.—*Grotius De jure belli et pacis*, c. 2. ss. 3 & 4. and *Mare liberum*, *passim*.—Lord *Hale*, c. 6. *p.* 78.—*Ibid.* c. 7. *de portibus maris*, p. 85.—*Cur. adv. vult.*

And now, there being a difference of opinion, the court delivered their judgments seriatim.

Best, J. The question in this case is, whether there be a common law right to pass over the shore for the purpose of bathing in the sea. It will not be disputed that the sea, which has been called the "Great highway of the world," is common to all. Bathing in the sea, if done with decency, is not only lawful, but proper, and often necessary for many of the inhabitants of this country. There must be the same right to cross the shore in order to bathe, as for any other lawful purpose. We are, therefore, now to decide, whether the public are precluded from passing, except at particular places, over the beach to the sea without the consent of some lord of a manor. That this will be the consequence of our deciding in favor of the plaintiff, has been already admitted at the bar, and must be conceded by every one. I am fearful of the consequences of such a decision; and, much as I dislike differing from the rest of the court, I have thought it my duty to declare that I cannot assent to it.

* The references are to lord *Hale's* treatises, as published by Mr. *Hargrave* in his Law Tracts.

We have been told that lords of manors will find it their interest to indulge the public with the privilege of going on or over the sands of the sea, and that judges and juries will check the vexatious exercise of the right to exclude them. But the free access to the sea is a privilege too important to *Englishmen*, to be left dependant on the interest or caprice of any description of persons.

It is agreed by all, that the sea shore was at first appropriated to the king, from whom the right to it must be derived. The present state of the shore shows the manner in which the Crown must have used it. Some parts of it were held exclusively by the Crown for the purposes of fisheries, harbors, warehouses, &c. But the greatest part was left open as a common highway between the sea and the land. This is the state in which it continues to this day, and in which, from its general sterility, it must ever continue. From the state of the greatest part, has arisen the general rule, or common law right, and the state of the portions exclusively occupied has occasioned the exceptions. The claim of the public to a right of way over the beach stands on the general law, and a person who will dispute this public right in any particular part of it, must establish his right to do so by showing, first, that the king had an exclusive possession of such part, and that a right to such exclusive possession has been conveyed from the Crown to such person. This has been the course in which persons have proceeded who have attempted to show any exclusive right, either in arms of the sea or in the shore. In lord *Fitzwalter's* case, 1 *Mod.* 105. lord *Hale* says, "An arm of the sea is *prima facie*, common to all, and if any will appropriate a privilege to himself, the proof lieth on his side; for in case of an action of trespass brought for fishing there, it is, *prima facie*, a good justification to say, that the *locus in quo* is *brachium maris, in quo unusquisque subjectus dom. regis habet et habere debet liberam piscariam.*" So, in *Bagott* v. *Orr*, 2 *Bos. & Pull.* 479. the court of common pleas held, "that if the plaintiff had it in his power to abridge the common law right of the subject to take sea-fish upon the shore within his manor. he should have replied that matter specially." The same doctrine is laid down in *Carter* v. *Murcot*, 4 *Burr*, 2162. It may be observed, that in the case now under consideration it is expressly found, that the soil of the *locus in quo* is in the plaintiff; but I say the soil must be in the plaintiff, as it was in the king; for the grantee cannot have a greater interest than the grantor had. The king had the right of soil in the shore in general; but the public had a right of way over it, and the king's grantee can only have it, subject to the same right. In the treatise of *De Jure Maris*, p. 22. lord *Hale* says, "The *jus privatum* that is acquired to the subject, either by patent or prescription, must not prejudice the *jus publicum* wherewith public rivers and arms of the sea are affected for public use." If the owners of the soil must claim by prescription, can they establish an exclusive right? Did they ever possess an exclusive right? For, as lord *Hale* says, the civilians tell us truly, "*Nihil præscribitur nisi quod possidetur*," *De jure maris*, p. 32. As the king might have granted a right in particular parts of the shore, so, either he or his grantee of the soil of any part of the shore, may take the products of the shore, provided their removal does not impede the public right of way. The owner of the soil of the shore, may also erect such buildings or other things as are necessary for the carrying on of commerce and navigation on any parts of the shore that may be conveniently used for such erections, taking care to impede, as little as possible, the public right of way. This is not more inconsistent with a public right of way over it, than the right of digging a mine under a road, or the erecting of a wharf on a river, are inconsistent with the right of way along such road or river. The former does not interfere with the use of the road; and although the latter, in order to be useful, must be carried out beyond the high-water mark, and, whilst the tide is up, must somewhat narrow the passage of the river; yet, such wharves are necessary for the loading and unloading of vessels, and the right of passage must be accommodated to the right of loading and unloading the craft that pass. The law in these, as in all other cases, limits and balances opposing rights, that they may be so enjoyed as that the exercise of one is not injurious to the other. The civil law, copying, in this respect, from the law of nations, allowed any one to build on the sea shore (there being, under that law, no lords of manors to claim the soil,) but imposed on the builders the condition that the law of *England* imposes on the owners of the soil; that is, that their buildings should not interrupt the right of way. *Digest, l.* 43. *tit.* 8. "*In littore jure gentium ædificare liceret nisi usus publicus impediret.*"

The universal practice in *England* shows the right of way over the sea shore to be a common law right. All sorts of persons who resort to the sea, either for business or pleasure, have always been accustomed to pass over the unoccupied parts of the shore with such carriages as were suitable to their respective purposes, and no lord of a manor has ever attempted to interrupt such persons. Goods could not be landed or loaded except at particular places, but this restraint was imposed by laws made for the protection of the revenue, and the security of the realm, and is not the consequence of any rights in the owners of the soil of the shore. Men have landed from boats, drawn their boats on the sands during their stay on shore, and embarked again in their boats. Persons have at all times, at their pleasure, walked or ridden on the sands. Men have, from the earliest times, bathed in the sea; and, unless in places or at seasons when they could not, consistently with decency, be permitted to be naked, no one ever attempted to prevent them. So far from the law allowing lords of manors to restrain persons from bathing, it will give them every facility for this recreation. Bathing promotes health. By bathing, those who live near the sea are taught their first duty, namely, to assist mariners in distress. They acquire, by bathing, confidence amidst the waves, and learn how to seize the proper moment for giving their assistance. It is found as a fact, in this case, that it has been the custom for the public to cross the spot in question on foot for the purpose of bathing. Bathing machines were used before my time, and I believe before that of the oldest person now alive, and I think the use of them is essential to the practice of bathing. Decency must prevent all females, and infirmity many men, from bathing, except from a machine. Attempts have been made to make those who use machines pay some acknowledgment to the lord of the manor where they were used: but I cannot find that any of those attempts have yet succeeded. I shall presently show from authority, that the right to fish is only a part of the general right of the subjects of *England*. Persons have also crossed the beach for the purpose of fishing in the sea, and have brought back their fish over the beach, both on horses and in carriages. These acts of the fishermen are instances in support of the common law right of way.

The practice of a particular place is called a custom. A general immemorial practice through the realm is the common law. Many of our most valuable common law rights have no other support than universal practice. In *Ball* v. *Herbert*, 3 *T. R.* 261. lord *Kenyon* says, "common law rights are either to be found in the opinions of lawyers, delivered as axioms, or to be collected from the universal and immemorial usage throughout the country." The instances put by me, sufficiently demonstrate the existence of a universal custom in favor of a public right of way over the sea shore.

It has been at all times the policy of this country to encourage navigation. The free passage of the sea shore is essential to the convenience and safety of navigation. Cases of immediate necessity or imminent danger may be said to form exceptions to general rules; but there are many cases in which there is neither immediate necessity nor imminent danger, in which boats must pass between ships at sea and the shore, letters and provisions must be sent, passengers require to land or to embark, intelligence necessary to the further prosecution of a voyage is desired, or a pilot is wanted. For many leagues of coast.

there is no public passage marked out, by which persons may go to or from the sea. But fixed places will not do. Winds or currents make it necessary, that the greatest part of the shore should be left open for persons to land on, and embark from. There is no statute, or rule of common law, that secures the right of passage over the shore for purposes connected with navigation; those who have passed over the shore for those purposes, have been trespassers, if they were not justified under the general common law right of free passage. Is it to be supposed, that, in a country, the prosperity and independence of which depend on navigation, that which is so necessary to navigation as a road for all lawful purposes to the sea, should not have been secured to the public, particularly when it might be done without injury to the interest of any individual?

There is no clear and express declaration on this point, either in the statutes or in the common law. But this right is so important to the best interests of the country, that had not the constant exercise of it been considered sufficient to establish it, the legislature would no doubt have declared it to be in the people of *England*. *Bracton, lib.* 1 *cap.* 12. *sec.* 6. says, "*Publica vero sunt omnia flumina et portus. Ideoque jus piscandi omnibus commune est in portu et in fluminibus. Riparum etiam usus publicus est de jure gentium, sicut ipsius fluminis. Itaque naves ad eas applicare, funes arboribus ibi natis religare, onus aliquod in iis reponere, cuivis liberum est, sicut per ipsum fluvium navigare: sed proprietas earum illorum est quorum prediis adherent, et eadem de causa arbores in eisdem natæ eorundem sunt: et hæc intelligenda sunt de fluminibus, perennibus, quia temporalia possunt, esse privata.*" This passage proves all that I am attempting to establish. It shows that all persons have a common right on rivers; that the right of fishing exists only as a part of that common right, and that the banks of rivers are as much open to the use of the public as the rivers themselves. The passage has been supposed to prove toc much, and therefore it has been said, that its authority cannot be relied on. Mr. Justice *Buller*, speaking of it in *Ball* v. *Herbert*, 3 *T. R.* 263. says, "that it plainly appears to have been taken from *Justinian*, and is only part of the civil law; and whether or not it has been adopted by the common law, is to be seen by looking into our books; and there it is not to be found." I admit that *Bracton* agrees with the civil law, and I must add, with the law of all civilized nations. *Selden*, who wrote his "*Mare clausum*," to prove that an exclusive right might be acquired in parts of the sea, admits that the sea was originally common to all, and in *lib.* 1. *cap.* 2. he has collected from the works of the learned of all nations, as well philosophers, divines, and poets, as lawyers, that the sea and its shores were common to all men, as much so as the air that blows over them. This I think proves, that the doctrine is reasonable, and ought to be adopted into our law, unless there be something in our particular situation to exclude it; and, so far from this being the case, there never was a country, the local situation of which, and the habits and interests of the inhabitants of which, so much required such a law.

But our books show, that this passage has been adopted into our law. Mr. Justice *Buller* tells us, that *Callis* quotes it as *English* law, and I have often heard lord *Kenyon* speak with great respect of that writer. *Bracton* has not stated this as civil law, he has made it part of his book, *De legibus et consuetudinibus Angliæ*. He was Chief Justice of *England* in the reign of *Henry* the Third; and lord *Hale* (*Hist. of the common law, ch.* 7.) says, that in his time the common law was much improved, and the pleadings were more perfect and orderly than in any preceding period of our history. Surely such a man is no mean authority for what the common law was at the time he wrote. In *Fortescue*, p. 408. lord Chief Justice *Parker* says, "As to the authority of *Bracton*, to be sure many things are now altered, but there is no color to say, that it was not law at that time, for there are many things that have never been altered, and are law now." As law is a just rule fitted to the exist ing state of things, it must alter as the state of things to which it relates alters. I do not say, that the whole of the passage in *Bracton* is now good law: it was all good law at the time he wrote, and all of it that is adapted to the present state of things is good law now. It is objected, that *Bracton* says, "that any one may, in any river, fasten vessels with ropes to the trees on the banks, and unload the cargoes on the banks." Undoubtedly the public cannot now pretend to claim this right in all navigable rivers. Many rivers have been rendered navigable since *Bracton* wrote, which in his time were private streams. The public have no greater right on the banks of such rivers, than the owners of the adjoining lands granted them when such rivers were made, from private streams, public rivers, and the extent of the grant must be ascertained from usage. This is the case with a new made road. If one dedicates to the public a right of way over his lands, the public must take the road with gates on such parts of it as the owner thinks proper to erect at the time he makes the dedication. But *Bracton* speaks not of newly made rivers, but of such as were always navigable, and the banks of which had been as open to the public as their waters. This I take to be the law with all inland navigations in the reign of *Henry* the Third. These, like the sea and its shores, were then the property of the public, and the right of the public in them was not acquired by any compromise with the interest of any individual. On some rivers that have been navigable from time immemorial, the public using but one of the banks for a towing path, the other has been usefully occupied by the owner of the adjoining land, and so an exclusive right has been established to the part so occupied. But the barrenness of the greatest part of the sea shore has prevented it from becoming the subject of exclusive property. It is useful only as a boundary and an approach to the sea; and therefore, ever has been, and ever should continue common to all who have occasion to resort to the sea. Thus, the case of *Ball* v. *Herbert* is distinguished from the present, and it must be recollected, that, in that case,

22

lord *Kenyon* said, "Some of the passages in lord *Hale* which seem to favor the common law right, are rather applicable to banks of the sea, and to ports; and it is part of the king's prerogative to create ports, which was lately exercised at *Liverpool*." In *Brooke's Abridgement, tit. Customs, pl.* 46. all the judges agreed, "that fishermen may justify going on the land adjoining the sea, to fish in the sea; for this is for the good of the commonwealth, affording sustenance to many persons, and is the common law." If the right of fishing is only a part of that more general right for which I am contending, as appears from the passage in *Bracton*, and will appear from lord *Hale*, then this is a decision in support of the general right.

The reason on which my judgment is grounded is public advantage. The right of bathing in the sea, which is essential to the health of so many persons, is as beneficial to the public as that of fishing, and must have been as well secured to the subjects of this country by the common law. That the right of using the shore for the purpose of fishing does not depend on any particular law applicable to fishing only, but is part of the more general right of the subjects to the sea and its shores, is proved by lord *Hale*, putting the practice of fishing as evidence of the general right. In part 1. *cap.* 8. *de jure maris, p.* 11. he says, "The king's right of propriety, or ownership, in the sea, and soil thereof, is evidenced principally in these things that follow: first, the right of fishing in the sea, and the creeks and arms thereof, is originally lodged in the Crown." This makes the judgment in *Brooke* bear directly on the point in dispute. Lord *Hale*, in his treatise *De Portibus Maris*, (*cap.* 6. *p.* 73.) says, "Before any port is legally settled, although the propriety of the soil of a creek or harbor may belong to a subject or private person, yet the king has his *jus regium* in that creek or harbor; and there is also a common liberty for any to come thither with boats and vessels, as against all but the king. And, upon this account, though *A.* may have the propriety of a creek or harbor, or navigable river, yet the king may grant there the liberty of a port to *B.*; and so the interest of propriety and the interest of franchise several and divided. And in this no injury is at all done to *A.*; for he hath what he had before, *viz.* the interest of the soil, and consequently the improvement of the shore, and the liberty of fishing; and as the creek was free for any to pass in it, against all but the king, (for it was *publici juris*, as to that matter before,) so now the king takes off that restraint, and by his license and charter makes it free for all to come and unload." Here, we have the distinct authority of lord *Hale*, that although a man has the soil under an arm of the sea, and the soil of the shore, yet the public have not only a right to navigate on the waters, but to *unload* on the shore; and that this right can only be restrained by the king's prerogative. If they have a right to unload, they must have the right to come over the shore; for the right to unload would otherwise be useless. The right on the shore is declared by this passage to be as common to the public as the right on the water: that the water is open to the public for all lawful purposes is not denied. What law, then, has narrowed the right of the public on the shore? Lord *Hale* then adds, "But if *A.* hath the ripa or bank of the port, the king may not grant a liberty to unlade on that bank or ripa without his consent, unless custom hath made the liberty thereof free to all, as in many places it is; for that would be a prejudice to the private interest of *A.* and which may not be taken from him without such consent. And, therefore, in the creation of a new port, either by proclamation or charter, it hath been the course to secure the interest in the shore beforehand, for the building of wharves and keys, for the application of the merchandize, and for the building of houses of receipt." Lord *Hale* makes the distinction between the shore of the sea and the banks of a river, which lord *Kenyon* points at in *Ball* v. *Herbert*; the former is free for all to come and unload, but the king cannot grant a liberty to unload in the latter, without the consent of the owner. I again repeat, that the shore is not free to unload from any particular law giving this freedom, but from the general right of passage over it, which the usage of the whole coast shows to have been reserved for the benefit of the public out of the grant of the the soil by the Crown. This is further proved to be the meaning of lord *Hale* by the concluding words of this passage, in which he says it was usual to secure the interest of the shore, not for a way to the sea, but for the building wharves, quays, and houses for the reception of goods. The right of way the public had, but the right of building was to be purchased. The cases of *Young* v. ———, *lord Raym.* 725. and *The Queen* v. *The Inhabitants of Cluworth*, 6 *Mod.* 163. are properly overruled by that of *Ball* v. *Herbert*; and I do not rely on those cases.

My opinion is founded on these grounds. The shore of the sea is admitted to have been at one time the property of the king. From the general nature of this property, it could never be used for exclusive occupation. It was holden by the king, like the sea and the highways, for all his subjects. The soil could only be transferred, subject to this public trust; and general usage shows that the public right has been excepted out of the grant of the soil. Our law books furnish us with little for our guidance on this subject; what is to be found seems to favor the common law right of way. But unless I felt myself bound by an authority as strong and clear as an act of parliament, I would hold, on principles of public policy, I might say public necessity, that the interruption of free access to the sea is a public nuisance. In the first ages of all countries, not only the sea and its shores, but all perennial rivers, were left open to public use. In all countries, it has been matter of just complaint, that individuals have encroached on the rights of the people. In *England*, our ancestors put the public rights in rivers under the safeguard of *magna charta*. The principle of exclusive appropriation must not be carried beyond things capable of improvement by the industry of man. If it be extended so far as to touch the right of walking over these barren sands, it will take from the people what is essential to their welfare.

whilst it will give to individuals only the hateful privilege of vexing their neighbors. It has been said, that lords of manors should have a right to prevent bathing, that they might hinder persons from doing it in places of public resort. Magistrates are armed with authority to bring to punishment such as bathe indecently. I would rather rely on disinterested and responsible magistrates, than on an interested and irresponsible lord of a manor. A lord of a manor might remove bathers from a part within view of his own house, but would he be equally active to protect his neighbors from offence? If he is not, I know no mode of forcing him to execute the power he derives from his property. For these reasons, I am of opinion that the defendant is entitled to the judgment of the court.

Holroyd, J. The question put in this case for our opinion, is the general question, whether there is a common law right for all the king's subjects to bathe in the sea, and to pass over the sea shore for that purpose, on foot and with horses and carriages. But, coupled with the facts stated in the case, the question really is, whether there is a common law right in all the king's subjects to do so in the *locus in quo*, though the soil of the sea shore, and an exclusive right of fishing there in a particular manner (namely, with stake nets,) are private property belonging to a subject, and though the same have been a special peculiar property from time immemorial. The plaintiff being stated to be the owner of the soil of the shore, and to have the exclusive right of fishing thereon, with stake nets, as lord of the manor, the soil, as parcel of or belonging to the manor, must according to 2 *Bl. Com.* 92. have been so from before the time of passing the statute, *Quia Emptores Terrarum, tempore, Edw.* 1. since which time no manor can have been created; and the plaintiff being stated to have the exclusive right of fishing, as lord of the manor, this can only be as appendant or appertenant to the manor. It must, therefore, be by prescription, and consequently there has been an exclusive right of fishing there from time immemorial. The question, too, is, as to the public right to the extent above stated, independently of usage and custom. The right is claimed on the pleadings, as founded not on usage or custom, but upon the supposed general law only; and the usage, as stated in the special case, is found to have been for the public to cross the sea shore on foot only, for the purpose of bathing, no bathing machines having ever been used in *Great Crosby*, where the *locus in quo* is situate, before the establishment of the present hotel. My opinion, therefore, on this case, will not affect any right that has been or can be gained by prescription or custom, either by individuals or by either the permanent or temporary inhabitants of any vill, parish, or district.

The claim upon the pleadings, respecting the public highway along the shore, and the verdict, and facts found in the special case respecting the same, make no difference, but leave the question, with respect to the right of bathing, and the right incident thereto (if any) of passing over the sea shore for that purpose, on foot and with horses and carriages, the same as if no such claim of a general public highway existed, or was put upon the record, as the jury have found a verdict for the plaintiff upon the new assignment, that the trespasses complained of were committed in the *locus in quo* on other occasions, and for other purposes than as a general public highway and out of the highway there.

It was contended in argument at the bar, that by the common law of *England*, all the king's subjects had a right, not only to traverse the ocean itself in every direction, as well for commerce, trade, and intercourse, as for every other lawful purpose; but, also, that they had a general public right of way over the sea shore to and from the sea, and that they had it, as well during the recess as during the flux of the tide, for all lawful purposes; and that the king could not grant the shore so as to supersede or to deprive the public of the exercise of that right over the sea shore. And it was further contended, that even if the public right was not so extensive, yet that, at all events, the king's subjects had a right of bathing on the sea shore, so that it be exercised in such a way as is conformable to decency; and that they had also, as incident thereto, a right to pass over the sea shore, not merely on foot, but with horses and carriages; that is to say, with bathing machines for that purpose, whether the sea shore belonged to the king as public property, or to any individual, as being now or even immemorially private property; and that such public right could not be superseded by the king's grant of the sea shore as private property. And the earliest authority cited for this purpose was from *Bracton*, who copied it from the civil law. But whatever may be found to be the civil law upon this subject, and whatever may have been stated by some of our law writers from the civil law, or may be found to have dropped as dicta from some of our judges; yet it appears, I think, that the civil law, as applicable to this subject, differs from the common law of *England;* that its principles have not only not been adopted into the common law, but are at variance with it, and are therefore no guide to us; that the public right, to the extent claimed in this case, is not only not found to be established by our law, but that the established principles of our law are inconsistent with it. The question is with regard to the shore; that is to say, the land between the high and low-water mark, and according to lord *Hale's* definition of the sea shore, between those marks at ordinary tides, that is to say, between the ordinary flux and reflux of the sea.

In *Bracton*, *l.* 1. *c.* 12. *s.* 6. it is thus laid down; "*Publici vero sunt omnia flumina et portus, ideoque jus piscandi omnibus commune est in portu et in fluminibus. Riparum etiam usus publicus est jure gentium, sicut ipsius fluminis. Itaque naves ad eas applicare, funes arboribus ibi natis religare, onus aliquod in iis reponere, cuivis liberum est, sicut per ipsum fluvium navigare; sed proprietas earum, illorum est, quorum prædiis adhærent et eadem de causa arbores in eisdem natæ eorundem sunt. Sed hæc intelligenda sunt, de fluminibus per-*

ennibus; quia temporalia possunt esse privata." This passage is quite general, and is not confined to tide or navigable rivers. The doctrine as to the banks of rivers, is contrary to the case of *Ball* v. *Herbert*, 3 *T. R.* 261. respecting the right of towing paths, where lord *Kenyon* says, "That there is such a custom on most of the navigable rivers no person doubts, but still the right was founded solely on the custom." And there the court determined against the general common law right claimed. It is, indeed, supported by the dicta of lord *Holt*, in *Young* v. ———, 3 *T. R.* 261. and *Rex* v. *Cluworth*, 1 *Ld. Raym.* 725. 6 *Mod.* 163. in the former of which cases he ruled, "that every man, of common right, may justify the going of his servants or his horses upon the banks of navigable rivers, for towing barges, to whomsoever the right of the soil belongs:" and in the latter, "that if one has land adjoining on a common river, every one that uses that river, has, if occasion be, a right to a way by brink of water over that land, or further in if necessary." But both these authorities were cited and commented on in the case of *Ball* v. *Herbert*, and expressly overruled by the court. The passage in *Bracton* is taken from *Justinian*, *Inst. lib.* 2. *tit.* 1. *ss.* 2. 4. and is in his very words, except with the addition of the last sentence. But besides the difference between our law and the civil law, in regard to what is even there laid down by *Bracton*, the variance between the common law and the civil law in other respects, as to marine properties and rights, shows, that the civil law cannot be any guide, or afford any illustration to us in these matters; and therefore, though *Justinian* in *s.* 1. of that book and title, says, "*Nemo igitur ad littus maris accedere prohibetur;*" yet his doctrine cannot have any weight or authority in that respect with us, unless it be found to be confirmed or adopted by our own lawyers, and particularly, if it be found, not to be consistent with, and conformable to the doctrines and principles of the common law. That there is this great difference between the civil and the common law, will appear from stating what is laid down in *Justinian*, in some of the other sections of that book and title, in comparing it with what is undoubtedly the common law, as to that species of property. In *Justinian*, the shore is thus defined, "*Est autem littus maris quatenus hybernus fluctus maximus excurrit.*" By the common law, we know it is confined to the flux and reflux of the sea at ordinary tides. In *Justinian*, this is laid down, *De usu et proprietate littorum, s. 5.* "*Littorum quoque usus publicus est et juris gentium, sicut et ipsius maris; et ob id cuilibet liberum est casam ibi ponere in quam se recipiat, sicut retia siccare, et ex mari deducere: Proprietas autem eorum potest intelligi nullius esse, sed ejusdem juris esse, cujus et mare, et quæ subjacet mari terra vel arena.*" By the common law, no such right exists in the public of erecting on the sea shore any building for drying their nets; and instead of the property in the shore being in no one, it is, *prima facie*, in the king, and may be in a subject; and so may even an arm of the sea, a *districtus maris*, as *Hale, De jure maris, p.* 31. says, "a place in the sea between such points, or a particular part contiguous to the shore, or a port, or creek, or arm of the sea;" though, as he also there lays it down, in the main sea itself, adjacent to his dominions, the king only hath the propriety, but a subject hath not, and indeed cannot have that property in the sea through the whole tract of it, that the king hath, because, without a regular power, he cannot possibly possess it. So by the civil law, *s.* 18. "*Lapilli et gemmæ et cetera quæ in littore maris inveniuntur jure naturali statim inventoris fiunt.*" By our law, we know that wrecks and things found upon the sea shore do not belong to the finder, but where the owner cannot be discovered, to the king or his grantee, or to some other person by prescription which presupposes such grant. So by the civil law, *s.* 22. "*Insula quæ in mari est, quod raro accidit,* (here he is speaking of an island newly rising from the sea,) *occupantis fit; nullius enim esse creditur.*" Lord *Hale, De jure maris, p.* 36. shows how the common law differs from this, "As touching islands arising in the sea, or in the arms, or creeks, or havens thereof, the same rule holds which is before observed, touching acquests, by the reliction or recess of the sea, or such arms or creeks thereof. Of common right and *prima facie*, it is true, they belong to the Crown; but where the interest of such *districtus maris*, or arm of the sea, or creek, or haven, doth, in point of propriety, belong to a subject, either by charter or prescription, the island that happen within the precincts of such private propriety of a subject, will belong to the subject, according to the limits and extents of such propriety."

By the common law, all the king's subjects have in general a right of passage over the sea with their ships, boats, and other vessels, for the purposes of navigation, commerce, trade, and intercourse, and also in navigable rivers; and they have also, *prima facie*, a common fishery there; but they may be excluded from the latter right, though not now by charter, at least by immemorial custom or prescription. These rights are noticed by lord *Hale;* but whatever further rights, if any, they may have in the sea, or in navigable rivers, it is a very different question whether they have, or how far they have, independently of necessity or usage, public rights upon the shore, (that is to say, between the high and low-water mark,) when it is not sea, or covered with water, and especially when it has from time immemorial been, or has since become private property. For the purpose of the king's subjects getting upon the sea, and upon the navigable rivers, to exercise their unquestionable rights of commerce, intercourse, and fishing, there are not only the ports of the kingdom, established from time to time by the king's prerogative, and called by lord *Hale* the *Ostia Regni;* but also public places for embarking and landing themselves and their goods. It was not by the common law, nor is it by statute, lawful to come with or land or ship customable goods in creeks or havens, or other places out of the ports, unless in cases of danger or necessity, nor fish or land other goods not customable, where the shore or the land adjoining is private property, unless upon the person's own soil, or with the leave of the owner thereof, who, lord *Hale* says, may, in such case, take amends for the trespass in unloading upon his ground, though he may not take it as a certain common toll; because, for so doing, it appears in lord *Hale's* Treatise *De portibus maris, p.* 51. that one *Morgan* was fined one hundred marks. No such amends could be taken, if there was a public right of coming there for that purpose in particular, or for purposes in general. In a case of necessity (as lord *Hale*, in his Treatise *De portibus maris, p.* 53. says) either of stress of weather, assault, or pirates, or want of provisions, any ship might put into any creek or haven. And he then further says, "In case of necessity, and for the supply of fishermen, all places were, to that purpose and end, ports:" that is, for the purpose of finding provisions for ships and mariners. This is not consistent with the general right contended for, as being in the public, of coming on the shore for their purposes in general, as and when they please. It is said, indeed, in *Fitzh. Barre*, 93. which cites 8 *Ed.* 4. 19. "*Nota* by *Danby, A. Puisne, Judge of C. P.* That the fishers who fish in the sea may justify their going upon the land adjoining to the sea, because such fishery is for the commonwealth, and for the sustenance of all the kingdom; wherefore this is the common law, which was granted, &c." But in *Bro. Abr. Customs*, 46. the same case is more fully stated, where the doctrine appears to have been laid down on a question which arose upon a custom. That was trespass for digging land; and the defendant pleaded, that it was four acres adjoining to the sea, and that all the men of *Kent*, from time immemorial, have used, when they have fished in the sea, to dig in the land adjoining and pitch stakes for hanging their nets to dry. *Nele, Counsel.* He ought to show what men. *Choke, C. J. of C. P.* and *Littleton, J. of C. P.* This is not the custom, for it is against common right and reason. *Danby, J. of C. P.* Fishers may justify going upon the land to fish, for this is commonwealth, and for the sustenance of man, and is the common law, which was granted. *Fairfax, Counsel.* "Dig ging is destruction of the inheritance, therefore it is not a custom, &c." But this appears more fully still by recurring to the year-book itself, and lord *Hale*, *De portibus maris*, 86. treats it as arising upon a custom; for he there says, "Look at the book of 8 *Ed.* 4. 18. for the custom of *Kent*, for fishermen to dry their nets upon the land, though it be the soil of private men." The case, as stated in the year-books, 8 *Ed.* 4. 18. 19. after stating the pleadings as in *Broke*, proceeds as follows: *Nele.* He hath said that the men have used, &c. and this is not a good prescription, being, he ought to show who, &c. *Choke.* This custom cannot be good; for it is against common right to prescribe to dig in my land; but there are other customs, which are used throughout the whole land, and such customs are lawful; as of innkeepers, &c. and also a neighbor negligently keeping his fire, &c. and such customs are good, &c. *Littleton.* A custom which runs through the whole land is the common law, as the cases that you have put are, &c.; and, Sir, such customs, which may stand with reason, shall be suffered, as in the case where the younger son ought to inherit; for there is a reason for this, &c. But this custom is against reason; for if he may dig in one place, he may dig in another place; and so, if a man hath a meadow adjoining the sea, they may, by such custom, destroy all the meadow, which would not be reasonable. *Dandy.* Those who are fishers in the sea may justify their going on the land adjoining to the sea; for such fishery is for the commonwealth, and for the sustenance of all the realm, &c.; wherefore this is common law, *quod fuit concessum.* (This, it may be observed, as far as it extends to the land above high-water mark, is contrary to *Ball* v. *Herbert*, unless where it is founded on custom. Such a custom may be good where a right to dig is not claimed, or the doing so may be justified under such circumstances as I shall afterwards state from lord *Hale.*) *Choke.* If I have land adjoining to the sea, so that the sea ebbs and flows on my land, when it flows, every one may fish in the water which has flowed on my land, for then it is parcel of the sea, and in the sea every one may fish of common right, &c.; and Sir, when the sea is ebbed, then in this land, which was flowed before, peradventure he may justify his digging, &c.; for this land is of no great profit to me, &c." It, therefore, clearly appears that this case proceeded entirely upon a particular custom, and the doctrine laid down by *Choke*, C. J. may be true, where there is such a custom; and such a custom, confined to the sea shore, may perhaps be good; but, if founded solely on the common law, is inconsistent with many passages in lord *Hale*. By the common law, though the shore, that is to say, the soil betwixt the ordinary flux and reflux of the tide, as well as the sea itself, belongs to the king; yet it is true that the same are also, *prima facie, publici juris*, or clothed with a public interest. But this *jus publicum* appears from lord *Hale*, to be the public right in all the king's subjects, of navigation for the purposes of commerce, trade, intercourse; and also the liberty of fishing in the sea, or the creeks or arms thereof, which lord *Hale*, *De Jure Maris*, *p*. 11. says, the common people of *England* have regularly, as a public common of pischary, and which, he says, they may not, without injury to their right, be restrained of, unless in such places, creeks, or navigable rivers where either the king or some particular subject has granted a propriety, exclusive of that common liberty. Neither in lord *Hale's* treatise, nor elsewhere, does it appear that there is a common law right in the king's subjects in general, or any of them, to appropriate the sea shore, or the soil even below the low-water mark, for general purposes, though temporary only, for their own use, without the king's grant or license, even where that can be done without nuisance to his subjects. Such an appropriation by any of the king's subjects, without his grant or license, though it were not in law a nuisance, would be (see lord *Hale*, *De Portibus Maris*, 85.) where the soil remains the king's, a purpresture, and encroachment, and intrusion upon the king's soil, which he may either demolish or seize, or rent, at his pleasure: and though it were even by building below the low-water mark, it would not, as lord *Hale* there says, be, *ipso facto*, a common nuisance, unless it be a damage to the port or navigation; but where it is a common nuisance, as he also there says, even the king himself cannot license it. This shows that by the common law the king's subjects have not a general right of using or appropriating the soil of the sea shore, or of the sea itself, as they please, even where the soil remains the king's, clothed with the *jus publicum*, and where that use or appropriation is effected in such a manner as not to be a nuisance to the public right of others.

But, further, such a general public right in all the king's subjects, to use the sea shore for all such temporary purposes as they please, would be, I think, inconsistent with the nature of permanent private property, or with the sea shore becoming such permanent private property. If, therefore, the right of bathing, and the right of passing over the sea shore on foot and with carriages, claimed as incident thereto, be claimed under the supposed general right of the public to use the sea, and the shore, for all such temporary legal purposes as they may please, such a public right of general appropriation is inconsistent with the fact of the *locus in quo* being private property, and of the fishing therein being also a private exclusive right, as stated in the case. And if the right of bathing, and of the incident foot and carriage way claimed for that purpose, cannot be established under such a general claim of right as I have before stated, it can only be supported under the specific claim of a public right of bathing, and of a carriage way, as incident thereto; for to that extent it must be established, in order to entitle the defendant to the judgment of the court. And then, I ask, where is such a right of bathing on the sea shore, where it has become private property, and may immemorially have been so, and of a carriage way for that purpose as incident thereto, when sought for, to be found as existing at the common law, independently of usage and custom; a right too which is here claimed beyond the extent of the usage actually found in the case?

Where the soil remains the king's, and where no mischief or injury is likely to arise from the enjoyment or exercise of such a public right, it is not to be supposed that an unnecessary and injurious restraint upon the subjects would, in that respect, be enforced by the king, the *parens patriæ*. Where there is, and has hitherto been, a necessity, or even urgency, for such a right, it must, or most probably will have, usage and custom in the place to support, regulate, limit, and modify it; for, whenever there has been a necessity for it, there, as far as such necessity has existed, some usage must have prevailed.

In *Ball* v. *Herbert*, 3 *T. R.* 261. lord *Kenyon*, in speaking of common law rights, says, "Common law rights are either to be found in the opinions of lawyers delivered as axioms, or to be collected from the universal and immemorial usage throughout the country." And *Ashurst*, J. says, "It seems extraordinary (if there be any such right) that it is not defined with greater certainty in any of our law books: for it is a right that in its nature must, if it existed, be subject to some restrictions, as, that it should be exercised only on one, and that the most convenient side of the river; for it would, in many instances, be a very oppressive right, if it could be claimed on both sides." And *Buller*, J. says, "This being claimed as a common law right, it can only be proved to exist by one of the means mentioned by my lord, as to general usage throughout the kingdom, of which the court is obliged to take notice: that clearly does not exist. Then the question is, whether in our books, or on records, that right is established for which the defendant contends. The case in lord *Raymond* is a very loose and inaccurate note. Another authority cited is a passage in *Bracton*, and quoted by *Callis*: that plainly appears to have been taken from *Justinian*, and is only part of the civil law; and whether or not that has been adopted by the common law, is to be seen by looking into our books, and there it is not to be found." The present claim, to the extent to which it is necessary to establish it on the part of the defendant, is not, therefore, as it appears to me, supported either by necessity, by general usage of the realm, which forms the common law, or by special usage in the particular place; nor is it to be found in our law books; nor, if it were, would it follow that it was such a common law right as might not, by prescription at least, be otherwise appropriated. That general common law rights are frequently so appropriated, we all know to be the fact; and that this may lawfully be established, by prescription at least, will appear from authority. The public common law rights, too, with respect to the sea, &c. independently of usage, are rights upon the water, not upon the land, of passage and fishing on the sea, and on the sea shore, when covered with water; and though, as incident thereto, the public must have the means of getting to and upon the water for those purposes, yet it will appear that it is by and from such places only as necessity or usage have appropriated to those purposes, and not a general right of lading, unlading, landing, or embarking where they please upon the sea shore, or the land adjoining thereto, except in case of peril or necessity. In *Carter* v. *Murcott*, 4 *Burr*, 2162. *Yates*, J. (speaking of a prescription for a several fishery, claimed in a navigable river,) says, "Such a right may be proved. By the law of *England*, what is otherwise common, may, by prescription be appropriated." *Grotius* owns that navigable rivers may be appropriated. The case of *The Royal Salmon Fishery in the River Banne*, in Sir *John Davis' Reports*, is agreeable to this; and it is a very good case."

Many passages in lord *Hale's Treatise* are inconsistent with the existence of such a general right of bathing, and of a passage over the shore with carriages, at common law, as is here claimed, and show that whatever the general public rights are, that they are only such as are upon and in the water, and not upon the dry land, unless in places sanctioned by usage, whether they be parts of the shore or not; at least, that they exist not upon the land, when not covered with water, where it has become private property, and, more especially, where it has immemorially been private or special property. I shall state a few of those passages. It appears from lord *Hale*, that the king may license the erecting of quays, or other buildings, on the sea coasts, even below the low-water mark, where they are not in fact annoyances or nuisances, *Hale*, *De portibus maris*, 85.; so wears, *Hale* 22. *De jure maris*. As to making of ports, and the threefold right therein, especially the right of an individual subject, by charter or prescription, in a port, and previously in a creek or haven, particularly in bringing in his own goods, where he is owner of the soil, *Hale*, 72, 73. As to the owner's right to improve the shore, it is laid down that the king cannot grant a right to lade or unlade on the ripa or bank, without the owner's consent; there cannot, therefore, be any common law right to lade or unlade on the quay or shore, or land adjacent in the port, *Hale*, 51, 76. Evidence to prove the shore parcel of a manor, &c. disproves the general right of all the king's subjects on the shore, at least when and where it is not covered with water. So, as to having the right of royal fish and wreck, it is a great presumption that the shore is part of the manor, or otherwise he could not have them, *Hale*, 26, 27. Now, this would not be the case, if the king's subjects had a prior general right to come when they pleased upon the shore. These passages from lord *Hale*, appear to me to be inconsistent with the general right contended for, independently of custom, for all the king's subjects to come as and when they please upon the shore, particularly where it has been either from time immemorial, or where it has since become private or special property, especially where it is not covered with the tide or water. Lord *Hale* notices and establishes the public right of navigating and fishing upon and in the water, and the right of resort to the ports, and of lading and unlading, landing and embarking therein, either at the public places appointed or by usage established for those purposes, or with consent, upon the land, either of the king or of individuals, but no further. This right of bathing, and of a carriage way, as incident thereto, is no where noticed; and it does not, I think, exist by the common law upon the *locus in quo*, the private property of the plaintiff, unsupported as it is by usage and custom. I am, therefore of opinion, in this case, that the plaintiff is entitled to the judgment of the court.

Bayley, J. The question in this case is, whether there is a common law right for all the king's subjects to bathe upon the sea shore, and to pass over it for that purpose, on foot, and with horses and carriages, notwithstanding the part on which the right is claimed, is, as to its soil, vested in a particular individual, and although that individual has an exclusive right of fishing in that place with stake nets, and of driving these stakes into the soil, that they may support the nets. And I am of opinion, that there is no such common law right. By the sea shore, I understand the space between the ordinary high and low-water mark, and the property in this is, *prima facie*, in the king. It may, indeed, by grant or prescription belong to a subject, but until the contrary is shown, the presumption is, that it belongs to the king. Many of the king's rights are, to a certain extent, for the benefit of his subjects, and that is the case as to the sea, in which all his subjects have the right of navigation, and of fishing, and it is so in highways, along which all his subjects have the right of passage, and the king can make no modern grants in derogation of those rights. I have mentioned the rights of navigation and of fishing, because I can find no trace of such a right as that now claimed recognized in any of our books. It is material to distinguish between the different descriptions of rights which is for the general benefit of all the kingdom; and the public may have a right of navigation, and a right of fishing, which tends to the sustenance and beneficial employment of individuals; but it does not thence follow that they have also the right of bathing. The existence or the extent of the subject's right is to be collected, in this as in other instances, from the manner in which the sea shores throughout the kingdom have from time immemorial been used, and from legal authorities upon the subject. The right, as claimed, is not confined to any particular place, if it exists at all, but it must exist upon every part of the sea shore. Every private building, then, erected upon the sea shore, and even wharves and quays, would be an obstruction to that right, and, of consequence, abateble or indictable. And yet, in how many instances are such buildings, wharves, and quays erected? Every embankment by which land is redeemed from the sea would obstruct the exercise of this right, and be a nuisance, and so would the erection of stakes for holding nets; and yet, how frequently are such embankments made, and such stakes set up? A distinction has, indeed, been contended for between wharves and quays, and other erections for public benefit, and for the interests of trade and commerce, and erections for private purposes; but in how many instances are there buildings for private purposes on the sea shore? Where an erection is made on the sea shore without authority, the Crown may treat it as a purpresture, and prosecute it accordingly; but it has never yet been held abateable or indictable, because it happens to interfere with a supposed common law right of bathing. Indeed, this is the first time, as far as I can learn, that such a right was ever stated upon any pleadings, or contended for in any court of law; and the inconveniences which would result from such a right afford to my mind a strong argument against its existence. In sea bathing, as it now prevails, particular regulations are desirable; the restriction of particular machines to particular spots; a separation of those which are for men from those which are for females; and the prevention of contests as to particular situations. Bathers who do not use machines should be in places of greater privacy, and at a distance from those parts which are generally used for the recreation of walking; and yet the existence of this common law right would be a great obstruction to any such regulations. Indeed, if an individual had the grant of the sea shore from the Crown, and were using it for recreation or bathing, he or his family might be interrupted and deprived of all privacy by the exercise of this common law right. Let it be observed, too, that the whole shore cannot be necessary for the exercise of this supposed right, and that it may be desirable to apply parts of the sea shore to other purposes. The king, for the public welfare, may suffer such a right to be exercised in those parts of the shore which remain in his hands to any extent which the convenience of the public may require; but may he not also allow other rights to be exercised on other parts? If the soil is vested in an individual, is he to be deprived of the right of saying how that soil shall be used, and of the privilege of making any regulations he may think fit? In those places in which convenience has required the right, and it has continued from the time of legal memory, there will be a right by custom; and, where that is not the case, the Crown, or its grantees, are not likely to withhold it, upon proper terms, and under proper regulations. The case of *Bagott* v. *Orr*, 2 *Bos. & Pul.* 472. seems to me to conclude nothing on the right in question. The defendant there justified trespassing on the rocks and sands lying within the flowing and reflowing of the tide, on the ground that every subject of the realm had the liberty and privilege of getting and taking away shell-fish and shells which had been left there by the tide. The general right of the public to take fish of the sea was admitted in argument; but the right to take shells cast on the shore was denied; and it was insisted, besides, that the general right was excluded where the shore was parcel of a manor. The court thought that the plaintiff should have replied specially to have raised the question as to excluding the general right; but they thought the claim as to the shells so questionable, that they offered the defendant leave to amend, by confining his claim to the sea fish, and that offer the defendant accepted. The claim, therefore, in that case, was very different from the present; it was a claim for something serving to the sustenance of man, not a matter of recreation only,—a claim to take, when left by the water, what every subject had an undoubted right to have taken whilst they remained in the water; and upon that claim there was no regular judgment. But it would by no means follow because all the king's subjects have a right to pick up fish on the shore, that they have, therefore, a right to pass over the sea shore for the purpose of bathing. The passages cited from lord *Hale's* treatise, *De jure maris*, *p* 22. and 36. in which it is laid down, "that the *jus privatum* that is acquired to the subject, either by patent or prescription, must not prejudice the *jus publicum*, wherewith public rivers or arms of the sea are affected for public use;" leave the question untouched; because the question in this is, what the *jus publicum* is: and that they do not define. Had lord *Hale* stated as part of the *jus publicum*, that the public might use the shore as they thought fit; that they might use it as a public highway, or for the purpose of bathing; then those passages would have been authorities applicable to this case. But lord *Hale*, in fact, only states that the *jus publicum* continues to exist, without defining what it is. *Bracton*, in *l.* 1. *c.* 12. *s.* 6. does state what the *jus publicum* is; and if that passage be good law, it is strong authority in favor of the defendant. The passage is as follows: "*Publica vero sunt omina flumina et portus. Ideoque jus piscandi omnibus commune est in portu et in fluminibus.*" Now, he does not even say navigable rivers, but I will assume that by *fluminibus* is meant navigable rivers, and so far as I have cited the passage, I concur in what is there laid down; but he goes on; "*Riparum etiam usus publicus est jure gentium sicut ipsius fluminis.*" That is, that the public have the same right to use the banks of the river that they have to use the river itself, and that, because the water is common to all mankind, the ripa is also common to all mankind. The passage then goes on, "*Itaque naves ad eas applicare, funes arboribus ibi natis relegare, onus aliquod in iis reponere, cuivis liberum est, sicut per ipsum fluvium navigare.*" The word "ripa" here applies to rivers and ports, and probably, also, to the land above the high-water mark; and, if it does, is this the law of *England?* Have all persons a right to fasten a ship to the banks of a river, or have they a right to tie ropes to the trees, or to land goods on the bank of every navigable river?

The case of *Ball* v. *Herbert*, 3 *Term Rep.* 262. is not a distinct authority upon this point, inasmuch, as in that case, the right of towing was claimed. But the general question as to the right of the public on the ripa of a navigable river was discussed, and the court appear to have been of opinion, that the ripa of a navigable river was not *publici juris*, and they therefore virtually overruled the authority of *Bracton*. Lord *Hale*, in his treatise, *De portibus maris*, *p.* 84. after citing this passage says, "as touching ports, and the public right of them, *Bracton* saith true; with this allay, that hath been before observed, that the law of *England* doth thus far abridge that common liberty of ports, that no port can be erected without the license or charter of the king, or that which presumes and supplies it, *viz.* custom and prescription." But in another passage, *page* 73. lord *Hale* says, "Though *A.* may have the propriety of a creek or harbor, or navigable river, yet the king may grant there the liberty of a port to *B.* and so the interest of the propriety, and the interest of the franchise, several and divided. And in this, no injury is at all done to *A.* for he hath what he had before, *viz.* the interest of the soil, and consequently the improvement of the shore, and the liberty of fishing; and as the creek was free for any one to pass in it against all but the king, (for it was *publici juris*, as to the matter before,) so now the king takes off that restraint, and by his license and charter, makes it free for all to come and unlade. But if *A.* hath the ripa or bank of the port, the king may not grant a liberty to unlade upon that bank or ripa without his consent, unless custom had made the liberty thereof free to all, as in many places it is; for that would be a prejudice to the private interest of *A.* which may not be taken from him without such consent." There may perhaps be a distinction between the ripa of the river where the soil has been long private property, and that space between the high and low-water mark, where the sea ebbs and flows, but if there be such a distinction what becomes of the authority of *Bracton*, where he says, "*Riparum etiam usus publicus, est jure gentium sicut ipsius fluminis*." No man can travel through this kingdom along the banks of rivers, without seeing that private rights, exclusive of public rights, exist there, and every one of those rights is at variance with the doctrine of *Bracton*, and with the supposed common law right now claimed. The practice of bathing may contribute to health, but it ought to be confined within reasonable limits, and it is by no means necessary, that the right should be co-extensive with the whole shore of the sea, or that it should extend to places where the right of fishing with stake nets exists. In the absence of any authority, to show that such right exists, and thinking that the authorities cited do not establish it, and that it would be attended with great inconvenience to the public, if a general right, free from all regulation by the owner of the soil was to be exercised throughout the whole of the kingdom, I am of opinion, that no such right exists, and consequently, that there ought to be judgment for the plaintiff.

ABBOTT, C. J. I have considered this case with very great attention, from the respect I entertain on this and all other occasions for the opinion of my learned brother *Best*, though I had no doubt upon the question when it was first presented to me; nor did the defendant's counsel raise any doubt in my mind by his learned and ingenious argument. This is an action of trespass, brought against the defendant for passing with carriages from some place above high-water mark across that part of the shore which lies between the high and low-water mark, for the conveyance of persons to and from the water for the purpose of bathing. The plaintiff is the undoubted owner of the soil of this part of the shore, and has the exclusive right of fishing thereon with stake nets. The defendant does not rely upon any special custom or prescription for his justification, but insists on a common law right for all the king's subjects to bathe on the sea shore, and to pass over it for that purpose on foot, and with horses and carriages; and this right is the only matter which, by the terms of the special case, is submitted to the opinion of the court. Now, if such a common law right existed, there would probably be some mention of it in our books; but none is found in any book, ancient or modern. If the right exist now, it must have existed at all times; but we know that sea bathing was, until a time comparatively modern, a matter of no frequent occurrence, and that the carriages, by which the practice has been facilitated and extended, are of comparatively modern invention.

There being no authority in favor of the affirmative of the question, in the terms in which it is proposed, it has been placed in argument at the bar on a broader ground; and as the waters of the sea are open to the use of all persons for all lawful purposes, it has been contended, as a general proposition, that there must be an equally universal right of access to them, for all such purposes, over land like the present. If this could be established, the defendant must undoubtedly prevail; because, bathing in the waters of the sea is, generally speaking, a lawful purpose. But, in my opinion, there is no sufficient ground, either in authority or in reason, to support this general proposition.

Commerce is a matter greatly favored in our law, by reason of the public and national benefits derived from it; but, even as to this favored matter, I have found no authority in the law of *England* in support of such a proposition. *Bracton*, in the passage so often referred to, speaks not of the waters of the sea generally, but of ports and navigable rivers. It may be admitted, that whatever is true of navigable rivers and their banks, may be true of the sea and of its shore. But the case of *Ball* v. *Herbert*, 3 *T. R.* 261. shows that the doctrine of *Bracton*, as to the banks of the navigable rivers, however warranted by the civil law, is not conformable to the law of *England*. "And as touching ports, and the public right to them," says lord *Hale*, *p.* 84. "*Bracton* saith true: but, with this allay, that the law of *England* doth thus far abridge that common liberty of ports, that no port can be erected without the license or charter of the king, or that which presumes and supposes it, *viz.* custom and prescription." So that even the privilege to be derived from ports cannot be in its nature universal. And, as to ports, lord *Hale*, *ch.* 6. *p.* 73. distinguishes between the interest of property and the interest of franchise, and says, that "if *A.* hath the ripa or bank of the port, the king cannot grant liberty to unlade on the bank or ripa without his consent, unless custom hath made the liberty thereof free to all, as in many places it is." Now, such consent as applied to the natural state of the ripa or bank would be wholly unnecessary, if every man had a right to land his goods on every part of the shore at his pleasure. And, if there be no general right to unlade merchandize on the shore, there can be no right to traverse the shore with carriages or otherwise for the purpose of unlading; and, consequently, the general proposition to which I have alluded cannot be maintained as a legitimate conclusion from the general right to navigate the water. I have spoken of merchandize, and not of fish; from the latter I studiously abstain, because no question of that kind is before the court, and it is unnecessary to say any thing upon it. It will be remembered, also, that I speak only of the general right, which is a matter perfectly distinct from those cases of necessity that often arise out of the perils of navigation. Having thus shown that the general proposition cannot, in my opinion, be maintained, I return to the particular right or privilege claimed in the present case.

One of the topics urged at the bar in favor of this supposed right, was that of public convenience. Public convenience, however, is, in all cases, to be viewed with a due regard to private property, the protection whereof is one of the distinguishing characteristics of the law of *England.* It is true, that property of the description of the present is, in general, of little value to its owner; but I do not know how that little is to be protected, and much less how it is ever to be increased, if such a general right be established. If there be a general right of passage across land of this description in the nature of a highway, by what law are stake nets, or other implements of fishing, to be placed there, or sand or stones to be taken away, whereby the exercise of the right which, as claimed, will, in its universality, extend itself over every part of the surface, may be obstructed, or rendered less convenient? By what law can any wharf or quay be made? These, in order to be useful, must be below the high-water mark, that vessels or boats may float to them when the tide is in; but when the tide is out, no carriage can pass them. In some parts of the coast, where the ground is nearly level, the tide ebbs to a great distance, and leaves dry very considerable tracts of land. In such situations, thousands of acres have, at different times, been gained from the sea and its arms, by embankments, and converted to pasture or tillage. But how could such improvements have been made, or how can they be made hereafter, without the destruction or infringement of this supposed right? And, it is to be observed, that wharves, quays, and embankments, and intakes from the sea, are matters of public as well as private benefit.

Another topic relied upon by the defendant, was usage and practice. The practice of modern times can be considered, at the utmost, in the nature only of evidence, more or less cogent according to its extent and uniformity. I am not aware of any practice, in this matter, sufficiently extensive or uniform to be the foundation of a judicial decision. It was said at the bar, that in some places a compensation is made to the owner of the shore; but I do not rely on this assertion as a ground of judgment. In many places, doubtless, nothing is paid. In some parts, the king is the owner of the shore; and it is not probable that any obstruction would be interposed on his behalf to such a practice. Of private owners, some may not have thought it worth while to advance any claim or opposition; others may have had too much discretion to put their title to the soil to the hazard of a trial by an unpopular claim to a matter of little value; others, and probably the greater part, may have derived or expected so much benefit from the increased value given to their own land above, by the erection of houses and the resort of company, that their own interest may have induced them to acquiesce in, and even to encourage the practice, as a matter indirectly profitable to themselves. But, further, the practice, as far at least as I am acquainted with it, differs in degree only, and not in kind or quality, from that which prevails as to some inland wastes and commons; and even the difference in degree is, in some instances, not very great. Many of those persons who reside in the vicinity of wastes and commons, walk or ride on horseback, in all directions, over them, for their health and recreation; and sometimes, even in carriages, deviate from the public paths into those parts which may be so traversed with safety. In the neighborhood of some frequented watering places, this practice prevails to a very great degree; yet no one ever thought that any right existed in favor of this enjoyment, or that any justification could be pleaded to an action at the suit of the owner of the soil.

The only remaining topic adduced for the defendant was, that the right may be considered as confined to those instances only wherein it can be exercised without actual prejudice to the owner of the shore, and subject to all modes of present use, or future improvement, on his part; but no instance of any public right, so limited and qualified, has been found. Every public right to be exercised over the land of an individual is, *pro tanto*, a diminution of his private rights and enjoyments, both present and future, so far as they may at any time interfere with or obstruct the public right.

But, shall the owner of the soil be allowed to bring an action against any person who may drive his carriage along these parts of the sea shore, whereby not the smallest injury is done to the owner? The law has provided suitable checks to frivolous and vexatious suits; and, in general, experience shows that the owners of the shore do not trouble themselves or others for such matters. But where one man endeavors to make his own special profit by conveying persons over the soil of another, and claims a public right to do so, as in the present case, it does not seem to me that he has any just reason to complain, if the owner of the soil shall insist upon participating in the profit, and endeavor to maintain his own private right, and preserve the evidence thereof. For these reasons, I am of opinion that there is not any such common law right as the defendant has claimed.

Judgment for the plaintiff.

EXAMINATION

OF THE

TITLE OF THE UNITED STATES,

TO THE LAND CALLED

THE BATTURE.

BY EDWARD LIVINGSTON, ESQ.

THIS title is supported—

First. By an incorrect and imperfect statement of facts.

Second. By an assumption, that the question is to be decided according to the principles of the *French*, not those of the Imperial or *Spanish* law.

Third. By an erroneous statement of that law.

The whole fabric of this imaginary title is founded upon the statement which supposes that in the year 1763, the sales of the *Jesuits'* property were made only to the road, and that they were bounded by a front line running on the inside of the levee and road. It will be clearly demonstrated that this position is totally unsupported; but that the contrary, to wit, that the sale of the *Jesuits'* property under which we claim, were bounded on *the river*.

In order to understand fully this point, it is necessary to remark that all the grants made by the *French* or *Spanish* governments, without, as it is believed, any exception, were bounded *by the river*, but all expressed under the general terms *face au fleuve*, or *face sur le fleuve*, or sometimes under the more general terms *face* alone, which, according to the testimony of all the surveyors, related to the place on which the lands were laid out, as the *river, bayou, &c.* So that if the lands lay on a *river* or *bayou*, the word *face* alone would, according to the general construction of the country, give a front on the *river* or *bayou*, unless there were some restrictive words which expressed the intention of the parties to be different.

It appears as well by testimony as by the express admission of the parties in this cause, that the *soil of this road* was not reserved to the king, but merely the *use of it*, vested in the public, since the proprietor made and changed it at his pleasure, as the encroachment or alluvion of the river, or as his own convenience required. There is every reason to believe that the grant to the *Jesuits* was in the usual form and was bounded by the river, but we are not left to presumption on this point. Though the original grants to the *Jesuits* be lost, yet in the proceedings which took place in the year 1763, preparatory to their division and sale, we find a certificate of the proper officer to the following effect:

"In the year 1763, on the 14th day of *July*, we the undersigned, counsellor of the king, inspector of the roads, and surveyor general of the province of *Louisiana*, certify that by virtue of the orders of Mr. *Dobadie*, commissary-general of the navy &c. dated this 13th instant, by which we were directed to transport ourselves to the habitations of the persons calling themselves *Jesuits*, &c. there to examine the titles and papers relative to the possessions of the aforesaid persons, which we found *ought to contain thirty-two arpents of front on the river St. Louis.*" And in the same proceedings, is a lease made by the *Jesuits* of a part of their land in which the leasee binds himself to make the levee and the road.

The original grant then was like all others bounded by the river, and the defendants in their case have taken pains to state that the batture or alluvion then existed. This perhaps was the fact,* but to a very inconsiderable extent. But this will make no difference in the case; for if there was an alluvion in the year 1763, whether it had prior to that belonged to the king or to the *Jesuits*, at that period the whole plantation with its batture became the property of the Crown by the forfeiture of the *Jesuits'* estate, and the king at that time ordered the estate, to be divided and sold....Did he grant the *whole?* or did he reserve the batture and the road?

Let us examine this point—

By the proceedings before referred to, it appears to have been the intention to divide and sell "all the said lands."

By the adjudication it is granted, with "all its members and appertenances without *reserving any thing*:" by the adjudication of the sixth lot (the farthest extremity of the land and not now in dispute) one acre was reserved to the king, so that it appears whenever the king wished to retain any part, his officers took care to insert the reservation in the deed.

Besides this, it is stated in the case, and proved on the trial, that governor *Carondelet* had at three several times directed *Gravier* to make the road and the levee, once by a letter which not only ordered him to repair the levee, but carries some evidence of his having done it before, because he speaks of his "*known exactitude.*" Now if the road and levee were reserved to the king, what had *Gravier* to do with working it? or if the road and levee were not comprehended in the sale of the *Jesuits'* property, and as they allege in this case, had been constantly considered as part of the demesne, how is it that *Baron de Carondelet* was ignorant of this circumstance?

It was therefore clearly the intention of the king not to re-

* Recent discoveries have made it probable that a great part of the land lying outside the levee, which was called alluvion by the witnesses, was really as much original soil as any other part of the country, since in digging a canal since the judgment, the stumps of a grove of cotton trees have been discovered in their natural position about three feet under ground, and measuring two feet in diameter.

serve any thing, but on the contrary, to sell the whole plantation, of which the alluvion formed a part. What motive could he have had for such reservation? The defendants and their counsel say, for the use of the city*—but a reservation to the Crown would have been of no use to the city, and if this had been the intent, the reservation would have been accompanied by a grant to their use. Let it also be remembered that the *Jesuits'* plantation consisted of thirty-two *arpents* in front, of which *Gravier* possessed only thirteen; the residue was sold to different persons at *the same time*, under *the same circumstances* and by the *same words* with those employed with respect to *Gravier's* part; yet the batture on the nineteen remaining acres, infinitely more extensive than that now in question, has been uninterruptedly held by the proprietors of the original soil; the public have never, that I have heard, pretended to it; nay the very persons most clamorous against my title, now hold property to a very large amount on those very battures. If, therefore, my title be defective and theirs good, we must look for the difference in something subsequent to *the sale* of the *Jesuits'* property under which we all hold.

The error (and when made by persons who so well know the customs of the country as the defendants, it deserves an harsher name;) the error, lies in representing the line always drawn in front, generally within the levee, as a front boundary; when they know, and their own witness (one of the defendants, the surveyor general of the province) stated that such front line was drawn not to mark a boundary between the plantation and the river, but to measure the extent of its front; which was always done on a direct line, and never followed the windings of the river; and that the stakes placed on the side lines were not intended to mark their extent towards the river, but to show the

* The Jesuits possessed a tract of land one league and a half above the town on the other side of the river. Unfortunately for this argument, it happens that this land is sold precisely in the same terms with those used with respect to the plantation near the city

direction of those lines, whether they opened, closed or were perpendicular to the river.

The certificates in note D. show this to have been the universal practice, in all the surveys under the *French*, *Spanish* and *American* governments.

But even if this line, contrary to the universal and uninterrupted usages of the country, to the whole course of evidence in the case, and finally, to the dictates of common sense; if contrary to all these, the line of *admeasurement* is to be turned into a line of *boundary*; yet it will avail them nothing, for it so happens that in this case the line of admeasurement crosses the levee a few toises from its commencement, and continues *on the batture outside of the levee during the whole of its course through the part now constituting the suburb St. Mary.** So that even if this notable discovery made by the corporation and their counsel be true, they will not derive from it the pleasure of disturbing *Gravier's* possession by claim from the *United States;* for their great argument of an intervening road and levee, totally fails them in this instance. But they will have the gratification of disturbing almost all the other titles in the country; for most of those lines of admeasurement are in other instances drawn within the levee and road: so that if this principle be admitted, scarcely a single plantation will be bounded by the river; and congress may make it inaccessible whenever they please to most of the inhabitants, for not one in an hundred have any exclusive possession between the road and the river.

A conclusive proof however, that the river was the front boundary of the *Jesuits'* plantation, as well since as before the division and sale of 1763, has been discovered since the trial.

Under the *French* government, a general plan was kept by the

*This appears from a map which has been carefully protracted by Mr. Lafon from the *proces verbal* of the *Jesuits'* survey; a copy of the map and *proces verbal* are filed for the inspection of those who may desire it in the office of Mr. Pedesclaux.

surveyor general, on which the lines of each concession were distinctly and accurately laid down. This was called the *Plan Terrier*, and the original or a copy was delivered to the *Spanish* surveyor general on the transfer of possession. He delivered copies of this plan to his deputies, and it was always considered by the *Spanish* government as an authentic record. On an extract of this map, which was thus delivered in 1795, the plantations above the town for the distance of about four leagues, are all delineated; in all of them the side lines extend to the river, which is laid down in every instance as the front boundary.

Among these plantations is that of the *Jesuits*—on the plan are marked the names of the persons who then held under the sales of 1763. But no such front line as Mr. *Derbigny* has imagined is found on this plan—no road as the boundary—nothing to distinguish it in this respect from the neighbouring plantations, which, as I have said, are all bounded on the river.

Yet this plan was given in 1795, at a time when the alluvion was considerable in extent, seven years after the suburb was laid out, and long after the time at which, as is now pretended, *Gravier* had abandoned his right.

This plan too, completely disproves the idea of a reservation of the front part by the sales of 1763. For it delineates, with great care and precision, the reservation of a small part near the town—designating minutely the difference between the old limits of the *Jesuits'* plantation on the side next the town, from those established in the sale of 1763. If then any reservation had been made by the king of the alluvion or land in front, would it not have been noticed with the same care as has been shown as to the lateral lines?

This document is alone so convincing that if an engraving can be prepared in time it shall be annexed to this work.

It is then I think proved—

First. That the ancient habitation of the *Jesuits* bordered on the river. And this fact is further proved by their having repeatedly changed the levee beyond Madame *Delar's*, in order to *take in* the alluvion.*

SECOND. That the sale of their property was made without any reservation.

THIRD. That by the sale of 1763, no new boundary was fixed between the front of the habitation and the river; in other words, that the several subdivisions as well as the original grant extended to the river.

It is therefore of no consequence whether there were or were not an alluvion formed at the time of the sale of the *Jesuits'* property. On either supposition, the grant going to the river gives us all within its lines, whether alluvion or original soil.

Second error in fact—

In the defendant's case, it is stated, that the batture called "the *Jesuits*" after the transfer of possession in 1767, continued to be considered as a part of the "*royal demesne;*" and as such was of public utility in supplying earth, without any claim being made to it by the proprietors or purchasers of the *Jesuits'* plantation, either before or after the cession.—And in the counsel's opinion, he says that it "never ceased to be part of the *sovereign's demesne*," and strangely asserts that "it is a fact *incontestably proved*, that neither *Jean* nor *Bertrand Gravier*, nor any of those through whom this claim is derived, ever possessed a single inch of the batture in question. It is further remarkable, that they never *set up any title* to that effect." p. 305.

It is somewhat extraordinary that this statement should be made by that very corporation, which for three years had been contending in a court of justice, that the premises belonged to the city of *New-Orleans*, and that the same counsel who during the whole of that period asserted in three several arguments, the unequivocal right of the corporation, should now as boldly pronounce that they never had any title, but that it always belonged to the *United States*.

* The existence of the old levee as well as the map above referred to, prove this fact.

Did the learned counsel give his true opinion to the corporation, when he was first called on to defend their cause?

If he did, how can the corporation justify the thousands of dollars they have expended in defence of a claim which their counsel must have told them was unjust?

Did the learned counsel suppress his true opinion, and flatter the city with the hope of gaining what he knew did not belong to them, but to the *United States?* A case not to be supposed.

Or has the learned counsel, after three years study of the cause, changed his opinion of its merits?

A revolution, then, of three other years, may perhaps prove that his second opinion was as erroneous as his first, and if the *United States* have the same confidence as the corporation, in the advice which is so kindly offered them, they may be induced to spend as many thousands as the city have done, and with equal success.

The error of this statement of facts appears—

First. By the allegation of the persons themselves, who make the statement, and those allegations, too, on record.

On the 16th of *March*, 1805, the mayor, in behalf of the city, filed a bill to perpetuate testimony in this case, in which they state, "that *Bertrand Gravier* was the owner of the plantation; that he had laid out the front part into lots, in 1788; that *after* the said lots had been sold, he considered himself as *no longer* bound to preserve the levee; that on being called on by the governor to repair the road, he declared that having converted his plantation into a fauxbourg, and sold the line of the lots on the side of the river, whatever intervened between those lots and the river belonged to the public, and was *no longer* his concern; that *in consequence of this formal relinquishment*, the *Spanish* government immediately caused the necessary repairs to be made, and the *inhabitants* of *New-Orleans have ever since*, without hindrance, &c. possessed and enjoyed the same premises, &c."

In their answer to the petition of *Jean Gravier*, the mayor, aldermen and inhabitants, repeat the same idea. After denying the right of *Jean Gravier*, they say, "that the truth is that sometime before the death of *Bertrand Gravier*, the first owner of the plantation on the front of which the suburb *St. Mary* was established, he the said *Bertrand Gravier had abandoned and himself acknowledged in an unequivocal manner to have abandoned* all the above mentioned parcel of land; that *in consequence of such abandonment*, the highway and levee have been maintained and repaired *then and afterwards*, till this moment, either by the *corvees publique*, or at the expense of the city; that *since that time* till now, the *inhabitants of this city* never ceased to have a peaceful enjoyment of the said parcel, either to place different wood-yards or for unloading flat bottomed boats and other rafts, *with permission* of the *corporation.*" And their answer concludes by avowing, that "the city council had erected a cabin on the land to lodge a guardian, and that they had caused the earth to be digged and carried away to repair the levee."

Yet with these allegations on record, in which they derive a title under *Bertrand Gravier* by virtue of an abandonment, in 1788; in which they say *the land belongs to, and is possessed by the city;* the corporation, in their statement, do not blush to assert, that the same land had continued ever since the year 1767, to be considered as part of the *royal demesne*, and that too, as they say, under the name of the "*Jesuits*' batture."

If it was royal *demesne*, how could the inhabitants of the city have enjoyed it? Was it not as strictly forbidden under the *Spanish* as under the *American* government, to intrude on the public property ? If it was royal *demesne*, how did it acquire the name of "*Jesuits' batture?*" If it was royal *demesne*, how could the corporation have the right to give *permission to the rafts and boats to unload*, or for the dealers in lumber to deposit their wood there ? Thus we see the allegation contained in the case, is not only at war with the truth, but is also expressly contradicted by the declarations of the defendants themselves *upon record*. Let us now examine the residue of this sentence, viz. "that no claim was made to the premises by the proprietors or purchasers of the *Jesuits'* property, either before or after the cession;" and the still stronger assertion of the counsel in his opinion, that it was "a fact incontestably proved that neither *Jean* nor *Bertrand Gravier*, nor any of those under whom this claim is derived, ever possessed a single inch of the batture in question. It is further remarkable that they never set up any title to that effect." I cannot comment upon the subject of this statement as it deserves, without departing from that rule of moderation which I have imposed upon myself in pursuing this enquiry: I will, therefore, simply state the proofs by which the reader will be enabled to appreciate the value of these allegations—allegations which ought to have been maturely weighed before they were hazarded by the corporation, or re-echoed by their counsel. They should have considered, not only from the regard always due to truth; but from the reflection that this case was to become the ground work of an application to the *United States*, to prosecute their claim at a great expense to them and with great inconvenience to the individuals concerned; that the doctrines contained in it, give rise to a most important and serious question, which, if resolved in the manner they seem to desire, will not only forever deprive the town of this species of property in the very city itself, but also ravish from the inhabitants all the alluvions that have been formed since the establishment of the country. It ought also perhaps to have occurred to the counsel, if not to his clients, that after the superior court had given an unanimous opinion in this important cause it was hardly treating the judges with proper candor not to state with more care the evidence upon which they pronounced. The corporation say that the purchasers of the *Jesuits'* plantation never *claimed* the batture in front of the suburb *St. Mary*; and their counsel asseverates the same thing as having been incontestibly proved. Why then in the passages I have quoted, did the corporation claim under *Gravier*, by virtue of his abandonment? Abandonment supposes right, possession, or at least claim of right. If *Gravier* never claimed, then *Gravier* never could abandon. Are the allegations of the corporation in their pleadings, or in their case to be believed? *Gravier* "never claimed," say the defendants and their counsel; yet he sold a lot on the batture on the 12th of *April*, 1794, to *C. F. Girod*, on the same day another to *Wiltz*, on the same day a third to *John Scott*, on the 12th day of *January*, 1795, two others to Mr. *Pierre Foucher:* reserving in the three first the right to dig earth for his brick-kiln. These deeds were *all on record*, were all produced on the trial, and could not have been forgotten. "*The batture was royal demesne, and Gravier never set up any claim to it.*" Yet governor *Carondelet*, in a letter dated the 10th of *March*, 1794, commands him to make the levee and compliments him on his former punctuality. He repeats this order at two different times; once by Mr. *Livaudais* and once by Mr. *Mentzinger*, and according to the uncontradicted testimony of Mr. *Segur* and Mr. *Laroche*, he thought it necessary to ask Mr. *Bertrand Gravier's* permission, and, after his death, that of *Jean Gravier*, to lay the rafts of royal masts on the batture.

What then becomes of this "fact so incontestably proved?" But I might have contented myself with the consultation itself, to show the error of its statements on this point. At page 300 of the opinion, the third position of the counsel, is, that between the alluvion and the land sold (viz. the sale in 1763) "lay a royal road, the same that still exists, and a levee, both which *were then and have still remained public property.*"

Here we find a broad assertion that the levee and the road were then, viz. 1763, and still are, public property; yet at page 305, of the same opinion, we find the old ground of *Gravier's* abandonment resorted to, and the date of the public title fixed to the laying out the fauxbourg, (1788.)

But a circumstance of "*still more weight*" (says the counsel) "is, that *Bertrand Gravier* himself, *when he converted the front of his plantation into a suburb*, declared that he considered himself discharged from the duty of repairing the roads and the levee" [what duty if the road and levee had ever since 1763 been public property? or how could he be *discharged* from a duty which according to the counsel's third position must have been always that of the public] because the front of the land was now become public property: so that *since that period*, the government and the city have been at the expense of keeping the road and the levee."

How difficult is the support of error! since even the acknowledged abilities of the learned counsel have not enabled him to write ten pages, without contradicting the witnesses, contradicting the records, and contradicting himself.

Third error in fact—

In the case stated, page 288, the defendants allege "that when the sales were made" (24th *November*, 1763) "*Louisiana* still belonged to *France*, and was under the dominion of the *French* laws." On the third day of *November*, however, in the preceding year, *Louisiana* had been ceded by *France* to *Spain*;* and although possession was not immediately taken, yet it will not be pretended that the king of *Spain* could acquire any rights

* If it should be objected that this argument injures the title of Gravier by showing that the king of France had no right to sell to those under whom he claims; there are four answers, all of them conclusive:

First—That the king of France may be considered, during the interval between the cession and the delivery of possession of the country, as only the trustee for the king of Spain; and that, therefore, all his acts, permitted and not revoked by the latter power on taking possession, are valid.

Second—That though not *de jure* yet *de facto*, France was sovereign of the country: therefore, all sales made by the actual possessor to a *bona fide* purchaser, are valid.

Third—That we are now in possession, and that the United States cannot prevail by the weakness of our title, but must show a conclusive one in themselves.

Fourth—That by the fundamental laws of Spain, the king could not acquire this species of property by virtue of the *French* laws, supposing them to be as they are stated by the defendants.

The whole then of the title in the *United States* so lately discovered, so contradictory to that which the parties who now support it, have alleged, must fall with the discovery, that at the time our title commenced, the king of *France* had abandoned the sovereignty, and of course could by virtue of this pretended prerogative claim no right to seize the alluvion, and shut out his subjects from the river on which he had bounded their grants.

Having pointed out some of the errors in fact in the defendants' statement, and shown that this cause is to be determined according to the *Spanish* laws; I ought, perhaps, from an examination of those laws to prove that they give the alluvion in all cases to the proprietor of the adjacent soil; but that point seems to be conceded, not only by implication in attempting to substitute the *French* for the *Spanish* laws, but expressly in page 303 of the opinion, where it is said that the alluvions formed since the cession, are the property of the front proprietors, by the *Spanish laws;* but to remove all doubt upon this point, I refer to the authorities cited in note F. *post.*

But although I have clearly shown, that this question is not to be decided by the *French* but the *Spanish* law, I can with ease deprive my opponents of evên the semblance of an argument, by showing thirdly, that both by the general laws of *France* and by special grants, the alluvions of the *Mississippi* belong to the proprietors of the adjacent soil, and not to the king.

The right of the adjacent proprietor is so consonant to the principles of natural law that it would require strong arguments to prove that any laws could permit a sovereign, after having bounded his grantee on the river, to cut him off from its use by seizing on the alluvion which might be formed on its banks. Let us examine carefully, before we pronounce that the *French* jurisprudence is liable to this reproach.

The laws relied on by the defendants, are the edicts of 1683,

1693 and 1710, and the opinion of *Pothier*. Of the edicts, the counsel has selected that of 1693, as the most favorable to his position. Let us examine this edict, without, however, subscribing to the doctrine, that any of the king's edicts could without further formality, change the general civil law of the kingdom, and with the observation that many of the provinces had their particular privileges, which they always preserved and which were enforced by the tribunals. In the very instance now before us, long after this edict, it is held by *Denizart*, by the authors of the jurisprudence of the *Encyclopædia*, and other authorities which I shall cite, that the law of the land is the reverse of that said to be enacted by the edict.

The ideas I had formed on this subject are confirmed and strongly expressed by *Portalis*, in his preliminary discourse to the civil code:

"Sous l'ancien régime, la loi étoit une volonté du prince—cette volonté étoit addressée aux cours souveraines qui étoient chargées de la verification et du dépôt des lois—la loi n'étoit point exécutaire sans un report avant d'y avoir été vérifiée et enrégistrée—La vérification étoit un examen, une discussion de la loi nouvelle. Elle représentoit la déliberation qui est l'essence de toutes les lois—l'enrégistrement étoit la transcription sur le régistre de la lois vérifiée—les cours pouvoient suspendre l'enrégistrement d'une loi, ou même la refuser—elles pouvoient modifier la loi en l'enrégistrant, et dès lors ces modifications faisaient partie de la loi même. Une loi pouvoit être refusée par une cour souveraine et acceptée par une autre—elle pouvoit être diversement modifiée par les diverses cours."

"Under the former government the law was the will of the prince—the expression of this will was addressed to the superior courts, which were charged with the verification and deposit of the laws. No law could be executed in any jurisdiction until it had been verified and registered therein. The verification was an examination or discussion of the new law—it represented that deliberation which is essential to all laws—the registry was the act of transcribing the law thus verified on the records. The courts might suspend the registry or even refuse it—they might modify the law when they enregistered it, and from that moment those modifications became part of the law itself. A law might be refused by one superior court and received by another—and it might be differently modified by different courts."

The edict declares that the king has an incontestable right upon *(sur)* all the navigable rivers, and that he and his predecessors, have caused researches to be made of isles and accretions *(crements qui s'y sont fait)* which had been made *therein*, and not *thereon*, as is translated in the opinion; and he confirms the ancient possessors of all islands, *atterissements*, *alluvions*, &c. in their possessions on paying certain dues to the Crown. Now, in this edict I can find no declaration of any thing but that the king had an incontestable right upon the navigable rivers of his kingdom,* and that he and his predecessors had claimed the islands and accretions or banks found therein, that is, in their channels or beds; but because the word alluvion is introduced in the list of property that is confirmed to the proprietors, I do not perceive that the king arrogates to himself a right to the alluvions which shall be formed upon the land which bounded on the river, and I can account for the word being introduced into this part of the edict, by supposing that it was the intent of the king to confirm to possessors of the islands not only original soil of these islands, but also the increase which they had gained or might afterwards gain by alluvion. This is a very natural construction, not only from the omission of this word in the declaratory part of the edict, but also because islands more frequently are increased by alluvions than even the banks of the rivers themselves. And thus the words of the edict will be satisfied without making it at war with the fundamental laws of the kingdom.

* Probably because the grants on those rivers, were not bounded by the river, as we have shown ours, in common with all the others in the country, to have been

The only remaining authority is that of *Pothier*. I confess that the part cited would lead the reader to suppose that this writer meant to decide the question in all cases of navigable rivers; but a closer attention will perhaps discover an inaccuracy of expression, or an error unavoidable in some instances, even by the most correct writer whose attention is turned to so many points as are embraced by the valuable work of *Pothier*.

I apprehend that what is laid down here as a general proposition, applicable to all navigable rivers in *France*, is true as to those only; (and this may be the case, perhaps, with the greater number) where the grants have not been bounded by the river but by a fixed front boundary. I believe so, because if the doctrine of *Pothier* were understood in the unqualified sense in which it is quoted, the other writers whom I shall cite, and who all without exception, give a contrary opinion, would at least notice that of so celebrated a writer, if they supposed it differed from theirs on so important a point.

I am also inclined to this solution from the passage which follows in the 160th article, where he gives the reason why, by the *Roman* law, the alluvion belonged to the adjoining proprietor :—

"It was (says he) by a kind of right of accession, that according to the *Roman* law the riparious proprietors, had, each one in his own right, the property of the islands which were formed in the river, and even in its bed, when the river abandoned it to take another course.

"The inheritances of these proprietors having towards the river an unlimited extent, and having no *other bounds but the river* and *which comprehended even the shores and all which was not occupied by the river*, the bed which had been covered when it ceased to occupy it was deemed to have made a part of those inheritances, and to be an accession to them. It was the same thing with respect to the islands which were formed in the river; these islands being nothing else but a part of the bed of the river which it had ceased to occupy."

"By the *French* laws the navigable rivers belong to the king; the islands which are formed within as well as the bed when it is abandoned to take a new course, belong to the king; the proprietors of inheritances on the bank cannot at all pretend to it, *unless they show titles of concession from the king.*"

From these citations I think it appears that *Pothier* makes the right of alluvion to depend on the fact of the concession or grant being bounded by the river, since he gives the existence of such boundary as a reason why, under the *Roman* law, the proprietor was entitled to the alluvion, and declares that unless he has a similar concession he is not entitled to it by the *French* law. I have endeavored, I know not with what success, to reconcile *Pothier* with the other *French* writers, some prior, and others subsequent to his work: every one of which, at least all that I have been able to consult, agree in the doctrine that the proprietor of land bounded by a river, whether navigable or not, is entitled to all the increase that may be produced by alluvion, but that *atterissement*, a word peculiar to the *French* jurisprudence, belongs in navigable rivers, to the king.

Alluvion is defined in the *French*, precisely as it is in the *Roman* and *Spanish* laws, to be an "increase of land, which is made by degrees *(peu à peu)* on the shores of the sea, of navigable and other rivers, by the earth which the water brings there." This definition is taken from *Guyot's Repertoire Universelle*, a work of great merit, compiled by upwards of forty counsellors, from different parts of the kingdom, and published in 1784. The whole article is transcribed in the margin, and I deduce from it these important consequences:

First. That the doctrine of *Pothier* is here shown, not to be the general law of France, but an exception to that law in the particular provinces, which are enumerated.

Second. From the part of these articles, which states the custom of Normandy to be, that the proprietors of the adjacent land shall have the alluvion, "*a lacharge des les bailler par aveu au signeur du fief et d'en payer les droits, seigneuriaux.*"

&c. that is, on condition that he shall make an acknowledgment (which is in the nature of homage in the *English* law) to the *feudal lord*, and pay his seignorial dues, &c. "The customs of *Sens, Auxerre nad Metz*, have similar dispositions, *and are admitted to serve as a rule in the French jurisprudence.*

Here then I think we may plainly discover, that if the king of France has any right to alluvions, he has them as *feudal lord*,* that even in lands held under this tenure, the proprietor would have a right to the property, paying the usual rents, and rendering the accustomed homage, but that in land not held under a feudal tenure, the king could have no pretensions to this accession of property, which would belong to the proprietor by the law of nature, to which this right is expressly referred by the Justinian code.

Should this reasoning be well founded, the dispute is at an end with respect to this property, which is expressly granted in *franc aleu*, or *allodial tenure*, as we should expresss it in the language of *English* jurisprudence. "*Franc aleu*," as appears from the following definition taken from the "*Coutume de Paris*," page 144 "is an inheritance which is subject to no seignorial rights or duties, either honorary as fealty and homage, or pecuniary as rent, fifth relief, or others that may be due as acknowledgments of the tenure from the superior lord; it is therefore that it is thus called *quasi liberum et solutum ab omnibus juribus*."

The authority of the *Encyclopædia* is also cited to show a difference between the *Spanish* and *French* laws on this point. A very cursory examination of the article will show its misapplication to the defendants' case. The whole text, (for the defendants have only quoted as much as they think suits their purpose) reads thus:

* Since the first publication of this work I have found my reasoning on this subject confirmed by the highest authority. Portalis in his preliminary discourse to the second book of the French code, expressly refers this claim of the Crown to a *feudal* origin. And moreover positively declares the whole law of alluvion to have been *settled* in favor of the adjacent proprietors long before the revolution

"Alluvion is an increase of the ground which takes place by slow degrees, on the shores of the sea, on the borders of *fleuves* and rivers; occasioned by the earth which the water conveys to it, and which becomes so consolidated with the contiguous land, that it forms a *whole with it—an identity.* The name of alluvion is also given to those lands which are slowly and imperceptibly left uncovered by the water.

"The *Roman* law places alluvions in the number of the means of acquiring according to the laws of nations, as being a kind of accession: that augmentation, being operated in a slow and imperceptible manner, remains to the inheritance to which it is found united.

"The portion which is thus added insensibly is not considered as a new land, it is a part of the old which becomes possessed of the same qualities, and it belongs to the same master —*in the same manner as the growth of a tree from parts of the tree*—and is the property of the proprietor of the tree. That right of increase by alluvion is grounded in the maxim of right, which bestows the profits and the advantages of a thing, to him who is exposed to suffer its damages and its losses.

"*The regulations of the Roman law on alluvion are generally followed in France*—the usages of *Metz*, of *Sens*, and of *Auxerre*, have on that subject precise regulations, which form their common law.

"But the province of *Frenche-Compte* must be excepted, where it is established as a maxim that the river *de Doux*, neither gives nor takes away—that is to say, that the person whose inheritance is diminished by the inundation of the river, may indemnify himself by possessing himself of the land which it has abandoned.

"The same thing takes place on the inheritances bordering on the river *de la Fère* in *Auvergne*, where the local *coutume* establishes the same right.

"The alluvions which the sea produces on the lands which it bathes, also belong, as a right of increase, to the proprietor of those inheritances, who may also make levees or dykes to secure them.

"We must observe, however, that to acquire by right of alluvion, two conditions are necessary—

"First. That the increase should be made slowly and imperceptibly, in such a manner that it cannot be discovered in what time each part of the alluvion has been formed to and consolidated with the inheritance.

Second. That the inheritance by virtue of which the right of acquiring by alluvion is claimed, be contiguous to the river, in such a manner that the bed on which it flows, seems as it were, to be a part of the same inheritance; for in case it did not bound exactly to the river, and that it was bounded by a cause-way or by a road, the parts left uncovered by the river between its bed and the road, cannot belong to the proprietor of the inheritance situated on the other side of the road. Those lands belong to the king in navigable rivers, and to the feudal lords in those that are not so."

Here we find the *Roman* law expressly recognized, as being generally followed in *France*, with the exception of the districts enumerated in the former authority, and then follow the passages selected by the defendants, which in no sort whatever, weaken the effect of the prior passages of this authority.

They are—

First. That the alluvion must be formed slowly and imperceptibly, so that the time of the incorporation of each part with the original soil, cannot be discovered. When the ingenious counsel can analyze the different deposits, separate the sands of the *Red* river, the rich mould of the *Missouri*, from the clay and other various soils which the *Mississippi* receives from a thousand tributary streams; when he can dive into its turbid eddies, watch the moment of the precious deposit, and date the existence of each stratum of its increase; then this first branch of the authority he has cited may be applicable to his cause.

The second point. *viz.* that no proprietor can claim any

alluvion, unless his lands are bounded on the river is true, not only in the *French*, but in the *Roman* and *Spanish* jurisprudence; and therefore it ought certainly not to have been cited in an argument to prove that they differed. As my adversary, however, can make no use of this part of his authority, it is a pity that it should be cited for nothing: I will therefore use it as a strong corroborative proof of the argument I used to show the reason why, on certain navigable rivers in *France*, the alluvion belonged to the king, to wit: that the grants there were bounded by the road, not by the river. The concluding lines may also serve to strengthen my reasoning, and to prove the feudal origin of the local variations which the *French* have made from the imperial law.

The opinion on this point concludes "that the *existence* of a public road or cause-way, forms an exception in favor of which all opinions may be reconciled;" but the authority says no such thing: the authority says, that the exception is formed by the road or cause-way being the *boundary;* not by its *existence*—an hundred roads and as many cause-ways might *exist*, yet if they were not the boundaries of the land, the alluvion would belong to the owner of the original soil.

Yet this is a fair specimen of the reasoning by which the government of the *United States* is gratuitously invited to harrass individuals with suits, and snatch their only support from the widow and the orphan.*

I might perhaps be excused from producing further authorities to show how untenable the ground is, on which the defendants have sheltered themselves under the *French* laws, even supposing them the guide of our decision. Take, however, in addition, the following respectable authorities:—

DENISART, *title* ALLUVION, *vol.* 1. *page* 74.—"1. L'ALLUVION est une accroisement qui se fait insensiblement, et peu-à-

* A large proportion of the batture was purchased by Mr. Delabigarre, and is now the property of his widow and infant children

peu sur les rivages de la mer, des fleuves et des riéières par les terres que l'eau y apporte.

"2. Lorsque par *alluvion*, un héritage se trouve insensiblement accru, et plus étendu qu'il ne l'étoit, l'accroisement appartient au propriétaire, et celui dont l'héritage est diminue par cette voie, ne peut pas revendiquer ce qui s'en manque.

"Cette maxime qui est puisée dans le droit Romain, A LIEU DANS TOUTE LA FRANCE, excepté en *Franche-Comt.* On y dit communément au contraire, que la riviére du Doux *n'ote ni ne baille.* Ainsi *l'alluvion* n'est point dans le cours de cette rivière, un moyen d'acquérir. Voyez la remarque de Dumoulin.

"Il faut encore excepter la rivière de Feère, qui, suivant une coutume locale d'Auvergne, *n'ote ni ne baille*, c'est-à-dire, que *lorsqu' elle prend d'anciennes possessions par inondations on autrement, petit-a-petit, de-ca on de-la l'ean, il est permis a celui qui perd, de suivre sa possession et de la revendiquer.*

"3. L'augmentation qui arrive dans un héritage par *alluvion*, est une seule et même chose avec l'héritage accru: [*fundus fundo accrescit, sicut portio portioni;*] il en prend toutes les qualitées accidentelles de fief et de roture, de propre et d'acquêt; il est sujet aux mêmes charges, fussentelles d'usufruit et de substitution.

"4. Il n'en est pas de même d'un accroissement subit, occasionné par un débordement, ou par quelqu'autre cas fortuit: la portion de ce terrien pourroit en ce cas être réclamée par le propriétaire. Voyez le coutume de Bar.

"5. La maxime est d'ailleurs afferme par l'arrét rendu au rapport de M. l'abbé de Vienne, en la quatrième chambre des enquêtes, le 15 Avril 1744, entre le marquis de Bouzols et M. de Chamflour, conseiller en la cour des aides de Clemont, rapporté par Guyot, traité des fiefs, tom. 6, chapitre *des rivieres*, page 673, n. 10; [et par arrêt du Mercredi 22 Février 1769, rendu en la grande-chambre, conformément aux conclusions de M. Seguir, avocat-général, la même chose a été jugée. La sentence qui avoit ordonné une visite des lieux, a été infirmée; et il a été ordonné qui par enquête respective, il seroit vérifié si le changement de cours de l'eau, sur la rivages de la mer, avoit été subit ou insensible. Me. Lochard pladoit pour le chopitre de Lucon, et Me. Caillou pour le sieur de Champagné.]

"6. Bourjon prétend que ce qui accroit par *alluvion* appartient au seigneur haut justicier; mais ni son opinion, ni l'avis des auteurs qu'il cité ne sont suivis dans l'usage. Voyez la contume de Normandie, art. 195, l'article 268 de celle d'Auverre, l'article 155 de celle Sens, et celle de Metz tit. 12, art. 28.

"7. Les attérissements formés subitement dans la mer ou dans les fleuves et riviéres navigables, apportiennent au roi par le seul droit de sa souverainté. Voyez la déclaration du moi d'Avril 1683, et M. le Bret, de la souverainté, liv. 2. chapitre 16; et les edits des mois de Décembre 1693, et Février 1710, concernant les attérissemens, isles et islots. On trouve ce doux édits dans le receuil de Néron, tome 2."

RENUSSON TRAITE' DES PROPRES, *p.* 39.

"It often happens that an inheritance which is bounded by *a stream or navigable river*, is augmented or diminished by the stream which forsakes its ancient bed, and makes for itself another. This augmentation or diminution, is a profit or loss to him *who has the adjoining inheritance.* The increase is an accessory, which belongs of common right, to the proprietors of the soil which is contiguous to it." *Ins. lib.* 2. *de rerum div. &c. &c.*

"This increase can have no quality different from that of the principal inheritance, according to *Argentée* on the custom of *Bretagne*, and *Dumoulin* on the ancient custom of *Paris*, who says *the increase of alluvion is acquired to us, in the same right by which the original soil belonged to us; nor is this increase considered as a new field, but as a part of the first.*

"But what shall we say of an island formed in a river, opposite to our soil, which is separate property? It would seem that an island being a thing separate from the inheritance which bor ders on the river, there would be no right of accession, and that the island ought not to be considered as of the same quality; nevertheless we may pronounce that IT IS OF THE SAME NATURE WITH THE INHERITANCE, *quia eodem jure alluviones accedit.* Common right requires that an island which arises in a river, should belong to the proprietor of the adjacent soil; or if it arises in the midst of a river, that it should belong in common to those who own the soil on the opposite sides, &c. 1 *Domat*, 268.

"The proprietor of an estate acquires the possession of whatever may be added to it by nature, which augments the land, and becomes as it were an accession thereto. Thus the insensible increase which may be gained by an estate joining to a river, by the operation of the water, is an acquisition gained by the proprietor of the estate.

"But if an inundation or the sudden change of the bed of the river, divides an inheritance, and joins it to another, the property of this part remains in its ancient owner."

Ferriere's Commentaries on the Institutes, Book 2, Title 1.

TEXT.

§ 20. *De Alluvione.*—"Moreover, whatever a *navigable river (fleuve)* adds by alluvion to our estate, is by the law of nature our own. By alluvion we mean an increase so imperceptible, that it is impossible to know how great an augmentation has been received at each instant of time."

FRENCH LAW.

"*The disposition of this section is observed among us.*"

TEXT.

§ 21. "But if by the impetuosity of its current, a river has carried off a part of your land, and joined it to that of your neighbor, this part does not cease to belong to you: however, if it has remained a long time joined to the inheritance of your neighbor, and the trees which it has carried with it have taken root, the soil shall belong to him."

FRENCH LAW.

"The provisions of this section take place in *France*, with this difference, nevertheless, that when the accessions which are thus *suddenly made*, are very considerable, and that they have remained joined to an inheritance for a long period of time without being claimed, it is said they ought to belong to the *kings*, or to the *superior lords*, as a kind of *vacant possession*, or a derelict which appears conformable to the royal ordinances by which the *islands* and *atterissements* which are formed in great rivers belong to the king."

A most persuasive, if not a conclusive argument that the law of *France* is as I have stated, may be drawn from the following circumstances and opinions. When the first consul undertook the great task of giving a general system of jurisprudence to *France*, he caused his digest or *projet de code* to be prepared by the first lawyers in the country—this was printed, and a copy sent to every superior tribunal in the republic for their consideration; and after a proper period it was returned with such remarks and amendments as had occurred to the different judges, that the legislature might, prior to its final adoption, have the benefit of the best legal advice on its different provisions.

The articles in this *projet* relating to the subject under discussion, are contained in the *2d sect. 2d title* of the *2d book*, and are as follows:

"15. The collection of earth *(atterissements)* and accessions which are annexed successively and imperceptibly to the land bordering on a river or navigable stream, are called *alluvion*. Alluvion belongs to the riparious proprietor, when it takes place on a river, whether it be navigable or capable of carrying rafts or not—under the condition in the first case leaving the path prescribed by the regulations.

"16. The rule is the same with respect to the running water, which retires insensibly from one of its banks, and encroaches on the other; the proprietor of the shore which is left dry, shall benefit by the alluvion—and the proprietor of the opposite shore shall not be permitted to reclaim the land which he has lost."

If this part of the project had made any change in the ancient laws of the country, some of the learned men to whom it was submitted, would have taken notice of the novelty, with marks either of censure or approbation—but we find them all either passing over the articles as merely declaratory of the old law, or else expressly acknowledging them as such, and stigmatizing the doctrine now contended for by Mr. *Derbigny* as an oppressive and ineffectual attempt to pervert the laws of the kingdom.

To begin with the tribunal of *Paris*, they set out with this general observation on the part of the code containing the provisions. "The rules proposed" (they say) "on the subject, are in general conformable to what has *always been practised*, and give occasion to but very few observations," and among those few are none on the subject of alluvion.

The tribunals of *Nanci*, *Nimes*, *Orleans*, *Rions*, *Liege*, *Metz*, *Montpelier*, *Agen*, *Aix*, *Grenoble*, *Poictiers*, *Rennes*, and others, pass over these provisions as matters of course, or recommend a slight alteration, to prevent disputes between the proprietors of lakes and the adjoining land.

The tribunal of *Rouen* has these strong expressions: speaking of the 19th article in the project of code, which declares islands in the middle of navigable rivers to belong to the nation, they say:

"The *Roman* law gave to the adjoining proprietors the islands which were formed in navigable rivers, a disposition which appears more equitable than this article of the code, and *more worthy of a great nation*, whose true interest is not to acquire property to the injury of individuals.

"The edicts and declarations of the former kings which claimed for the domain the islands of navigable rivers and *fleuves* (primary rivers) were only exchequer laws; these laws were founded on the false pretext that the islands were an appendage of the river, which they considered as belonging to the king. But,

"1. The river itself is not a national domain, but a thing of which the public have the use; it belongs to the nation, not in full property, but as an appendage of its sovereignty.

"2. The islands are not appendages to the waters of the river, but to the bed of the river: the right of individuals to which is acknowledged when the river abandons it.

"An island cannot be formed without increasing the width of the river at the expense of the adjoining land—and the damages to which the proprietors of these lands are exposed, should entitle them to the islands, as an indemnity for the risks and losses they incur.

"The principle which we propose would not at all invade the public right to the islands, which the nation possesses, or for which they have positive titles—but it would tranquillize those individuals, who FOR AGES have possessed islands in the rivers, as the true owners—and whom the agents of the domain HAVE ALWAYS VEXED WITHOUT HAVING EVER SUCCEEDED IN DESPOILING THEM OF THEIR ESTATES."

"La loi Romaine au digeste *de acquirendo rerum dominio*, attribuaient aux propriétaires voisins, les iles qui se formaient dans les fleuves—disposition qui parait plus equitable que cet article du code, et plus digne d'une grande nation, dont le veritable intérêt n'est point d'acquérir des propriétés nouvelles par preference aux particuliers.

"Les edits et déclarations des ci-devant rois qu'attribuaient au domaine les iles des fleuves et rivières navigables, n'etoient que des loix bursales. Ces lois se fondaient sur le faux pretexte que ces iles étaient un accessoire du fleuve qu'on regardoit comme appartenant au roi.

"1. Le fleuve lui même n'est point un domaine national, mais une chose publique; il appartient à la nation non a titre de propriete, mais à titre de souverainete.

2. L'ile n'est pas un accession des eaux du fleuve, mais bien du lit du fleuve, sur le quel les droits des particuliers ne sont pas me connus lorque le fieuve l'abandonne.

3. Il ne peut guère se former une ile sans que le fleuve s'olargesse aux Depens des terrain voisins; et le ravage aux quels sont exposes les proprietaires des ce terrains, doivent leur faire obtenir les iles qui se forment dans le fleuve, comme une juste indemnite des risque q'uils courent et des pertes qu'ils epronvent.

Le principe que nous proposons ne porteroit aucune atteinte à la propriete dominiale des iles que la nation possede ou sur les quelles elle à des titres d'engagement; mais il servirait à tranquilliser les particuliers qui depuis des siecles possedent des iles dans les fleuves comme veritables proprietaires, et que les agents du domaine ont toujours vexes, sans pourtant parvenir à les depoullier de leur fonds.—*Observations du tribunal d'Appel de Rouen*, p. 15.

Here we have the positive declaration of a learned tribunal speaking to the collective legal wisdom of the nation, and in the performance of a solemn and disinterested office, deciding that the edicts did not extend to *alluvions*, but only to islands in navigable rivers.

That even in that strong case, the edicts were considered as EXCHEQUER LAWS, *(lois bursales)* founded on FALSE PRETEXTS, which were NEVER EXECUTED, served only for the purposes of VEXATION, and that the proprietors have IN SPITE OF THEM kept possession of their islands FOR AGES.

The tribunal of *Toulouse* recommends the same provisions in favor of isles and islands. And that of *Lyons* expressly declares that the claims of the Crown to the "*islands in navigable rivers*," never considering the edicts as even claiming alluvions, were founded on no other law than that of force, *(le droit du plus fort.)*

Portalis, in his preliminary discourse to this part of the Code, repeats the same ideas; asserts that the language of the Code on the subject of alluvion, is that of the ancient law, as SETTLED LONG PRIOR TO THE REVOLUTION; refers the claims of the Crown to obsolete feudal principles, and finally declares that the edicts were only fiscal attempts to oppress the subject.

I should not have multiplied these authorities, had it not been for the respect I bear to that of *Pothier*. None of those I have cited, at all accord with the doctrine the defendants suppose him to maintain. Many of them are posterior to his work, and of those none mention his opinion as differing from their own. This notice his acknowledged respectability would have required, had they thought this difference existed. I think, therefore, I may fairly infer from their silence, that they have construed the passage cited in the way that I have done: of course that there is a perfect coincidence between these eminent writers on this point, and that the laws of *France*, except in the particular enumerated districts, are conformable to the *Roman* and the *Spanish* codes.

But as I am determined not to leave my adversaries a single recess in which they can hide a doubt, or from which they can bring out an argument, I will suppose that I have wholly failed in this division of my cause; that the laws of *France* are to govern, and that they are as laid down by the defendants; yet the alluvions of the *Mississippi* have not since the first settlement, belonged to the Crown of *France*.

First. Because I have shown, we hold the lands in *franc aleu* or allodial tenure.

Second. Because, if the king of *France* had this right, he has expressly *renounced it*, and the authority in *Pothier*, as well as the edicts, admit that a grant of alluvion shall be good against the Crown.

In *September*, 1712, *Louisiana* was first granted, by the Crown, to Mr. *Crozat*. I have never seen a copy of this grant, but there is reason to believe from a subsequent recital, that it was extremely liberal. This however is immaterial, for having surrendered his grant, the same country was conceded to the *West India* company, by letters patent, dated in *August*, 1717, the 5th article whereof is in the following words: "In order to provide the said *West India* company with the means of making a permanent establishment, and to execute all the plans they may form, we have given, granted, and conceded, and by these presents do give, grant and concede to them, forever, all the lands, coasts, ports, havens and islands which form our province of *Louisiana*, as well, and with the same extent as we had granted it to Mr. *Crozat*, by our letters patent, dated 14th *September*, 1712, to enjoy the same in full property, *lordship and justice, reserving to ourselves, but only fealty and homage*, which the said company shall render to us and the kings our successors, with a Crown of gold of the weight of twenty marks."

By the 8th article the company are expressly authorized to grant lands in *franc aleu* or allodial tenure.

Under this ample grant, all the titles of the *Jesuits* were derived,* and after reading it, I fancy nothing more will be said of the *royal right* to the alluvions of the *Mississippi*, under the *West India* company.

Again, by the fifteenth article of the charter, the custom of *Paris* is expressly introduced and established *unchangeably* as the fundamental law of the territory. Whatever then may the laws

* The title to the *Jesuits*, is dated in 1726, near six years before the patent to the company was resumed by the Crown

of the other part of the *French* dominions be, unless alluvions can be shown to be the property of the Crown by the *custom of Paris*, the argument with respect to this property is at an end. This has not been attempted; for it was known that it could not have been done with success. As however, I have not the same reasons to shrink from this research, I will refer to *Ferriere's* folio edition of the custom of *Paris*, and its commentary, 4 *vol. p.* 917, *nos.* 37, 38, 32. "Alluvion is an imperceptible increase to an inheritance, produced, insensibly diminishing the neighboring lands; for the augmentation cannot otherwise take place. This increase is so intimately united to the inheritance, that it assumes all its qualities, and consequently becomes separate property, if the inheritance were so. According to *Demoulin*, on the first article of this custom, *gloss.* 5, *nos.* 115, 116, where he says, *incrementum alluvionis nobis adquiretur, eo jure quo ager augmentatus primum ad nos pertinebat, nec illud incrementum sentitur novus ager sed pars primi.*

"It would not be the same case, if the river should add to the inheritance of an individual, an island or an entire parcel of soil, although it should be united to the inheritance, THIS WOULD BE CONSIDERED AS A PART OF THIS INHERITANCE; but not with the quality of separate property." See also the same work, *vol.* 1, *p.* 886.

These authorities prove much more than is necessary for my purpose, not only that alluvions strictly so called, which are made imperceptibly, belong to the proprietor of the soil to which it is attached; but that the *custom of Paris*, in conformity with the *Roman* and the *Spanish* laws, give to him the islands and portions of land formed in a river or on its banks, by a change of its course, or other sudden accident.

But the custom of *Paris*, as I have shown, was declared by the charter, and I might have added by an express edict of "*Louis* the XIVth," to be the law of this colony.

So that I think I have fully demonstrated that even if the general law of *France* would have given this kind of property to the king, yet on the *Mississippi*, it belonged to the adjoining proprietor, as well by the laws of the province as by the actual grant of the king.

Before I conclude, I ought perhaps to make some observations on the relinquishment, alleged to have been made by Mr. *Gravier*, of his title, and the notorious acts of ownership which are stated to have been done by the *Spanish* government. Let it be remembered that proof of these very acts was produced by the corporation of the city as evidence of *their title*, and that it has not been until after they despair of making any title in themselves, that they now appropriate the same evidence to make out one for the *United States*. What reliance can the *United States* have on such accommodating proof, that will fit any claim and serve any occasion? That first used to establish the interests of the corporation is now set to work as the engine of their malice and resentment. But it is not from its general character that I would stigmatize it. Let us do justice and examine it fairly. What are these proofs?

1. *Gravier* abandoned his right to the public.

2. Governor *Carondelet* ordered the sheds on the batture to be pulled down.

3. The cabildo refused permission to erect any buildings thereon.

4. The inhabitants of the town dug earth there, and the public used the batture as a landing.

5. The auditor gave it as his opinion that the ground between high and low-water mark belonged to the public.

1. *Gravier* abandoned the batture to the public.

A point materially relied on both in the case and in Mr. *Derbigny's* opinion, to show this relinquishment of *Gravier* is, that by depositing a plan, in which this part of his farm was not laid out into lots, he had virtually declared that it was a common for the public—the case indeed goes further, and says that in this plan the batture *was marked as a space which is to remain free and not subject to be built on.* This in the literal acceptation of the terms is UNTRUE, for there is *no such mark* on the plan, and therefore I presume Mr. *Moreau*, who drew the case, meant that it should be understood with the qualification that follows, that it was marked as free only because it was not divided into lots, that is to say, because it was *not marked at all.* The same wise reasoning would vest all the rear as well as the front part of *Gravier's* farm in the public, because the line of lots occupied but a small part of the farm fronting on the road. But it is said Mr. *Gravier* declared that he had abandoned his right to the public. If the evidence of these declarations had been as full, as certain, and circumstantial, as it is contradictory, vague, and frivolous, yet without writing, and recording, it would give no title to the *United States*, according to the laws of the country at the time it was said to have been made, [see the discussion of this point in the report of the case.] But the proof itself is wholly uncertain—one witness says it was to *the public*, another to the inhabitants of the town, and a third to those of the suburb—none of them pretend to relate with precision the time, conditions or consideration of the supposed abandonment. But can it possibly escape the attention of the most superficial reasoner, that this branch of the argument is directly at war with all the others, and that the very allegation of it is an express admission of our title? The same may be said of the *Baron de Carondelet's* and governor *Gayosa's* orders to repair the roads by the public convicts—for it was in both instances said to be founded on this supposed abandonment, of which both the governors know so little that they always considered *Gravier* as the owner of the land, and sent the order for repairs in the first place to him. These very facts too, stated and relied on by those who advocate the title of the *United States*—completely contradict the unblushing assertion that "*the batture never ceased to be part of the sovereign's domain.*" If this was the case, why did *Carondelet* and *Cayosa* both send to *Gravier* to repair the roads, and why, according to Mr. *Derbigny's* showing, did they undertake the task only when informed that *Gravier* had abandoned his right.

2, 3, 4, and 5. Governor *Carondelet* ordered the sheds built on the batture to be pulled down. The cabildo refused permission to build others—the auditor gave it as his opinion that the public had a right to the land, and they actually used it for a public landing.

There is proof that the demolition of the buildings arose from their being in the range of the fort guns. *See the deposition of Mr. Pedesclaux.* But admitting these facts to be proved in the fullest manner, no other inference can be drawn from them, than one incident to the nature of the property. By the civil law, the public have a right to the use of the banks of navigable rivers, though the property remains in the owner of the adjacent soil; on the *Mississippi*, by usage and the nature of the ground, the bank comprehended the levee, and all the space between it and the river. When the river encroaches, the levee is brought nearer in; when it retires, or forms an alluvion, the proprietor extends his levee, encloses the new made ground, and leaves the public the enjoyment of the new bank and that part lying outside of it, for the purposes of navigation. On this space it is unlawful for the proprietor to erect any thing that may interfere with the use secured to the public. The governor therefore would have had a right to order the sheds to be demolished, because they must have interfered with the public use. The cabildo, who were the governor's council, were right in refusing permission to erect any buildings—the auditor was perfectly correct in the opinion he is said to have given, and the public had a right to the free use of the property for the purposes of navigation. They were all right *then*, because *Gravier* had not enclosed the alluvion land, and by making a new levee and tow path on the bank of the new made ground, given the public the accommodation the law required. But they would have been perfectly wrong if *Gravier* had at that time offered, as the proprietors do now, to reclaim the land from the inundation of the river, and by erecting a tow path, a levee, and commodious wharves, give the public ten-fold the convenience to which they were entitled by law. Thus we see, that all the material facts proved by the advocates for the title of the *United States*, confirm and strengthen that which I assert to be in *Gravier* and those who claim under him, and I may, without flattering myself, believe that I have fully established the following points:

I. That the *Jesuits'* plantation was like all the others on the river, bounded in front by the river itself.

II. That no alteration took place in the front boundary of any of the subdivisions of that plantation by the sales of 1763.

III. That the alluvion formed in front of that plantation belongs to the proprietors of the several subdivisions:

1. By the general law of *France*.
2. By that of *Spain*.
3. By the particular laws of this province while under the *French* government.
4. By virtue of the allodial tenure by which they were held.

IV. That the alleged relinquishment by *Gravier*, is too uncertain to give title: and if proved, only serves to destroy the other arguments used by the advocates of the *United States*.

V. That the acts relied on as possessory by the government, are perfectly consistent with my title, and rather serve to strengthen than destroy it.

The view I proposed to take of the arguments urged in favor of the claim of the *United States* to this property is now finished. Let it be read with attention. Let those whose duty or inclination calls them to decide on these pretensions, examine carefully the principles and study the authorities cited to show that this was never of right a part of the sovereign's demesne. Let this be done without prejudice or partiality, and though all my prospects of fortune are involved in the decision, I shall await it without anxiety. I have hesitated long before I resolved on its publication; but the unwearied pains which are daily taken to slander my title, and render my property useless, require that I should take some steps to counteract them.

This must be my apology for discussing a legal question before the public.

EDWARD LIVINGSTON.

December 10, 1807.

3 Durn. & East. 253.

BALL *v.* HERBERT.

[The insertion of this case in the alphabetical order, was omitted by mistake.]

TRESPASS for breaking and entering the plaintiff's close, being part of an artificial bank adjoining to the river *Ouze*, at *Wiggenhall* in *Norfolk*, and treading down the grass with men and with horses, and fixing lines, &c. to certain barges, and drawing and towing those barges.

Plea, that the port of *King's Lynn*, in the said county, hath been immemorially a common and public port for all the king's subjects; and that the river *Ouze* hath been immemorially a public king's highway and navigable river, where the tide flows and reflows, leading between the port of *King's Lynn* and the village of *Stow*, in the same county, to wit, at *Wiggenhall*, for boats, barges, and lighters, &c. at all times of the year, &c. That the close in which, &c. hath been immemorially part of the banks of and adjoining the said highway and navigable river. That the defendant at the time when, &c. was possessed of the several boats, barges and lighters, in the declaration mentioned, which were laden with goods and merchandizes, and passing up and down the said highway and navigable river, and going to and from the said port of *King's Lynn*; by reason whereof, &c. he entered with his said horses, &c. and drew and towed his said boats, &c. as stated in the declaration.

To this there was a general demurrer, and joinder.

Graham for the plaintiff. The general question is, Whether, at common law, the public have a right to tow vessels on the banks of either side of a navigable river? If any such right existed, its importance would certainly have caused it to have been treated of in some of our law-books, under a specific head, and the right itself would have been defined with precision; but no such head of law is to be found. Neither can the extent of this right be any where traced; and whether it extends to both sides or only to one, whether to horses as well as men, and what number of horses, or who is bound to keep the banks in repair, the books are altogether silent. In the case of highways in general, to which the claim in question bears the greatest analogy, all matters of this sort are clearly ascertained, and are set forth in pleading by the party claiming a right of way. The question, however, is not entirely new in point of fact; for it arose in respect of this very river, and was discussed in the year 1747, before Lord Ch. J. *Willes*, in the case of *Vernon* v. *Prior*. That was an action of trespass, like the present, against one of the navigators of the river, by the owner of the adjoining land, for towing upon the banks. The defendant justified under a custom to tow with horses, which was negatived by the verdict. Now though that case so far differed from the present, that the issue was taken on a custom, yet several *dicta* were mentioned by the defendant's counsel, at the trial in support of the common law right now claimed, which were over-ruled by Lord Ch. J. *Willes*, who delivered it as his opinion that no such right could be maintained. It appears too, in that case, that Serjeant *Prime* drew the plea: now it is plain that, if he had entertained any idea that such a right existed at common law, he would not have run the risk of pleading a custom which might not be supported by the evidence. In consequence of this determination, the proprietors of the barges applied to parliament in the next year for an act to enable them to navigate in this manner; and one of the grounds stated for the application was, that Lord Ch. J. *Willes* had been of opinion that they had no other remedy. An opinion to the same effect was also incidentally given by Lord *Hardwicke*, in the case of *Pierse* v. Lord *Fauconberg*, where he directed a second issue to try whether the plaintiff had a right to a track path on either side of the river *Tees*, for the convenience of towing without paying any acknowledgment to the owners of the soil; after having directed a former issue to try whether the river *Tees* was a navigable river from *Yarumbridge* to *Low Worsall*, which was found in the affirmative. Now, unless his lordship had been of opinion that no such common law right existed, the second issue would have been totally nugatory; for when once it was determined to be a navigable river, the common law right would have immediately attached. Few of our rivers, besides the *Thames* and the *Severn*, were naturally navigable, but have been made so under different acts of parliament. And even in those two it was never left to the discretion of the navigators to make towing paths on the banks wherever and on which side they pleased, but those paths have always been ascertained, and confined to one or other side of the river. Two statutes have been passed relative to the navigation of the *Severn*; 9 *H.* 6. *c.* 5 and 19 *H.* 7. c. 18. the latter of which allows a towing path to the navigators upon making reasonable compensation to the owners of the land for the hurts they may thereby receive; which negatives the idea of any common law right to go without paying. And if it should be contended that the subjects have a right to go on the banks upon making a reasonable satisfaction, infinite difficulties will arise in ascertaining what that reasonable satisfaction shall be: it must necessarily vary according to circumstances, and the value of the damage can only be settled by action, for as it is said in *Litt. s.* 212. no man can be entitled to damage at his will. The same argument may be drawn from the 14 *Geo.* 3. *c.* 91. and several other acts relative to the *Thames*, which give a right to certain commissioners to purchase towing paths, with an exception in favour of pleasure grounds, where the owners have enjoyed the land down to the water's edge for a certain number of years. But even supposing there were such a common law right, it could not be extended to a case like the present, where the banks are artificial, and have been raised within time of memory, and are kept in repair at a very considerable expense, to prevent the overflowings of the river, which had formerly inundated a large tract of land. And as to this particular case the right claimed is of the more importance to be resisted, because the banks are made of such materials as are not calculated to resist the constant tread of horses: which must necessarily endanger the country. Several acts of parliament have been passed since the time of *Hen.* 8. for securing these banks, and putting them under the care of the commissioners of sewers; one of which makes it felony to destroy them.

Wilson, for the defendant, (after observing that, as it was stated in the plea that the close in which, &c. had been immemorially part of the old banks of the navigable river, all argument respecting their being artificial banks, as stated in the declaration, was done away,) insisted that persons using this ancient river had a right by the common law to tow on the banks with men and horses, as often as was necessary for the purposes of navigation: not indeed to dig the soil, for that would be an injury of another nature; but to exercise this right, doing as little damage as possible. As fishermen may justify going on land adjoining the sea to fish; for it is for the common good; though they cannot justify digging there for the purpose of fixing stakes to dry their nets upon. *Bro. T.* "*Custom,*" *pl.* 46. And whenever private rights interfere with public convenience, they must give way. *Com. Dig. T.* "*Pleader,*" 3. *M.* 37. But, in a case like the present, it is begging the question to say that it is an injury to the plaintiff's property; because if the common law right does exist, it is paramount his title, and he never had any title but subject to the public right. It is like an highway, where the soil is in a private person; or, like the soil in an arm of the sea in a private person by prescription: *Hale's Tr.* 36. And it is to be observed that by the civil law, which prevails in the greatest part of Europe, the banks of public rivers are public. *Just. Inst. l.* 2 *Tit.* 1. *s.* 4.; which shews that such a law cannot be attended with any great inconvenience. The authorities on the common law right of towing are collected by lord *Hale* in his tract *De Portibus Maris*, *c.* 7. The first passage is taken from *Bract. l.* 1. c. 12. *s.* 6. "*Quod publica sunt omnia flumina et portus, ideoque jus piscandi omnibus commune est in portu et in fluminibus. Riparum etiam usus publicus est jure gentium, sicut ipsius fluminis.*" And though *Bracton's* authority is impeached in *Fitz. Abr. t.* "*Garde,*" *pl.* 71. and *Plowd.* 357. it is to be observed that the passage in *Fitz. Abr.* refers to one of the year-books, which does not warrant it; and in *Fort.* 408. it was said that he was a good authority when speaking of our law: and *Stamf. P. C.* cites *Bracton* continually, and makes him his text. No objection can arise from lord *Hale's* treating on this subject in his chapter *On Ports*, because, in the preceding chapter *about rivers*, he makes an express reference to this; and it is evident that the authorities are applicable to navigable rivers as well as to ports. Lord *Hale* then mentions two strong cases on this subject; the one against the prior of *Tynemouth*, the other the *Nottingham* case. One of the articles of complaint against the former by the burgesses of *Newcastle*, who sued for the king and themselves, was that "*Rex debet habere towagium batellorum majorum et minorum in aquâ de* Tyne, *ascendendo á mari liberè pe, terras dominorum quorumcunque, prædictus prior non permittit, hujusmodi transitum facere volentes terras suas ingredi,*" &c. To which it appears by 1 *Parl. Rol.* 26. that the prior pleaded, "*Quod quoad towagium in aquâ de* Tyne, *nunquam hujusmodi officium exercentes in terram suam adjacentem impedivit, preterquam in pratum suum de* Astwyk, *quod est et fuit liberum hactenus et exemplum, et hoc par. ver.*" There are several issues taken, but the replication does not mention towage. And the judgment given was *(inter alia)* "*Quod portus ille remaneat domino regi et hæredibus suis liberè cum prisis et* towagio, *et omnibus libertatibus ad portum spectantibus.*" In the *Nottingham* case, the custom was claimed to go *liberè* on the banks of the *Trent*, between *Hull* and *Nottingham*; and the complaint was that the owners had made exactions for the liberty of passage, which were prohibited in future. Lord *Hale* then (speaking of the nuisances to which ports are subject by law) mentions "towage or haleing of ships or vessels up or down a river or creek, to or from the port town." And "the impediment or hindrance of mooring ships in the ground adjacent, if it hath been so anciently used, without paying any thing for it. Or, if it be a new port, it seems the mooring of ships being for the "general good of commerce, must be suffered upon reasonable amends." After commenting upon all which, Lord *Hale's* own opinion seems to be, that the subject has a right to go on the banks, making nevertheless a reasonable compensation to the owner, unless there be a custom to go without paying anything; and it appears from the prior's plea in the *Tynemouth* case, that a special custom may exempt the land from the general right of towing-paths. [Lord KENYON, Ch. J. The defendant claims a common law right, *without making any compensation.* If he has only a *qualified* right, he should have adapted his plea to it. For if he were to obtain judgment, it would ascertain his right to the extent claimed on this record, namely, a *general right without making any compensation.*] But if the defendant has a common law right to go on the banks for the purposes of navigation, on paying a reasonable satisfaction, then the plaintiff has mistaken his action, which ought to have been brought for the compensation, and not an action of trespass: and the judgment on this record would be no bar to an action to be brought by the plaintiff for a reasonable compensation. The statute 19 *H.* 7 *c.* 18. declares the passage *upon* the river *Severn* to be free, with a proviso that the owners of the lands adjoining shall be satisfied for the damage they receive by haleing. Now this does not *give* the right of haleing, but pre-supposes it, and gives the right of demanding recompense. And the 23 *H.* 8. *c.* 12. (reciting that the subjects had immemorially had a path on each side the *Severn* for towing, but that of late years certain tolls had been taken by the owners of the land) enacts that no person should thereafter receive any such toll.—These statutes are also noticed by Lord *Hale*, just before he gives his opinion on the common law right before mentioned. *Callis*, in his reading on the stat. of *Sewers*, says, "the use of the banks is common to all the king's liege people, as to tie the ships and boats to the trees, and to tow them to and fro," *&c.* In *Young* v. ——, it was ruled by Lord *Holt*, at *nisi prius*, "that every man of common right may justify going with horses on the banks of navigable rivers for towing barges," *&c.* And this does not appear to be a hasty opinion, for Lord *Holt*, a few years afterwards,d elivered an opinion to the very same effect: 6 *Mod.* 163. This precise question came solemnly before the court, in *Zangers* v. *Whiskard*. It was an action of trespass for breaking and entering the plaintiff's close at *Holmeade, &c.*; to which the defendant pleaded a justification, that the river *Lee* was an ancient navigable river between *London* and *Ware*, to which the *locus in quo* was adjoining, and that the stream of the river there was so weak that he could not pass with his boat without towing, &c. To this the plaintiff demurred. On the first argument, the defendant's counsel contended that the navigation was for the public good; and that the defendant, having a right to navigate on the river, had in consequence, a right to every thing necessary to the enjoyment of it: which questions were met fairly by the plaintiff's counsel. But on the second argument, the plaintiff's counsel shifted his ground, and resorted to eight formal objections to the plea. The defendant's counsel concluded the second argument by saying, "that this manner of drawing barges was used on the banks of the *Thames*, *Severn*, *Ouze*, *Exe*, and all the great rivers in *England*; and no question was ever made of it; which was not controverted by the plaintiff's counsel in reply. And though this case was adjourned, and no determination appears to have been made in it, yet it is a strong authority in favor of the common law right; for the circumstance of the plaintiff's counsel resorting, on the second argument, to objections of form, is an admission by him that he thought the right could not be resisted. Thus this right stood at common law; and it will not be found that any of the statutes relating to the towing on particular rivers have varied it. It may be observed that many of them were not *ancient* navigations, and when they were made navigable, some of them perhaps cut through private property, it became necessary to provide for the towing. Besides, in acts of this sort it is very common to insert a clause giving a right which existed before, especially in a doubtful matter, *ex majori cautelâ.* The first statute relating to the *Thames* is that of 3 *Jac.* 1. *c.* 20. which is perfectly silent as to the right of towing. Now as towing at that time was as necessary on the banks of the *Thames* as at present, it is a fair inference that the legislature did not think it necessary to give such a right. Then followed the 21 *Jac.* 1. 1. *c.* 32. "for making the *Thames* navigable from *Bercot* to *Oxford;*" which gave a right of towing: but that was because it was a *new* navigation. And it appears by the preamble to the 24 *Geo.* 2. *c.* 8. that the *Thames* had been *immemorially navigable* from *London* to *Bercot,* but not from *Bercot* to *Oxford.* And the navigation on the *Thames* has, since the time of *James* the first, been entirely regulated by statutes. There are also two statutes for improving the navigation of the *Trent;* the one from *Welden Ferry* to *Burton,* the other to *Gainsborough,* both which give a right of towing: but the first navigation was entirely new, and the other was partly so; so that it became necessary to insert clauses in those acts to give towing-paths, on paying a certain satisfaction for them. And with respect to the provisions in the several statutes alluded to for purchasing towing-paths, they give power to purchase the *soil* itself, and not merely the *right* to use it. This right is of great importance, as affecting the public, and particularly several counties through which the river in question runs. And no inconvenience can arise from allowing the right; because, according to lord *Hale's* opinion, a reasonable recompense is to be made to the owner whose soil is injured, which will be sufficient guard against any abuse. The objection, that that reasonable recompense is not sufficiently ascertained, and that it will be productive of great litigation in the courts of law, is not a sufficient answer to the right; because the same objection will equally apply to every case where the law admits a reasonable satisfaction to be tendered to the party aggrieved in bar of his action. As in the case of replevin, or for any irregularity in a distress by 11 *Geo.* 2. c. 19. or in case of actions against justices; in which cases, reasonable satisfaction is to be ascertained by a jury. As to the case of *Vernon* v. *Prior*, in 1747, the issue was *on a custom;* and whatever was said by *Willes*, Ch. J. on the general right, was extra judicial, and not applicable to this point. And with respect to *Peirse* v. *Lord Fauconberg*, one issue was to try whether there was any custom *without paying*, which accords with lord *Hale's* opinion; and it was material to the parties to establish such a right.

Graham, in reply, was stopped by the court.

Lord Kenyon, C. J. I remember when the case of *Peirse* v. *Lord Fauconberg* was sent here from the Court of Chancery, it was the current opinion of *Westminster Hall*, that the right of towing depended upon usage, without which it could not exist. It has been said that this right now in question is of great importance to the navigation through several counties; now if this navigation has been carried on for a series of years, and this right of towing constantly exercised, there would be abundant usage on which it might be supported. But that is abandoned, and the defendant resorts to the common law right. Now common law rights are either to be found in the opinions of lawyers, delivered as axioms, or to be collected from the universal and immemorial usage throughout the country. That the right now in question is not to be collected from the unanimous current of authorities is manifest. Very little is to be found in the books upon the subject, the whole of which, down to his time, lord

Hale has collected; and after commenting upon it, he seems to have formed an opinion against the right: for he says that, where private interests are involved in the question, they shall not be infringed without a satisfaction being made to the parties injured. But on what ground can a common law right stand, if satisfaction is to be made for the enjoyment of it, and that satisfaction not ascertained? it must resolve itself into an agreement between the parties, and cannot be considered as a right to use the banks *indefinitely*. And some of the passages in lord *Hale*, which seem to favor the common law right, are rather applicable to banks of the sea, and to ports; and it is part of the king's prerogative to create ports, which was lately exercised at *Liverpool*. Then is this bottomed on immemorial usage: the right is not claimed on one side or the other, as is most convenient, but on both sides of the river. But that is directly contrary to common experience; for if we look at any of the great public rivers, we shall find that it is not used, although it would be highly convenient to the persons using the navigations. On the contrary, the navigators are obliged, at several places, to pass from one side of the *Thames* to the other with great inconvenience and delay; that is the case by the duke of *Montague's* gardens, between *Richmond* and *Kew*, and in various other parts. Such is the right on that river, the *quantum* of which is ascertained by the usage. That there is such a custom on most of the navigable rivers, no person doubts, but still the right is founded solely *on the custom:* but here the claim is set up without any custom at all. The authorities which have been mentioned are very few. The case in lord *Raymond*, though before an eminent judge, was only a *nisi prius* decision. It is a short note taken by lord *Raymond* when he was very young; not even the name of the case is given; and it does not appear what the case was, or how the question arose: I rather think the principal question there was whether, when a right of passage was ascertained, and that was founderous, the party entitled might not go on the adjoining land. However, at most it is only an opinion delivered at *nisi prius;* opposed to which is that of lord Ch. J. *Willes*, in the case cited. And lord *Hardwicke's* opinion was against the right, as is evident from the manner in which he sent the case of *Peirse* v. *Lord Fauconberg* into this court, which was very fully considered. Therefore, on these authorities, on the silence in the books respecting this common law right, and on account of the extreme inconvenience to which individuals, having lands adjoining the public rivers, would be subject, I cannot bring my mind to say that the defendant's justification can be supported. Perhaps small evidence of usage before a jury would establish a right by custom on the ground of public convenience: but the right here claimed extends to every bank of every navigable river throughout the kingdom.

Ashhurst, J. I am of opinion, first, that no such *general* right exists as that claimed; and, secondly, if *any qualified* right could be supported, the defendant's plea is not adapted to it. As to the first; it seems extraordinary (if there be any such right) that it is not defined with greater certainty in any of our law books. For it is a right that in its nature must, if it existed, be subject to some restrictions; as that it should be exercised only on one, and that the most convenient, side of the river; for it would, in many instances, be a very oppressive right if it could be claimed *on both sides*. The state of property on the *Thames* is strong evidence to shew that no such general right exists; for there is no instance in any part of the banks of that river where the right is claimed *on both sides;* and yet the defendant's claim would go to establish a right on both sides. The instances which have been mentioned where the right of towing has been given by several acts of parliament, also negative the idea of general right; for we are not to suppose that rights should from time to time have been given by the legislature which existed before; and it is no answer to say that such provisions were inserted *ex abundanti cautelâ*. And the reason assigned by the defendant's counsel why such a right was given by the 24 *Geo.* 2. *c.* 8. namely, because that part of the river was not navigable before, is not satisfactory, for when once a river becomes navigable, or, in other words, when it is made a common highway for all the king's subjects, that right would immediately attach. On the general ground, therefore, I think no general right of towing exists. But then it was contended that a right might be supported on making reasonable compensation to the owner of the land. Lord *Hale* touches this right very tenderly; for he says that it does not exist without making a reasonable satisfaction. But it is not necessary to enter into that question here; because, if it were a right *sub modo*, it ought to have been so claimed in pleading. And even if such a right existed, the party should either pay or tender a reasonable satisfaction, in order to give them that right. For it would be to no purpose to give the owner merely a right of action to recover that compensation, when it is to be enforced against strangers passing by, whom the owner cannot know, and who perhaps may be foreigners.

Buller, J. The defendant's plea on this record rests wholly on a general common law right; in deciding which it is not necessary to go into the question, which has been made respecting the mode of pleading. This being claimed as a common law right, it can only be proved to exist by one of the ways mentioned by my lord. As to the general usage throughout the kingdom, of which the court is obliged to take notice, that clearly does not exist. Then the question is, whether in our books, or on records, that right is established for which the defendant contends. The case in lord *Raymond* is a very loose and inaccurate note. Another authority cited is the passage in *Bracton*, and quoted by *Callis:* that plainly appears to have been taken from *Justinian*, and is only part of the civil law; and whether or not that has been adopted by the common law is to be seen by looking into our books; and there it is not to be found. *Callis* compares a navigable river to an highway; but no two cases can be more distinct. In the latter case, if the way be founderous and out of repair, the public have a right to go on the adjoining land: but if a river should happen to be choaked up with mud, that would not give the public a right to cut another passage through the adjoining lands. I therefore am of opinion that no common law right of towing exists. But I wish not to be precluded by this determination from giving an opinion on the question, which has been made on the pleadings, whenever it shall arise in future. At present I cannot agree with what has been said on that head. This is not like the case of toll thorough. The distinction, which has been made between toll thorough and toll traverse, is not where the question arises on a defence merely, but where the right itself of taking toll has come in question. And the distinction taken is, that the party who claims toll thorough, must shew a consideration for it, because it is against common right: but in the case of toll traverse, no consideration need be shewn, because that is not against common right. Then if the defendant is right in saying that by the common law he has a right to go on the banks of navigable rivers, he need not shew any consideration, and the owner of the land would not be entitled to any satisfaction till after the defendant had used the towing path. Customs, which are consistent, may be pleaded against each other. And the party pleading a general custom need not shew the modification of it, which is not inconsistent with the right claimed by him. The case of *Kenchin* v. *Knight*, is strong to this point: there the defendant pleaded a custom to put swine upon a common; to which the plaintiff replied that he could only put in such swine as were rung, without traversing the custom set up in the plea: and the replication was held good on demurrer, because the customs were not inconsistent. Now here, if every subject has a right to tow on the banks making a reasonable satisfaction, it is not necessary for the party to plead such satisfaction, because that claim arises afterwards. And if it were otherwise, it would be attended with manifest inconvenience; because, the sum not being ascertained, it would be a perpetual dispute between the owners of the barges and the land owners, how much should be paid, which would be destructive of the right of the public, and the navigation would be stopped till the quantum was ascertained. I have said thus much on the subject, lest I should be precluded from considering the question, whenever it should arise: but in the present case, I am of opinion against the common law right. In addition to the observations made on the cases cited, I think that the instances of the three great rivers alluded to are very strong against the right. From what passed in the case of *Vernon* v. *Prior*, it seems as if lord Ch. J. *Willes* entertained a wish that the public should have this right, and yet he could find no legal ground on which to support it; for the application to parliament in 1748 is said to have been made with his approbation. On the river *Trent* there have been some claims of this sort of a more recent date not unworthy notice. The persons passing there with barges, endeavoured to set up this right, in consequence of which several actions were brought against the barge owners, who, on being advised that they could not support the right, suffered judgment to go by default. But they still continued their towing, on which actions were again brought against sixty or seventy persons at the same time, and then they abandoned their claim. The state of the banks of the *Thames* also affords a strong argument against this common law right; for if it exist, all the houses built on those banks must be considered as nuisances.

Grose, J.—It is enough for me at present to say that I perfectly agree in the general position, that there is not any *general* common law right of towing.—Judgment for the defendant.

INDEX

TO THE

TREATISE.

www.ingramcontent.com/pod-product-compliance
Lightning Source LLC
La Vergne TN
LVHW090259210926
848480LV00001B/75
* 9 7 8 1 5 8 7 9 8 1 0 5 0 *